Courtroom Ethnography

Lisa Flower · Sarah Klosterkamp
Editors

Courtroom Ethnography

Exploring Contemporary Approaches, Fieldwork and Challenges

palgrave
macmillan

Editors
Lisa Flower
Lund University
Lund, Sweden

Sarah Klosterkamp
University of Bonn
Bonn, Germany

ISBN 978-3-031-37984-0 ISBN 978-3-031-37985-7 (eBook)
https://doi.org/10.1007/978-3-031-37985-7

Cover credit: Marina Lohrbach_shutterstock.com

This Palgrave Macmillan imprint is published by the registered company Springer Nature Switzerland AG
The registered company address is: Gewerbestrasse 11, 6330 Cham, Switzerland

Foreword

Law can be slippery and evasive. It is often couched in obscure language, and involves stuffy rituals and forms of address that only those "in the know" seem to truly understand. A lot of law is text-heavy too: decisions, laws, statutes, submissions—all rely on text. It can mean that the law seems to exist in a reified, theoretical form that is hard to engage with in a human and relational way. Law that is composed of arguments, ideas, and concepts gives the impression of not only disembodiment, but a general meta-physical existence. What is more, this impression is typically useful to legal processes, because, with this sense of above-ness, it is easier to cultivate the appearances of rationality, objectivity and impartiality. These, in turn, are often seen as crucial in ensuring perceptions of fairness, confidence in the law, and, ultimately, obedience to it.

We can understand legal abstraction as the process by which disputes, which always happen in context, get packaged and readied for legal consideration. It involves stripping narratives about arguments and fears, difficulties and indignities, down to the legally relevant essentials[1]. It allows diverse situations to be rendered comparable, which facilitates the application of rules, the utilisation of analogies, and the identification of precedents. For many academics in disciplines in the humanities, arts, and social sciences, though, a

[1] Law "drops almost everything" in Latour's (2010, 264) terms, in order to "go everywhere and make everything coherent" (Latour 2010, 264)

certain ruthlessness accompanies the act of abstraction—the violence of truncation—because it is often in the context, background, sociology, history, anthropology, and psychology surrounding events that we arrive at a full understanding of them. Via abstraction, law claims monopoly over relevance itself.

Court hearings are sites of abstraction. Their purpose is to hear testimonies, narratives, and representations, and extract from them what is legally relevant and astute. Judges, and the other legal professionals involved, are hearing for resonances between the accounts given and their legal ways of ordering the world (whether this is really *listening* is an interesting question—see Back 2007).

As this core work of court hearings proceeds, the impression of law as rational, objective, and impartial must be maintained. This is immensely challenging because it is in court hearings that the humanity and fallibility of the law comes into view in the person of the judge, as well as the other people involved: the court hearing involves exposure of the law as a human institution. Furthermore, it is in court hearings that the reliance of the law on a myriad spectrum of forms of cooperation, coproduction, and material assemblages can be seen. The disruption of the law is a common occurrence in courts, from delays, recesses, and adjournments, to contempt of court. The fragility of the law, which is always there in its textual form but hidden behind the authority of words and the impersonalism of documents, is most at risk of showing itself in the court.

Consequently, efforts to portray the law as separate from social life reach their greatest intensity via the symbolism of the courtroom and courthouse: their micro-geographies, architecture, forms of address, modes of speech, etiquette, routines, and schedules. The paraphernalia of the court can arguably be viewed as compensatory: a sort of prop to shore up the very valuable and important image of the law in a situation in which it is at risk.

It is for these reasons at least that court ethnography offers such promise and is such an exciting prospect to a researcher. Firstly, observing court hearings allows the observer to see something legally fundamental take place, which is often hidden away on laptops and in offices: namely the process of sorting—rejecting and connecting—explanations of real-life events to legal provisions. Via the window that court hearings offer onto legal processes, the observer can glimpse the realities of the abstractive process: not only its subjectivity, but the labour, skill, emotions, and power-dynamics involved, including gender and racial dynamics. Secondly, situating oneself in a court to conduct research is to be located at the epicentre of the struggle between abstract law and law in real life, law as separate and law as fragile, self-contained, and contingent. Court ethnography foregrounds this very struggle, a feature of the approach that legal minds and established ways of thinking might not always welcome (Darian-Smith 2004). It is disruptive and constructively critical (Flood 2005). In particular, court ethnography offers a very different "way in" to understanding the law to that offered by legal texts. One is able to view the constant efforts to construct the image of the law and in particular the various failures and slippages of these very efforts. From the behind-the-scenes glimpses of judges having their lunch and driving into and out of the car park, to the complex sociology of the waiting areas and the banter between security guards, the courthouse offers a view of the underbelly of the law, a vision of its mechanics in "abundant, concrete detail" (Bochner 2000, 270).

We might refer to these mechanics as the logistics of law, a concept which I think holds a good deal of promise. By legal logistics I mean the complex assembling, keeping going, moving and flowing, service work, making safe, procuring, transporting and gathering, notetaking, interpreting and translating, visiting and arriving that makes a court hearing, and hence many legal processes, possible (Gill et al. 2022). Legal logistics set the rhythm of courthouses and courtrooms, and determine their spaces and schedules, both in virtual, online contexts and physically. Viewed logistically, courts resemble legal factories, with inputs, speeds, quality controls, and outputs. In military parlance, logistics refers to the auxiliary, ancillary functions of supply crews and teams who provide the combatants with ammunition, fuel and food (Neilson 2012). In the social sciences there is a keen (if rather belated) interest in logistics, ranging from insights into capitalist supply chains all the way to the logistification of border control processes in Europe (Coe 2020; Vianelli 2022). An appreciation of logistical activities that facilitate and make possible "frontline" legal functions like judging and lawyering is important to understand the way law is shaped by financial, economic, and social factors, the conditions that give rise to good and bad quality law and, ultimately, the prerequisites for justice. Many of these prerequisites are material, which speaks to recent interest in legal materiality. Court ethnography enables researchers to glimpse not only the edifice of structures—material, social, cultural, psychological, linguistic, corporeal—that enable the law to function but also the investment that goes into them (or doesn't), betraying the fact that, after all and as we always knew, the law is nothing more than an effect produced by a constant effort to assemble, conjure, mimic, perform, enact, and stage the law itself.

Court ethnography, of course, is no panacea. It can be extremely demanding work both emotionally and physically (court houses not being known for their comfy seats). It can offer a very partial view of the law without access to legal papers, or even, necessarily, the viewpoints of the people involved in the research questions. Court ethnography might also, arguably, be exposed to the risk of basing understanding of legal processes on precisely the projected impression of the law that is visible from courtrooms and courthouses. Given the controlled and performed nature of legal hearings, court ethnography needs to be conducted critically and thoughtfully, aware of not only what can be seen in the court but also what is missing and made invisible (Gill et al. 2020). It can also struggle to find legitimacy amongst those who might look for "Black Letter" reasons to change things, or statistical insights into legal processes as the basis for redesigning them. Aside from all this, it can be extremely time intensive, tedious occasionally, and frustrating (when, for example, sessions do not run or are delayed).

Nevertheless, court ethnography does many things and holds immense potential, especially in current times as Sarah Klosterkamp and Lisa Flower's eloquent introduction to this volume amply demonstrates. It usually lets judges and other legal actors know they are being watched, which can be important for holding legal systems to account. And it can offer a view of legal systems and processes back to legal decision makers and actors who are often so embedded and immersed in legal matters that they can struggle to see themselves and the systems in which they operate through fresh eyes. As such, the method is rich and promising. "[D]eep and thick ethnography is one of the best routes we have in comprehending the complexity of law and legal processes in a changing society" Starr and Goodale (2002, 8) write. The chapters contained in this book are exemplary in demonstrating its effectiveness and the helpful, practical tips that the chapters offer to researchers doing court ethnography will be invaluable for future research. The range and breadth of topics in the volume is impressive, the organisation of the chapters and sections is thoughtful and effective, and the editors and authors can be congratulated on making an important advance in this field.

June 2023

Nick Gill
University of Exeter
Exeter, England

References

Back, Les. 2007. *The Art of Listening*. Berg.

Bochner, Arthur P. 2000. Criteria Against Ourselves. *Qualitative Inquiry* 6(2): 266–272.

Coe, Neil M. 2020. Logistical Geographies. Geography Compass 14(10) e12506.

Darian-Smith, Eve. 2004. "Ethnographies of law" in Sarat, Austin (ed.). 2004. *The Blackwell Companion to Law and Society*. Blackwell, 545–568.

Flood, John. 2005. "Socio-legal ethnography" in Banakar, Reza and Max Travers (eds.) *Theory and Method in Socio-Legal Research*. Hart, 33–48.

Gill, Nick, Jennifer Allsopp, Andrew Burridge, Daniel Fisher, Melanie Griffiths, Jessica Hambly, Nicole Hoellerer, Natalia Paszkiewicz, and Rebecca Rotter. 2020. What's Missing From Legal Geography and Materialist Studies of Law? Absence and the Assembling of Asylum Appeal Hearings in Europe. *Transactions of the Institute of British Geographers*, 45(4): 937–951.

Latour, Bruno. 2010. *The Making of Law: An Ethnography of the Conseil d'Etat*. Polity.

Neilson, Brett. 2012. Five theses on understanding logistics as power *Distinktion: Journal of Social Theory*, 13(3): 322–339.

Starr, June, and Mark Goodale. 2002. "Introduction: Legal ethnography: New Dialogues, Enduring Methods" in Starr, June, and Mark Goodale (eds.). 2002. *Practicing Ethnography in Law: New Dialogues, Enduring Methods*. Palgrave Macmillan, 1–10.

Vianelli, Lorenzo. 2022. Warehousing Asylum Seekers: The Logistification of Reception. *Environment and Planning D: Society and Space*, 40(1): 41–59.

Acknowledgements

We would like to thank all the contributors who have been involved in this project and whose hard work, enthusiasm, and spirit of curiosity have consistently inspired us in our own research. In particular, the generosity of all those involved in giving precious time, composing thoughtful insights on each other's contributions at the authors' workshop, formulating and providing critical feedback, and showing support to fellow contributors throughout this process has been wonderful to be a part of.

This project includes an exciting range of contributors from a broad span of disciplines who have come together in their united interest in courtroom ethnography. By giving insight into each other's work, they have shaped this project into the interdisciplinary and collaborative process we had envisioned. Not least the support shown to early career researchers who may find themselves at a particularly precarious point of their career has been fantastic to behold.

Thank you to Greta Wierichs for your help and assistance in compiling the index for this volume. Your open eye for all the hidden nuances and details within each chapter was especially helpful to get started.

Thank you also to Palgrave for providing us with the opportunity to work on this project. As early career researchers, we truly appreciate your continuous support and trust in us throughout the entire process: from proposal submission to final publication.

Lisa Flower
Sarah Klosterkamp

Contents

Notes on Contributors

Tasniem Anwar works as an Assistant Professor at the Department of Criminology at the Vrije Universiteit Amsterdam. She conducted her Ph.D. on the prosecution of terrorism financing at the department of political science at the University of Amsterdam. The findings are published in academic journals including *Security Dialogue* and *The Journal of Law and Society* and the *European Journal of International Relations*. Her current research interests include counter-terrorism financing, terrorism trials, and emerging security technologies for countering terrorism. She is co-convenor of the webinar series "Decolonising Europe" and a senior organiser of the Doing IPS seminar series in the Netherlands.

Moa Bladini LLD is a Senior Lecturer in criminal law at the Department of Law, University of Gothenburg. Bladini's research expertise covers both criminal law, in particular gender-based violence on and offline, and criminal procedure law, including court room ethnography. Her research is defined by a theoretical and methodological interest, including feminist legal theory, sociology of emotions, interdisciplinarity, and ethnographic methods.

Kerstin Bree Carlson is Associate Professor at Roskilde University, where she teaches law and society-related topics. She is also affiliated with iCourts at the University of Copenhagen and The American University of Paris. She is the author of Model(ing) Justice: Perfecting the Promise of International Criminal Law (CUP 2018) and The Justice Laboratory: International Law in Africa (Chatham House/Brookings 2022), and co-editor of The President on Trial: Prosecuting Hissène Habré (OUP 2020) and Transitional Justice in Aparadigmatic Contexts: Accountability, Recognition and Disruption (Routledge 2023) as well as several articles and book chapters on topics in international criminal law and transitional justice. She writes frequently for The Conversation blog. Her current research focuses on justice constructions in terror law in France, Denmark, and Colombia.

Fiona Donson is Senior lecturer in the School of Law, University College Cork, Ireland. She is Director of the Traveller Equality and Justice Project, an EU funded project on access to justice for Travellers in relation to denial of access to goods and services (TEJP) which she runs with her colleague Dr. Samantha Morgan-Williams. Fiona's research includes access to justice, administrative justice, and human rights. Her publications include *Parental Imprisonment and Children's Rights* (with Dr. Aisling Parkes—eds. Routledge, 2021) and *Law and Public Administration in Ireland* (with Dr. Darren O' Donovan, Clarus, 2015). Before joining UCC in 2007 Fiona worked as a human rights practitioner and child rights advocate for a number of years in Cambodia. Fiona is also chair of the Free Legal Advice Centre's "Equal Access Project", which provided equality law training to minority group community advocates.

Lisa Flower is currently an Associate Senior Lecturer at the Department of Sociology, Lund University. Her research expertise covers law and emotion along with the digitalisation of the courtroom with particular focus on court reporting and the use of video links in trials. Flower's publications have explored courtroom interactions and the emotions within (*Interactional Justice: The role of emotions in the performance of loyalty,* Routledge 2019), live blogging of criminal trials, and a forthcoming book which presents a sociological examination of the digital courtroom (*The Digital Courtroom: Participation, attendance, engagement and consumption,* Routledge 2024).

Tea Fredriksson earned her Ph.D. in criminology at Stockholm University in 2021. She currently works at the Department of Criminology at Stockholm University, as an Assistant Lecturer and postdoc researcher. Her main research interests are spaces of punishment (such as prisons and courtrooms), cultural (re)presentations of crime, punishment, and victimhood, and interdisciplinary research using intersectional frameworks. She has published in book and article form, on topics ranging from prison autobiographies and victim-survivors in film to how women's desistance from crime can be understood as uncanny. Largely, her research can be said to be at home in criminology's spectral turn, taking an interest in what lies beneath sociocultural (re)presentations and imag(inari)es of crime.

Jessica Hambly is a Senior Lecturer and Co-Director of the Law Reform and Social Justice programme at the Australian National University College of Law. She is a socio-legal scholar with interests relating to asylum and refugee law and procedure. Jessica's Ph.D. "*Advocates in Asylum Appeals*" (2017, University of Bristol) was funded by a UK Economic and Social Research Council Studentship. She is co-author (with Nick Gill, Nicole Hoellerer, and Dan Fisher) of *Inside Asylum Appeals: Access, Participation and Procedure in Europe* (forthcoming, Routledge). Jessica worked with a number of grassroots refugee and migrant rights organisations in the UK, France, and Greece before moving to Australia in 2020.

Anita Heber was promoted to Associate Professor in criminology in 2012, and she works at the Department of Criminology at Stockholm University. Her main research interests are victimology, the victim–offender overlap, sex trafficking, and organised crime. She has published a number of articles, reports, and books on these subjects, and she has led several research projects within these areas. Heber has also been teaching for two decades at both an undergraduate and a postgraduate level; her main teaching areas are qualitative and quantitative methods, criminological theory, victimology, as well as media and crime. She is a member of several scientific boards and is also the director of studies for the Ph.D. programme and the advanced level in criminology at Stockholm University.

Jeanne Hersant is an Assistant Professor at the School of Social Work of the Pontificia Universidad Católica de Chile. Her research includes studies of access to justice and access to science. She has research pieces published in *Current Sociology, Law & Social Inquiry, Notices of the American Mathematical Society*. She is the co-author with Hilary Sommerlad, Nina Holvast, Luca Verzelloni, Stefanie Gustafsson, Rebecca Sandefur, and Tom Clarke of "Paralegals and the casualization of legal labour markets" in Rick Abel et al. (eds) *Lawyers in Twenty First Century Societies, vol. 2 Comparisons and Theories*, Hart Publishing. She also published "Proceso penal inquisitivo y acceso a la justicia en Chile: un estudio socio-histórico de los empleados judiciales y sus quehaceres en el marco de la práctica de la delegación de funciones (1974-2012)" in *Política Criminal* (2022). Between 2018 and 2022, she was the lead researcher of two research programmes funded by the Chilean research agency (ANID): an ethnographic study on "Judicial reforms and access to justice in Chile (2000-2020)" (Fondecyt Regular 1180038) featuring Fabiola

Miranda-Pérez as an associate researcher, and "Women in mathematics in Chile. Sociology of a scientific field from an interdisciplinary and gender perspective" (PIA-ANID ANILLO SOC180025). She is currently the coordinator of the group on Gender, Science and Technology within the Latin American Interdisciplinary Gender Network (LAIGN).

Alex Jeffrey is Professor of Human Geography at the University of Cambridge and a Fellow of Emmanuel College. Alex's research has explored state building and law making in the wake of mass violence, in particular in Bosnia and Herzegovina and, more recently, in Myanmar. His publications have examined the nature of state institutions constructed through international instruments (*The Improvised State*, Wiley Blackwell, 2013), the legal geographies of court spaces (three progress reports in *Progress in Human Geography*, 2019, 2020, and 2021), and the political and legal implications of attempting to construct a new legal institution in the wake of war (*The Edge of Law: Legal Geographies of a War Crimes Court*, Cambridge University Press, 2020).

Louise Victoria Johansen is an Associate Professor at the Faculty of Law, University of Copenhagen. She works within the area of Law and Anthropology and is theoretically inspired by the field of sociology of knowledge, intersectionality, and the role of emotion in law. Her research focuses on knowledge processes across different criminal justice institutions such as the police, the prosecutor's office, the judiciary, and the prison and probation service. Using ethnographic methods, she has studied the production and use of pre-sentence reports; lay adjudication and lay participation; victims' perceptions of the criminal justice process; and remand prisoners' expectations of a "fair trial". Some of the analytical perspectives from these different studies have resulted in the following articles:

(2023) The power of professional ideals: Understanding and handling victims' emotions in criminal cases. *International Review of Victimology*, 29(2): 236–258.

(2022) Between Remand and Verdict: Ethnic Minority Prisoners' Legal and Penal Consciousness. *The British Journal of Criminology*, 62(4): 965–981.

(2019): Lay participation in Danish Crime Trials: On the Interaction Between Lay and Professional Judges During Deliberation. *Journal of Law and Society* 46(4): 586–611.

(2019): "Impressed" by feelings: How judges assess defendants' emotional expressions in Danish courtrooms. *Social & Legal Studies* 28(2): 250–269.

Sarah Klosterkamp is a feminist urban, political, and legal geographer, currently employed at the University of Bonn, Germany. Her work investigates how the law proceeds and multiplies classed and racialized geographies of inequalities within and through state-driven institutions such as courts, asylum facilities, employment offices, and carceral spaces. Within her current project as a PostDoc, she spotlights eviction processes and the housing crisis in Germany and the UK. Furthermore and within the scientific community of Human Geography, she is committed as an Editorial Board Member for Political Geography Open Research,Law & Space (un)Journal and *ACME: An International Journal for Critical Geographies*, she holds the position of vice-chair of the *Legal Geography Speciality Group* at the *American Association of Geographers* and serves as the chair of the *AK Feministische Geographien.* Beyond academic researching and publishing, she is also passionate about teaching, data visualisation, and open-science communication, some of which she also undertakes as a freelancer at DER SPIEGEL and SPIEGEL International.

Julie Laursen is an Assistant Professor and Marie Sklodowska-Curie scholar at the Faculty of Law, University of Copenhagen. In her previous position as a Research Associate at the University of Cambridge, she examined the Nordic exceptionalism thesis—put at its simplest, the idea that punishment practices in the Nordic (inclusionary) countries are more liberal and humane than those in neo-liberal (exclusionary) nations. Together with colleagues, Julie compared prison practices in Norway with prisons in England & Wales and published extensively in the field of comparative penology (see for example Crewe et al 2022; Crewe, Laursen & Mjåland 2022; Laursen 2022; Laursen, Mjåland & Crewe 2019; Mjåland & Laursen 2021). Julie's current research project entitled "Indeterminate sentencing and imprisonment – an interdisciplinary study of the experiences of court processes and prison practices" is based in Denmark and provides an in-depth examination of the experience of being indeterminately sentenced by a court and of serving an indeterminate sentence in prison. Julie's broader research interests are prisons, comparative penology, indeterminate sentences, and the moral aspects of punishment.

Sara Lembrechts is a doctoral researcher in the Migration Law Research Group at Ghent University. Her Ph.D. (FWO.OPR.2020.0017.10, 2020–2024) focuses on the position and rights of children, young people, and families in appellate asylum proceedings in Belgium. Her research is multidisciplinary in combining a case law analysis with legal ethnography, qualitative interviews and co-creative workshops with children, young people, judges, and other stakeholders in the appellate asylum procedure. Sara has a Master's in Children's Rights and Childhood Studies, an LLM in International Laws and a Bachelor's in European Studies. She has worked as a researcher and policy adviser for the Children's Rights Knowledge Centre (2012–2020) and was involved in several research projects about children's rights and child abduction at the University of Antwerp (2016–2021). Her publications and research interests cover children's rights, child participation in legal proceedings, child abduction, and knowledge management. She co-authored the *Children's Rights Legal Commentary on the UN Convention on the Rights of the Child and its Protocols* (Edward Elgar, 2019) and was co-editor for the *Routledge International Handbook of Children's Rights Studies* (2015).

Fabiola Miranda-Pérez holds a Ph.D. in Political Science from the University of Grenoble Alpes, France, she is currently a faculty member at the Faculty of Health and Social Sciences of the Universidad de las Americas in Chile. Her recent work includes "Psychosocial Professionals in Chilean Justice Institutions. Reflections based on the experiences and practice of psychologists and social workers". The *British Journal of Social Work* (2022) and "Adaptaciones metodológicas y etnografía virtual en una investigación sobre profesionales psicosociales en justicia: desafíos del aprender haciendo". *Antípoda. Revista de Antropología y Arqueología* (2022). Between 2019 and 2022, she was the lead researcher of the Fondecyt Iniciación grant from the National Agency for Research and Development of Chile (ANID) N°11190123 "New repertoires of public action: psychosocial professionals in the context of family and criminal justice reform in Chile".

Samantha Morgan-Williams is a Lecturer at the Centre for Criminal Justice and Human Rights in the School of Law, University College Cork and coordinator of the TEJP Legal Clinic which provides free legal advice to Traveller victims of discrimination. Samantha and Dr. Fiona Donson will publish "*Traveller Law in Ireland*" with Clarus Press in 2023.

Samantha's current research focuses on access to justice for the Traveller Community and non-discrimination law. Samantha also has a community development background having previously groups. In this capacity, Samantha provided legal training to Traveller women's groups focused on empowerment and education on discrimination in accessing goods and services. As part of this participatory and community-led research, Samantha has received funding from Travellers of North Cork to establish the "Traveller Court Support Initiative" training programme, the first of its kind in Ireland, training Traveller women to act as peer-supports for other Traveller non-discrimination litigants.

Axel Pohn-Weidinger is an Associate Professor in the Department of Sociology at the University of Strasbourg. His research focuses on the sociology of the welfare state, the sociology of law, and the ethnography of literacy. He is currently conducting research on public ombuds institutions from a comparative perspective.

Emma Rowden is a Senior Lecturer in Architecture at Oxford Brookes University. An internationally recognised expert on courthouse design, for the past fifteen years her research has focused on how the built environment impacts upon perceptions of procedural fairness. She has published widely in this field, reporting on several research projects, including her doctoral research into the impact of videolink use on legal proceedings and courthouse design. More recently, she has collaborated with Professor Linda Mulcahy (University of Oxford) on a series of award-winning user-tested public information films designed to support court users navigate the online justice system, as well as the book The Democratic Courthouse (Routledge, 2020) which charts an untold modern history of ideas about court design in the UK.

Thomas Scheffer studied sociology in Bielefeld. Professor of Sociology with an emphasis on interpretative social research at the Institute for Sociology, Goethe University Frankfurt. Member of the Konzil of the German Sociological Association. His research fields are political ethnography, discourse studies, sociology of law, political sociology, case study method, and qualitative methodology. Scheffer developed the trans-sequential analytics (TSA) as a critical ethnomethodology, in order to link event and process of discourse work. At the moment, Scheffer works on a Sociology of existential problems. His main publications are: Asylgewährung (2001), Adversarial Case-Making (2010), Criminal Defence and Procedure (with Kati Hannken-Illjes and Alexander Kozin, 2010), and Polizeilicher Kommunitarismus (with Christiane Howe, Eva Kiefer, Yannik Porsché and Dörte Negnal, 2017).

Sara Uhnoo is Associate Professor of Sociology at the Department of Sociology and Work Science, University of Gothenburg. Her expertise covers criminology and youth research, and issues related to control and prevention of different types of crime and disasters. Recently she has been particularly interested in the implementation of consent-based rape legislations, feminist criminology, sociology of emotions, youth crime, and voluntary policing.

Åsa Wettergren is Professor in Sociology at the Department of Sociology and Work Science, University of Gothenburg. Wettergren is a recognised scholar in the Sociology of emotions, and since 2012 working in research projects on

Law and Emotions, and on Emotions in the environmental & climate movement. She has published extensively on these topics in both international journals and books at international publishers.

List of Figures

1

Introduction to Courtroom Ethnography

Sarah Klosterkamp and Lisa Flower

Courtrooms are sites where both the mundane and the life-changing are deliberated, evaluated and decided upon. Child custody battles, traffic violations, asylum appeals, contractual disputes, war crimes, climate actions, murder, defamation, even pigeon-related damage claims, all are handled in courtrooms. The courthouse, as the bigger unit of this socio-legal setting, can be understood as an arena and symbol of justice and democracy yet concomitantly perceived as a site where power is exercised over culturally and economically disadvantaged groups (Banaker and Travers 2013; Burridge and Gill 2016; Crenshaw 1989, 1991; Nader 1972). It is clear that the courthouse as a whole, and the courtroom in particular, can be understood as the center of societal, national and global conflict resolution (Faria et al. 2020; Jeffrey 2019; Walenta 2020). It is therefore paramount to understand questions of how the law shapes, renders, undermines and uplifts justice within society? What do we learn by observing the settings where the law is put into action? Which individuals, themes and prompts are most prominent within

S. Klosterkamp (✉)
University of Bonn, Bonn, Germany
e-mail: s.klosterkamp@uni-bonn.de

L. Flower
Lund University, Lund, Sweden
e-mail: lisa.flower@soc.lu.se

L. Flower and S. Klosterkamp (eds.), *Courtroom Ethnography*,
https://doi.org/10.1007/978-3-031-37985-7_1

legal settings, and which remain absent? And which jurisdictional settings and sites are most prevalent to investigate this nexus?

For us, as Editors of this volume, the courthouse and the legal proceedings within represent a vast and vital multi-disciplinary research field regarding a wide array of empirical questions and fields of study. Moreover, we consider the courthouse to be a nexus of situated and grounded knowledge stemming from the multitude of actors that inhabit court spaces such as the judiciary, lawyers, juries, scholars, activists, defendants, plaintiffs, witnesses, family members and many more. Ethnography is frequently drawn upon to access the social-legal entanglements inside and with this edited volume we hope to provide a broad overview of contemporary approaches, fieldwork and challenges.

The starting point for this edited volume is that ethnography enables us to focus on social activity in situ (Atkinson 2015; Cicorel 1995; Hammersley and Atkinson 2019; Roach Anleu and Mack 2019) sharing social actors' everyday lives. It gives us insight into the routines and practices, the symbolism and social identities, and the day-to-day interactions, happenings and occurrences taking place around us (Paik and Harris 2015; Jeffrey 2019; Roach et al. 2016). In short, it helps us to attain understanding and insight into processes and interactions which are otherwise difficult—perhaps even impossible—to attain from other methods (Herbert 2000). The courtroom ethnographer thus observes interactions, events and scenes, seeking out patterns and rhythms, always striving to find the exception that reveals the underlying rule. Typically, observations have entailed participating in people's daily lives in a physical sense—shadowing lawyers to court, sitting in the public gallery, hanging out in the waiting areas and have thus entailed participating in a traditional face-to-face sense, deemed necessary for the researcher to perceive the rich ebb and flow of social information and the facilitation of nonverbal feedback (Goffman 1963, p. 17, also Collins 2004). However, with current shifts in many jurisdictions away from physical trials taking place in the courtroom, to certain aspects—even entire trials—being held remotely via video link, the work of the courtroom ethnographer is also shifting, moving towards that of the remote ethnographer (Postill 2015). Indeed, we are in the midst of a reterritorialization of court processes as they become distributed across legal, carceral and domestic spaces (Jeffrey 2020, personal correspondence). The road ahead for the courtroom ethnographer is truly an exciting one!

Ethnographic studies of courtroom interactions have a long history dating back to Pound's (1910) notions on the advantages of studying law in the books versus law in action, the work of Cicourel (1968), Emerson (1969) and Bortner (1982) on juvenile justice, Carlen's (1976) study of magistrates' courts in action, Warren's (1982) research on insanity hearings and Rock's (1993) analysis of the social world of the criminal court and Latour's (2010) extensive ethnography of the Conseil d'État (which included ethnographic observation of the aforementioned pigeon-related damage claims). Alongside this we find ethnomethodologically informed studies such as Garfinkel's (1956, 1967) on degradation ceremonies and jurors, and Atkinson and Drew's (1979) work on verbal interactions in courts.

However—and importantly—we believe that the courthouse and, in particular, trials, are currently seeing a revival of interest, perhaps even a legal turn, as reflected in the rise of ethnographic studies of the law and its enactment in the courtroom (Faria et al. 2020). This, in turn, presents a need to focus on the ethnographic eye currently observing these settings—an eye that may be ethnographically honed for the first time, or which may belong to the more experienced ethnographer observing novel interactions—perhaps even sensitive interactions—or facing ethical or methodological issues. In short, a deeper exploration of the research being conducted in courthouse settings has contemporary interest to a wide range of disciplines and actors. This is particularly pertinent as the trials and tribulations within the courtroom tend to mirror core debates in the social and cultural sciences. These investigations—of which we unite a wide variety within this edited volume—help us to understand how the law works, how it is contested over social struggles and how it renders and challenges the society as a whole—and how to investigate these shifts and challenges over time and united with longstanding approaches as well as along more recent research topics, prompts and point of scholarly debates. We therefore hope this book can serve as a timely contribution to the rapidly growing field.

By bridging the gap between disciplines and empirical foci, this edited volume presents an overview of how to do courthouse ethnography including methodological challenges, grounded empirical insights and best-practice examples, by fusing together different themes and scopes of expertise, whilst also presenting the current state of the art for courthouse ethnography as a field—a theme running throughout the book. As such, we offer an extensive range of current research, practices and knowledges of the field, which currently remain unexplored in a cohesive and comprehensive text. Moreover, our aim for this book beyond a tool for teaching ethnography as a research method, is to provide a deeper and wider understanding of what goes on in the courtroom. In this book, we therefore showcase the work of an international range of more than 24 scholars from a multitude of disciplines including sociology, feminist legal geography, law and architecture and beyond. The contributions also reflect an international range of authors spanning Australia, the EU, the UK and Chile and include up-and-coming researchers alongside established academics and practitioners. In the following chapters, we join these contributors as they face hurdles and obstacles, unexpected events and deep insights. We follow them as the trials and tribulations of courtroom ethnography are divulged, dissected, discussed and demystified. We learn how to overcome boundaries and uplift marginalized voices, how to ethnographically investigate within different fields, and how to relate to the broader societal and political debates surrounding trials currently taking place. With such a range of contributions, our hope is to elevate the vibrant field of courtroom ethnography and present new perspective and future directions.

The textbook is organized into two thematically aligned Parts. The first part entitled "Doing and Teaching Courtroom Ethnography" focuses on how to conduct ethnographic research in the courtroom and its antechambers, including questions of positionality, reflexivity, practicalities, access and more. This part closes with a bonus chapter which expands the scope of the book to encompass teaching courtroom ethnography, provided by Axel Pohn-Weidinger. In Part II, "Contemporary and Critical Aspects of Courtroom Ethnography", the contributions dive more deeply into a selection of methodological, technical and ethical issues the courtroom ethnographer may face when conducting ethnographic fieldwork and offer glimpses into new directions and debates within the field. In Part I, each chapter concludes with practical tips and in Part II, each chapter concludes with further readings, making the book handy and vibrant both for ethnographic beginners and for experienced ethnographers with an interest in other perspectives, methods or modes of doing and experiencing courtroom ethnography in research and teaching.

We would like to uplift and highlight the rich and illuminating tradition of ethnographic accounts from four conceptual points of origin, namely by focusing on accounts that center on: the law and legal pluralism; legal legislation, knowledge and jurisdictions; the courtroom and its architecture and finally; the courtroom as a social sphere, before offering a closer look at what this volume and its contributions offer.

Starting with the law and legal pluralism, both the choice of the field of observation and the focus on what lawyers call "legal reality" follow a long tradition of work in the ethnography of justice, for which Roscoe Pound's (1910) maxim still applies: instead of studying "law in books", it is better to study "law in action" (see also Travers and Manzo 1997; Pollner 1987).

Whilst sociologists, geographers, anthropologists and other social scientists have long been interested in the law, the methodological step into the courthouse to actually observe law in action was only taken recently. This is perhaps surprising as it is precisely the gathering of "grounded data-sets" (Faria et al. 2020: 1107) that provide information for ethnographic research questions in different ways. Such data-sets enable us to critically reflect upon the narratives, sense-making and micro-interactions taking place within different court settings (Bennett and Layard 2015; Sylvestre et al. 2015; Walenta 2020). Empirically there is much to gain from such an approach, since court files remain inaccessible in many legal jurisdictions, but are revealed in the physical legal proceedings taking place in the courtroom (Jeffrey 2019, 2020; Klosterkamp 2021; Klosterkamp and Reuber 2017). By conducting ethnographic observations of court proceedings, not only can the details of these files be accessed, but also the ways in which they are performed, negotiated, constructed and conveyed. This has been done in past decades by research engaging with scholarly debates on different analytical frameworks and as such, by taking into account transactional analysis from thick description to discourse analysis towards processual/procedural approaches. These analytical approaches privilege different aspects of the ethnography and court specifics at place, and illustrate the rich and multiple ways of engaging with legal evidences contested, examined and negotiated in courts (Ahmed 2013; Berti and Bordia 2015; Darian-Smith 2017; Eppert and Roth 2021; Hannken-Illjes et al. 2006; Jeffrey 2021). Hence, by entering the court, an array of information and evidence contained within court files—such as witness reports, tapped phone calls, GPS data-sets, moving patterns and social service records—including how they are evaluated by those participating in proceedings, become accessible and are accessed by us, as researchers (Klosterkamp and Reuber 2017). However, it should be remembered that all of this data is also largely shaped by the level of jurisdiction and state law which brings us to the second aspect.

With regard to ethnographically informed courtroom accounts that center on legal legislation, knowledge and/or jurisdiction, the unit of inquiry is usually one specific type of case, followed by a sequence of other similar cases or points of focus within a particular jurisdiction. Specific procedures and the rules for participation and public access form the particular setting in which each type of case is negotiated and evaluated by the legal experts in the courtroom and shape the observability of each trial for the ethnographer (Klosterkamp and Reuber 2017: 258). Within these settings, linguistic forms may be important to attend to as they reveal strategic narratives through which the case is (re)constructed as an aggregate of collective, asymmetrically distributed knowledge (Hoffmann 2014: 290). For instance, by conducting sequential analyses focusing on "information processing, perspectivizations, interpretations and reinterpretations, fade-ins and fade-outs, weighting and preparation, arguments and counter-arguments" (Hoffmann 2014, 287; Scheffer 2010) the production of each court case by legal experts can be revealed over time (Anwar 2020). In this respect, the negotiation over a case outcome and its contribution to legal reasoning of a case constitutes a historical—and partially coincidental—composition of disparate parts. This contribution is sometimes subtle, sometimes expressed explicitly. Nevertheless, and within this analytical framework of the examination of legal legislation in action, the scope and valuation of the individual parts and outcomes may differ—sometimes considerably—depending on the legal system, type of court and prevailing law of evidence (see Scheffer et al. 2010 for a comparative approach of legal systems; see Márquez Porras 2021; Paik and Harris 2015 for specific aspects within the same legal system; see Keane and McKeown 2022 and Jeffrey 2021 for laws of evidence). Once again, this makes the courthouse a compelling arena for ethnographic investigation.

Leaving the courtroom and its legal proceedings, other researchers have focused on the courthouse itself and its architecture. These approaches use ethnographies to study the materialities of courts (Jeffrey 2019), including courthouse buildings, courtroom architecture and furniture design (Kumar 2017; Resnik and Curtis 2011; Rowden 2011; Klosterkamp 2021) along with design-induced courtroom atmospheres (Bens 2018; Gill et al. 2021; Klosterkamp 2023) and the associated sensory experiences (Flower 2020). These courtroom material environments and atmospheres at place also expand and deepen our insights of the courtroom itself, its national security framings, threat perceptions, aims and possibilities for seeking justice, by bridging the local and national to more global notions of the law and its different shapes and objectives (Burridge and Gill 2016; Brickell et al. 2021; Brickell and Cuomo 2019; Faria et al. 2020; Flower 2019a, b; Jeffrey 2020; Klosterkamp 2023; Ramirez et al. 2021). Such geopolitical aspects are crucial for understanding legal spheres because, as Mulcahy (2011: 1) writes that "the environment in which the trial takes place can be seen as a physical expression of our relationship with the ideals of justice". Moreover, going forward in an age where trials are rapidly moving towards the digital sphere also entails increasing our understanding of how the ceremony of a trial can be upheld in the absence of key symbols (Rossner and Tait 2021). Courtroom ethnography plays a vital role in this.

Another key theme of research is understanding the court as a social sphere (e.g. Bergman Blix and Wettergren 2018; Flower, 2016 2019a; Jacobson et al.

2016; Mann 1985; Roach Anleu and Mack 2017). These studies use ethnography to enable a "disciplined unravelling" (Rock 2001: 31) of the practices, performances and understandings legal actors and lay participants engage in, and with, in the courthouse. Nevertheless, most studies on courtroom spaces and experiences privilege the immediate moment and local, and have a tendency to focus on audiovisual aspects to the detriment of the other senses, also reflecting the law's wider occularcentrism. In turn, although attention to "the local" and to audiovisual aspects is vital to an instructive ethnography, it must not deflect us "from connecting to past and present structures of power, the very structures that are mirrored, sustained, or disrupted in courtrooms" (Faria et al. 2020: 1097). In this way, we are able to understand the social construction of the courtroom as a society in miniature, with regimes and rules, scenes and sanctions, deviancies and even dullness.

In resonance with this rich scholarly work, we aim to connect long-standing (Herbert 2000; Stiles 2009) and more recent calls for ethnographies of the law (Atkinson 2015; Bennett and Layard 2015; Billo and Mountz 2016; Braverman et al. 2014; Klosterkamp 2022, 2023; Márquez Porras 2021; Travers 2021), by bridging them to feminist, practitioner and activism-engaged interventions (Brickell and Cuomo 2019; Faria et al. 2020; Gill and Hynes 2021) and by opening up for broader and indeed, thicker, empirical focus (Coffey 2018; Flower 2020; Gorman 2019; Ramirez et al. 2021; Walenta 2020). Whilst the current corpus has much to offer to an analysis of the law, in the chapters to come, we gather various lineages and fields in order to present a comprehensive and international overview of current research and methodological considerations when planning and conducting ethnographic research in the courthouse.

Part I is committed to the overarching theme of "Doing Courtroom Ethnography". The first contribution, "Framing the View", written by Jess Hambly, introduces us to the theme by taking the reader back to the questions of what we see, how we decide what is important and what to focus on when planning and conducting an ethnography of courtroom trials. The next chapter, "Negotiating Access", written by Sara Uhnoo, Moa Bladini and Åsa Wettergren, deepens these insights by presenting different strategies and best-practice approaches on how to negotiate access to the courthouse, in particular when attempting to gain access to specific court proceedings centring on sensitive topics. Questions of navigating ethical challenges and power disbalances when doing courtroom ethnography by amplifying feminist methodological thinking, positionality and politics of fieldwork, are then discussed by Sarah Klosterkamp and Tasniem Anwar in Chapter 4, "Positionality and Research Ethics". This is followed by Alex Jeffrey's work on

"Challenging the Authority of Sight" which explores what is knowable using courtroom observation and the limits to understanding trial processes using ethnography in Chapter 5. Chapter 6 is written by Thomas Scheffer and focuses on "Doing a Trans-Sequential Analysis of Courtroom Proceedings". The final chapter of this part, "Teaching Courtroom Ethnography", written by Axel Pohn-Weidinger, serves as an additional bonus chapter as it sets the stage for those interested in teaching courtroom ethnography for undergraduates and graduates and includes a step-by-step approach to planning and conducting such teaching.

Part II, "Contemporary and Critical aspects of Courtroom Ethnography", aims to deepen the forementioned aspects of doing courtroom ethnography by enriching it with more empirical sites and foci. This part begins with "Video Links and Eyework" by Lisa Flower, Sarah Klosterkamp and Emma Rowden which explores how courtroom ethnography can aid understanding of the importance of eye contact in a time when video links are rapidly moving towards becoming a commonplace form of participation in trials. Chapter 9, "Hate Crimes, Institutional Racism and Reverse Engineering" written by Kerstin Bree Carlson, focuses on the subtle institutional ways of discrimination depicted by drawing on a recent example of hate crime in Denmark. This is followed by "Children and Families in Asylum Processes", a deep dive into the architectural and structural setting unaccompanied children and families in asylum processes are facing in Belgium, written by Sara Lembrechts. "Moral Communication in Courts" is then illustrated by Julie Laurson and Louise Victoria Johansen in Chapter 11, which examines how judges in Denmark communicate punishment to defendants. Chapter 12, "The Court as a Site of Rediscrimination" by Samantha Morgan-Williams and Fiona Donson takes us to a particularly novel topic, namely how the court may serve as a site for re-discriminating members of marginalized and deprived community members, such as the Irish Travellers in the UK. The penultimate chapter of the book, written by Jeanne Hersant and Fabiola Miranda Perèz, explores "Courtroom Observations in Contexts of Exceptionality" and the plethora of challenges the courthouse ethnographer faces when conducting ethnography in extraordinary times, such as during Chilean uprisings and pandemics. The final chapter of the book examines how "Courtroom Performances of Masculinities and Victimhood" are performed in the Swedish courtroom and is provided with insightful empirics collected and analysed by Tea Fredriksson and Anita Heber.

This book should be read as a flowing account of the current state of play of courtroom ethnography. Each contributor has been invited to reflect upon the themes in their own chapter and those emerging in their fellow authors' chapters in order to ensure an organic and cohesive line to the book, regardless of the breadth of multi-disciplinarity and wealth of empirical focus. In short, we hope that this book can be read and enjoyed by scholars and students, criminologists and criminal lawyers, sociologists and civil rights activists alike. We are convinced, that this rich collection of emerging trends, challenges and new fields of inquiry proposes much to learn and depart from, for further research and/or collaborations. In short, there is so much more to do!

And finally, we would like to thank all of the marvellous contributors who have made this book project a fantastic editorial journey for us. The collegiality, encouragement and support that has emerged throughout this process have been inspiring and we salute you!

References

Ahmed, Fauzia E. 2013. The compassionate courtroom: Feminist governance, discourse, and Islam in a Bangladeshi Shalish. *Feminist Formations* 25 (1): 157–183.

Anwar, Tasniem. 2020. Unfolding the past, proving the present: Social media evidence in terrorism finance court cases. *International Political Sociology* 14 (4): 382–398.

Atkinson, J. Maxwell, and Paul Drew. 1979. *Order in court: The organisation of verbal interaction in judicial settings*. London: Macmillan.

Atkinson, Paul. 2015. *For ethnography*. Londres: Sage.

Banaker, Reza, and Max Travers. 2013. *Law and social theory*. Oxford: Hart Publishing.

Bennett, Luke, and Antonia Layard. 2015. Legal geography: Becoming spatial detectives. *Geography Compass* 9 (7): 406–422.

Bens, Jonas. 2018. The courtroom as an affective arrangement: Analysing atmospheres in courtroom ethnography. *The Journal of Legal Pluralism and Unofficial Law* 50 (3): 336–355.

Bergman Blix, Stina, and Åsa Wettergren. 2018. *Professional emotions in court*. Abingdon: Routledge.

Berti, Daniela, and Devika Bordia. 2015. *Regimes of legality: Ethnography of criminal cases in South Asia*. New Delhi: Oxford University Press.

Billo, Emily and Alison Mountz. 2016. For institutional ethnography. *Progress in Human Geography*, 40 (2): 199–220.

Bortner, Marvelm. 1982. *Inside a juvenile court: The tarnished ideal of individualized justice*. New York & London: New York University Press.

Braverman, Irus, Blomley, Nick, Delaney, David and Alexandre Kedar. 2014. *The expanding spaces of law*. Palo Alto: Stanford University Press.

Brickell, Katherine, and Dana Cuomo. 2019. Feminist geolegality. *Progress in Human Geography* 43 (1): 104–122.

Brickell, Katherine, Alex Jeffrey, and Fiona McConnell. 2021. Practising legal geography. *Area* 53 (4): 557–561.

Burridge, Andrew, and Nick Gill. 2016. Conveyor-Belt justice: Precarity, access to justice, and uneven geographies of legal aid in UK asylum appeals. *Antipode* 49 (1): 23–42.

Carlen, Pat. 1976. *Magistrates' justice*. London: Martin Robertson & Company Ltd.

Cicourel, Aaron V. 1968. *The social organization of juvenile justice*. New York: John Wiley.

Cicorel, Aaron. 1995. *The social organization of juvenile justice*. New Brunswick: Transaction.

Crenshaw, Kimberlé. 1989. Demarginalizing the intersection of race and sex: A black feminist critique of antidiscrimination doctrine, feminist theory and antiracist politics. *University of Chicago Legal Forum* 1989 (1): 139–167.

Crenshaw, Kimberlé. 1991. Mapping the margins: Intersectionality, identity politics, and violence against women of color. *Stanford Law Review* 43 (6): 1241–1299.

Coffey, Amanda. 2018. *Doing ethnography*. London: Sage.

Collins, Randal. 2004. *Interaction ritual chains*. Princeton: Princeton University Press.

Darian-Smith, Eve, ed. 2017. *Ethnography and law*. Abingdon: Routledge.

Emerson, Robert M. 1969. *Judging delinquents: Context and process in juvenile court*. Chicago: Aldine de Gruyter.

Eppert, Kerstin, and Victoria Roth. 2021. Radical men and sympathizing women? Gendered constructions of agency in charges of terrorism in Germany. *New Journal of European Criminal Law* 12 (4): 5.

Faria, Caroline, Sarah Klosterkamp, Rebecca M. Torres, and Jayme Walenta. 2020. Embodied exhibits: Toward a feminist geographic courtroom ethnography. *Annals of the American Association of Geographers* 110 (4): 1095–1113.

Flower, Lisa. 2016. Doing loyalty: Defense lawyers' subtle dramas in the courtroom. *Journal of Contemporary Ethnography*. 47 (2): 226–254.

Flower, Lisa. 2019a. *Interactional justice: The role of emotions in the performance of loyalty*. Abingdon: Routledge.

Flower, Lisa. 2019b. Emotional defence lawyers. *History, Culture, Society* 3 (2): 282–299.

Flower, Lisa. 2020. Rumbling stomachs and silent crying: Mapping and reflecting emotion in the sensory landscape of the courthouse. In *Sensory penalties*, ed. Katy Herrity, Bethany E Schmidt, and Jason Warr, 159–174. Bingley: Emerald Publishing.

Garfinkel, Harold. 1956. Conditions of successful degradation ceremonies. *American Journal of Sociology* 61: 420–424.

Garfinkel, Harold. 1967. *Studies in ethnomethodology*. Englewood Cliffs, NJ: Prentice-Hall.

Gill, Nick, Jennifer Allsopp, Andrew Burridge, Daniel Fisher, Melanie Griffiths, Natalia Paszkiewicz, and Rebecca Rotter. 2021. The tribunal atmosphere: On qualitative barriers to access to justice. *Geoforum* 119: 61–71.

Gill, Nick, and Jo Hynes. 2021. Courtwatching: Visibility, publicness, witnessing, and embodiment in legal activism. *Area* 53 (4): 569–576.

Goffman, Erving. 1963. *Behavior in public places: Notes on the social organization of gatherings*. New York: The Free Press.

Gorman, Cynthia. S. 2019. Feminist legal archeology, domestic violence and the raced-gendered juridical boundaries of U.S. asylum law. *Environment and Planning A*, 51 (5): 1050–1067.

Hammersley, Martyn, and Paul Atkinson. 2019. *Ethnography: Principles in practice*. Abingdon: Routledge.

Hannken-Illjes, Kati, Livia Holden, Alexander Kozin, and Thomas Scheffer. 2006. Trial and error—Failing and learning in criminal proceedings. *International Journal for the Semiotics of Law* 20 (2): 159–190.

Herbert, Steve. 2000. For ethnography. *Progress in Human Geography*, 24 (4): 550–568.

Hoffmann, Ludger. 2014. Der Fall des Rechts und wie er zur Sprache kommt. In *Der fall bielefeld: Transcript* ed. Oberzaucher Frank, Bergmann Jörg, and Ulrich Dausendschön-Gay, pp. 287–344.

Jacobson, Jessica, Gillian Hunter, and Amy Kirby. 2016. *Inside crown court: Personal experiences and questions of legitimacy*. Bristol: Policy Press.

Jeffrey, Alex. 2019. Legal geography 1: Court materiality. *Progress in Human Geography* 43 (3): 565–573.

Jeffrey, Alex. 2020. Legal geography II: Bodies and law. *Progress in Human Geography*, 44 (5): 1004–1016.

Jeffrey, Alex. 2021. Legal geography III: Evidence. *Progress in Human Geography* 45 (4): 902–913.

Judith Resnik and Dennis Edward Curtis. 2011. *Representing justice: Invention, controversy, and rights in city-states and democratic courtrooms*. Yale: Yale University Press.

Keane, Adrian, and Paul McKeown. 2022. *The modern law of evidence*. Oxford University Press.

Kumar, Shailesh. 2017. Interpreting the scales of justice: Architecture, symbolism and semiotics of the supreme court of India. *International Journal for the Semiotics of Law—Revue Internationale de Semiotique Juridique* 30 (4): 637–675.

Klosterkamp, Sarah and Paul Reuber. 2017. Im Namen der Sicherheit—Staatsschutzprozesse als Orte politisch-geographischer Forschung, dargestellt an Beispielen aus Gerichtsverfahren gegen Kämpfer und UnterstützerInnen der Terrororganisation "Islamischer Staat". *Geographica Helvetica*, 72 (3): 255–269.

Klosterkamp, Sarah. 2021. Geographien des Ein- und Ausschlusses: Strafvollzug und -Prozesse Im Kontext der Aufarbeitung von Beteiligungshandlungen im syrischen Bürgerkrieg. *Geographica Helvetica* 76 (2): 205–219.

Klosterkamp, Sarah. 2022. Legal ecologies of climate change: How farmers are advancing environmental justice in the German Courts. *Law & Space (un)Journal*. Accessed January 24, 2023. https://lawandspace.com/legal-ecologies-of-climate-justice/.

Klosterkamp, Sarah. 2023. Affectual intensities: Toward a politics of listening in court ethnography. *Gender, Place & Culture. A Journal of Feminist Geography*, 30 (11): 1529–1555.

Latour, Bruno. 2010. *The making of law: An ethnography of the Conseil d'Ètat*. Malden: Polity.

Márquez Porras, Rául. 2021. A call for ethnographying the judiciary (beyond the courtroom). *The Journal of Legal Pluralism and Unofficial Law* 53 (3): 419–423.

Mann, Kenneth. 1985. *Defending white-collar crime: A portrait of attorneys at work*. New Haven: Yale University Press.

Mulcahy, Linda. 2011. *Legal architecture*. London and New York: Routledge.

Nader, Laura. 1972. Up the anthropologist: Perspectives gained from studying up. In *Reinventing anthropology*, ed. Dell Hymes, 284–311. Ann Arbor: University of Michigan Press.

Paik, Leslie, and Harris, Alexes. 2015. Court ethnographies. In *The Routledge handbook of qualitative criminology*, ed. Heith Copes and J. Mitchell Miller. Abingdon: Routledge.

Pound, Roscoe. 1910. Law in books and law in action. *American Law Review*, 44, 12–36.

Postill, John. 2015. Digital ethnography: 'Being there' physically, remotely, virtually and imaginatively. Retrieved from https://cva.unifr.ch/content/postill-2015-digital-ethnography-%E2%80%98being-there%E2%80%99-physically-remotely-virtually-and, Last Access: November 8th, 2023.

Ramirez, Olimpia M., Caroline Faria Valdivia, and Rebecca Maria Torres. 2021. Good boys, gang members, asylum gained and lost: The devastating reflections of a bureaucrat-ethnographer. *Emotion, Space and Society* 38 (4): 100758.

Roach Anleu, Sharyn, and Kathy Mack. 2017. *Performing judicial authority in the lower courts*. London: Palgrave Macmillan.

Roach Anleu, Sharyn, and Kathy Mack. 2019. Law and sociology. In *The Routledge handbook on socio-legal theory and method*, ed. Naomi Creutzfeldt, Marc Mason, and Kirsten McConnachie, Chapter 11. London: Routledge.

Roach Anleu, Sharyn, Stina Bergman Blix, Kathy Mack, and Åsa Wettergren. 2016. Observing judicial work and emotions: Using two researchers. *Qualitative Research* 16 (4): 375–391.

Rock, Paul. 1993. *The social world of an English Crown Court*. Oxford: Oxford University Press.

Rock, Paul. 2001. Symbolic interactionism and ethnography. In *Handbook of ethnography*, ed. Paul Atkinson, Amanda Coffey, Sara Delamont, John Lofland, and Lyn Lofland. London: Sage.

Rossner, Meredith, and David Tait. 2021. Presence and participation in a virtual court. *Criminology & Criminal Justice* 23 (1): 135–157.

Rossner, Meredith, David Tait, Blake McKimmie, and Rick Sarre. 2017. The dock on trial: Courtroom design and the presumption of innocence. *Journal of Law and Society* 44 (3): 317–344.

Rowden, Emma. 2011. Remote participation and the distributed court: An approach to court architecture in the age of video-mediated communications. PhD Thesis, University of Melbourne; Melbourne, Australia.

Scheffer, Thomas. 2010. *Adversarial case-making: An ethnography of English Crown Court procedure*. Leiden: Brill.

Scheffer, Thomas, Kati Hannken-Illjes, and Alexander Kosin. 2010. *Criminal defence and procedure: Comparative ethnographies in the United Kingdom, Germany and the United States*. New York: Palgrave Macmillan.

Spiegel, Samuel J. 2021. Climate injustice, criminalisation of land protection and anti-colonial solidarity: Courtroom ethnography in an age of fossil fuel violence. *Political Geography* 84: 102298.

Stiles, E. Erin. 2009. *An Islamic court in context. An ethnographic study of judicial reasoning*. Basingstoke: Palgrave Macmillan.

Sylvestre, Marie-Eve, William Damon, Nicholas Blomley, and Céline. Bellot. 2015. Spatial tactics in criminal courts and the politics of legal technicalities. *Antipode* 47 (5): 1346–1366.

Travers, Max. 2021. Court ethnographies. In *The Oxford handbook of ethnographies of crime and criminal justice*, ed. Sandra. M. Burcerius, Kevin. D. Haggerty, and Luca Berardi. Oxford Handbooks Online: Oxford University Press.

Travers, Max, and John F. Manzo. 1997. *Law in action: Ethnomethodological and conversation analytic approaches to law*. London: Dartmouth Press.

Warren, Carol. 1982. *The court of last resort: Mental illness and the law*. Chicago: University of Chicago Press.

Walenta, Jayme. 2020. Courtroom ethnography: Researching the intersection of law, space, and everyday practices. *The Professional Geographer*, 72 (1): 131–138.

Part I

Doing Courtroom Ethnography

2

Framing the View

Jessica Hambly

Introduction

In her book *Creative Ecologies*, architectural scholar Helene Frichot begins by taking us to an image of the mathematician and anthropologist Maria Reiche (Frichot 2019). The image shows Reiche balancing precariously at the top of a ladder, her dress billowing up in the wind as she faces out towards a big sky and barren landscape. Frichot suggests this tableau signifies a state of being 'attached to the empirical ground, in situ, but with just the right amount of distance to achieve criticality from within her local environment-world' (Frichot 2019, 3–4).

This chapter considers a principal challenge of ethnographic research—the daunting task of deciding how to frame your view. Ethnography, some might say, is characterised by an 'anarchic atmosphere', where 'constant surprise' is par for the course (Flood 2005). But this does not mean leaving everything to chance, nor does it relieve the researcher of having to make choices about what ethnographic data to capture. If, as Flood suggests, 'the core of ethnography is to be alert and attentive to everything around you' (Flood 2005, 34), such sensory overload can overwhelm and overburden both the researcher(s)

J. Hambly (✉)
Australian National University College of Law, Canberra, ACT, Australia
e-mail: Jessica.Hambly@anu.edu.au

L. Flower and S. Klosterkamp (eds.), *Courtroom Ethnography*,
https://doi.org/10.1007/978-3-031-37985-7_2

and the research project itself. Confronting and navigating choices around what you are seizing, and how, is a key challenge for ethnographers.

'Framing' has received significant attention across disciplines (for example the enormous body of work generated by Goffman [1974]). In this short chapter, I use 'framing the view' to encapsulate some of the lines along which we can delineate and organise ethnographic inquiry. Even then, we encounter multiple meanings. In one sense, framing the view implies deciding what to focus on and what to 'grab' from the scene. In a distinct but related sense, view framing also implores us to reflect on our place in the scene, mode of participation, analytical familiarity, and distance from what is being studied (Duch and Rasmussen 2021). We come at methodological choices from our individual, situated standpoints (Haraway 1988); our ethnographic gaze filters through our gendered, racialised, and other intersectional social identities (Faria et al. 2020) alongside our political commitments and academic and disciplinary milieus.

This chapter presents questions encountered in the course of two courtroom research projects. Each focused on immigration courts, but they differed in notable ways. The first, my PhD project, was a small-scale comparative study of two asylum tribunal locations in the UK.[1] I was the sole researcher, and responsible for all aspects of planning, data collection, and writing up. For the second, I was employed as a post-doctoral researcher within a multidisciplinary team, undertaking a much larger scale international project comparing asylum appeals around Europe, and the ethnography was a collective endeavor.[2] Drawing on these experiences, this chapter offers some prompts for how to approach decisions around what to focus on, and reflects on how choices are inflected by our personal and scholarly lifeworlds.

I start by outlining the background to my research, locating it within a body of ethnographic work in socio-legal studies, and discussing, more specifically, ethnography in asylum courts. I then go on to discuss the non-linear, iterative process of frame selection, navigation, and capture, particularly relating to the challenge of working at the boundaries of law, itself a contested terrain (McDermont and Clarke 2017). While our frames may shift throughout research, the chapter argues that conducting robust, ethically responsible, and practically manageable ethnography requires holding

---

[1] 'Advocates in Asylum Appeals' (2017) University of Bristol, funded by UK Economic and Social Research Council Studentship.

[2] 'ASYFAIR', Principal Investigator: Professor Nick Gill. Funded by EU Horizon 2020 grant StG-2015_677917.

ourselves continually accountable to our research communities and to ourselves (Naber 2014).

Ethnography in Asylum Courts

The field of socio-legal studies, where I situate my work, has produced rich ethnographies of law (on development of socio-legal studies, see Thomas 1997; Wheeler 2020). Pat Carlen's (1976) ground-breaking work on Magistrates' courts and spaces of justice continues to scaffold discussions of cultural and class hierarchies in courtrooms (Henderson and Duncanson 2018). Other influential work has focused on language and communication (Conley and O'Barr 1990); interacting social worlds of courthouse participants (Rock 1993); emotions and interactional dynamics (Flower 2020; Mack and Roach Anleu 2010; Moorhead and Cowan 2007); relationships between courtroom workgroups (Eisenstein and Jacob 1977; Young 2013); physical surroundings (Mulcahy 2007); and construction of cases (Scheffer 2010). The impact of this work has been to provoke novel ways of seeing, studying, and theorising vibrant perspectives on the life of law that doctrinal and other text-based legal research may not broach (see also Chapter 1).

There is a growing body of ethnographic research in asylum courtrooms (Gill and Good 2019). Influential ethnographies from the UK, where I began my work, included Travers' (1999) interpretive account of the British immigration courts, Good's (2007) anthropological take on expertise and credibility assessment, Anderson et al.'s (2014) Bourdeusian theorisation of a 'culture of disbelief' in tribunals, Gill et al.'s (2018) geographic analysis of asylum appeals, and Campbell's (2017) dive into the bureaucratic dystopia of the UK asylum system. With the expansion of this literature comes greater opportunity for international comparison (European contributions are brought together in Gill and Good [2019]). Recent studies from Sweden and Germany have looked in particular at asylum judges (Johannesson 2022; Vetters 2022). Outside the European context, Torres (2018) examines legal space in US immigration courtrooms from a feminist geopolitical perspective.

Stepping into asylum courtrooms gives us a view of the day-to-day practices, mundane routines, and often time-pressed interactions of workgroups involved in making extremely high stakes decisions where an erroneous decision can result in sending a person back to a country where they face persecution, serious harm, or death (Hambly and Gill 2020). Asylum courts, argue Gill and Good, are particularly ripe for ethnographic study, given the complexity of matters at play, and also their status as 'boundary organisations'

(2019, 17). Asylum determination is often characterised as quasi-judicial (Hambly 2019), taking place at the intersection of law and administration (Thomas 2011), and exemplifying the kinds of legal pluralism set out by Moore (1973) in her study of semi-autonomous social fields. Only ethnography, it is suggested, can 'capture the current, contested reality of claiming asylum (…) laying bare the confusion, improvisation, inconsistency, complexity and uncertainty inherent to the process' (Gill and Good 2019, 21). Indeed, ethnography has been fundamental to unpacking some of the underlying dynamics and mechanics of asylum decision-making, and has offered fresh, and often disturbing, insights into the 'messy, contingent, discretionary, unreliable, inconsistent and unjust processes through which legal doctrine is translated into bureaucratic practice…' (Gill and Good 2019, 308).

This brief discussion of ethnography in asylum courtrooms highlights the strength of interdisciplinary, empirical legal studies when it comes to producing new knowledge and understandings of complex legal environments. Ethnography can provide the means to investigate the tangle of ecologies that construct and influence the life of law. However, this comes with associated challenges. Courtroom ethnographers come from a wide spectrum of disciplines, and bring with them different methodological insights (Coutin and Fortin 2015). Working in multidisciplinary research teams carries obvious benefits where members bring diverse expertise. But still, this can become overbearing when framing our view, as we straddle different strands of literature and our conceptual frameworks become 'muddied' (Frichot 2019, 183). Situating ethnography within a scholarly conversation means acknowledging the partiality of that conversation. This does not mean reifying disciplinary boundaries or siloing areas of research. Rather, recognising the genealogies of one's work assists in framing the view, and promotes research integrity by signalling blindspots and guarding against overstating the novelty of our contribution (Liboiron 2021).

Selecting Frames

> Well there appears to be this big drive to stop people coming into the country and I think maybe that's just seeped in to the decision-making process really…
>
> I think there's certain cultures that grow around hearing centres… and they're not really applying the law, they're applying the kind of culture that is in that particular place.
>
> [Interviews with asylum lawyers during PhD fieldwork, UK, 2014–2015]

I began my doctoral research in 2012 just as the so-called 'hostile environment' was announced by then-Prime Minister Theresa May as an explicit, central pillar of asylum law and policy in the UK. This was a package of measures intended to make life as difficult and unbearable as possible for people seeking asylum (Canning 2017). Using ethnography, I analysed how the hostile environment played out in asylum appeal procedures, and how the force of international refugee law, which the UK pledged to uphold, was constructed and shaped by its environments, including official policy and procedures, and also physical settings, local decision-making cultures, and competing fields of professional and organisational practice.

As Gill and Good (2019, 16) remind us, courtroom ethnographers may need to understand legal frameworks, but those are not the whole picture. Overly doctrinal legal mindsets can be critiqued for isolating law from its socio-political context (Anders 2015, 413). Ethnography invites us to reflect critically on understandings of 'the law' and legal procedures, and bridge some of the 'chasms' between legal and other worldviews (Good 2007, 147). Socio-legal ethnographers such as Merry (1990), Ewick and Silbey (1998), and Darian-Smith (2017) destabilised definitions of law, pushing understandings beyond rules, statutes, regulations, and decisions, to law's pluralistic, cultural forms (see Chapter 9). My theoretical framing was influenced by a perspective on law as social process (Bourdieu 1987) and legalities operating within expansive webs of power relations replete with more-or-less institutionalised rules, procedures, meanings, materials, and cultural resources (Ewick and Silbey 1998, 17).

Building on Hawkins' (2002) ethnographic theorisation of the complex, multi-layers of legal and regulatory decision-making—'surround, field, frame'—I studied how the promises, expectations, and commitments of refugee law were brought to life in UK asylum tribunals. The approach I took sought to go beyond actors' day-to-day practices and unpack what was going on in relation to a wider social, political, and cultural landscape. Ethnography under this view is capable of cutting deeper than participant-observation (Flood 2005, 43; Gibb 2019), and going beyond the 'tellable', 'visible', or 'reportable' features of daily life as it is experienced by actors in the field (Travers 1997, 7–9). Moreover, this went beyond the zone of 'gap' studies (Gould and Barclay 2012) which had focused on interrogating what Roscoe Pound, in 1910, had termed the space between 'law in the books' and 'law in action', and strove for a more innovative inhabitation of the 'hyphen-space' of socio-legal studies (Wheeler 2020). Similarly, in my postdoctoral role, where I was responsible for conducting ethnography at the French National Asylum Court ('CNDA') as part of the ASYFAIR project, the research sought to build a distinctly geographic account of differences in asylum appeal procedures between countries under the Common European Asylum System by exploring a 'grey zone of implementation' (Gill et al. 2022, 2). Ethnography, in both projects, was a tool for unpacking the socio-spatial, material, and environmental enactments of law's promises.

Selecting frames requires not only thinking through social and theoretical parameters, as above, but also, relatedly, spatio-temporal boundaries of the courtroom. In this sense, ethnography is not only capable of revealing the 'micro-geographies' (Gill and Good 2019, 314) of courtroom environments, for example layouts, furnishings, and atmospheres, it can also extend well beyond the room. This more 'macro' sense could apply to social fields and contexts (as discussed above), what Eisenstein and Jacob (1977) characterise as the 'ecology' of courtrooms and for Hawkins (2002) is the 'surround', also the wider physical environs (waiting rooms, car parks, local neighbourhoods), and, notably in contemporary times, to hybrid forms where 'digital and physical landscapes touch, overlap, and blend' (Liu 2022; see also Chapter 8). The temporal aspirations of ethnography often seek to combine witnessing immediate events with an appreciation of slower, unravelling currents, requiring development of relationships and immersion over a period of time (Fassin 2013, xi). However, a feminist approach may 'rethink and extend the very boundaries of the courtroom itself' (Faria et al. 2020, 1098), inviting radically expansive dimensions, not only reaching for transcripts, files, legislation, and other text-based sources, but also linking to wider, intersectional power relations and decentring the traditional ethnographic focus on face-to-face interactions (Klosterkamp 2023; Coutin and Fortin 2015, 78–79).

Contemplation of our political and ethical commitments is a fundamental part of view framing. Ethnography itself—in the sense of witnessing and constructing social description of otherwise unseen spaces—might be considered a political act (Coutin and Fortin 2015, 77). For me, alongside PhD research, I was volunteering in local refugee rights organisations and grassroots legal aid clinics. I made no secret of my commitment to feminist, anti-racist politics, and found, like Faria et al. (2020, 1108), that if anything, this actually strengthened the depth and quality of research, and facilitated access to networks and information. I was open about these lines of access and the role they played in framing my inquiry during the ethics approval process and writing up of my work. Entering the field with a commitment to social justice, engaged ethnography makes 'no pretense of objectivity' (Graeber 2009, 12), and this does not undermine the academic integrity or rigour of a project, so long as the researcher remains critical and reflexive of positionality. Not only do we frame the view; we are part of the scene.

Navigating Frames

> Courts are to most people exceptional worlds which they avoid if possible. Indeed, one of the most alienating environments is the court. The court is strange, hostile, threatening, and distant. (Flood 2011, 336)

Courtroom ethnography may not fit the traditional 'exotic' view of ethnography, but it is still capable of transporting readers to a location many would never otherwise have occasion to visit. As ethnographers entering the courtroom, the degree of strangeness may depend on our backgrounds and training. Fassin suggests that the more proximate, or complicit, you are with the social world you are studying, the more that people will let you in (2013, 25). Above, it was suggested that one's political stance can influence access. Whether one has a legal or other background can also play a significant role in how actors respond to you in the courtroom. When I was conducting research in the UK tribunals, I would often be asked by lawyers and judges who I was and where I was from. I answered that I was a student from Bristol University. My impression was that I was seen as relatively innocuous—'just a student'. But it also seemed to matter that I was a *law* student, this bought me a degree of insider currency, reflected in the kinds of remarks participants offered me (for example, speaking in deliberate 'legalese', quoting from cases, talking about Inns of Court and high-profile judges). Particularly in courtroom settings, designed to construct and amplify hierarchies between law/non-law (Mulcahy 2007), one's place in the scene can be impacted by the 'legal capital' one is presumed to carry. In my subsequent role at the CNDA, I was also questioned by judges as to who I was and what I was doing. There, I used '*universitaire*' (academic) and emphasised the interdisciplinary nature of inquiry. I was aware that a number of the adjudicators were also '*universitaires*', some drawn from disciplines outside of law specifically for their geopolitical and sociological expertise (Laacher 2018; Hambly et al. 2020). Changing how I presented myself in the scene reflected the change in research context. Contrasting with what was said above, not being *seen* as a lawyer, and indeed not *being* a lawyer, can bring its own advantages in courtroom ethnography when one's view is capable of transcending some of the strictures of legal conventions and expectations. While a background in law might open up shared legal knowledge, conversely, a degree of estrangement from courtroom environments can be a more discerning vantage point for taking a critical view of law in action. That said, negotiating 'insider–outsider' status (Flood 2005, 33) will continually change as ethnographers spend more time and gain familiarity in the courtroom.

Balancing and navigating relationships in, and to, the field means adapting to shifting frames. Some aspects of the view are framed for us. A major thematic shift I made early in my doctoral project was from focusing on judges to focusing on lawyers. Having applied to the tribunal service for permission to interview judges about their day-to-day work, I was told I could interview judges as long as I did not 'touch on the judicial role'. This would not have made for very interesting interviews. I decided I could still get at my research questions from a different angle by interviewing lawyers. I made the most of what was available in terms of access, even if it was not what I had initially envisaged. Access may be restricted in other ways. When at the courthouse, autonomy in terms of where you can go and what you can observe may be curtailed. For example you may be limited to the public areas, and even then you might be controlled (told to sit in certain places) or asked to leave some hearings. Even with hearings that were not strictly 'behind closed doors', occasionally I would be asked to leave due to sensitivities in the case and a perceived risk from my presence. Sometimes ushers at the court, knowing I was there for research, would try to funnel me into particular courtrooms for the 'interesting cases' or 'good judges'. At the start of the research, I was interested to see what their idea of an interesting case or good judge entailed. However, as the project progressed I felt more able to discern which courtrooms or cases I wanted to observe as I was gradually developing and narrowing down my themes.

Embracing elements of surprise alongside 'disciplined and deliberate witness-cum-recording' (Willis and Trondman 2000, 5) is part of the balancing act for ethnographers. While in the field, some of the most interesting ethnographic findings may come from unexpected happenings. Indeed, deviation from what is anticipated can alert us to an underlying convention (Goffman 1963). In framing our view, even though our eyes might be trained towards a particular target it is important to preserve our peripheral vision, and sometimes soften our gaze to allow the unexpected in.

Capturing Frames

The previous section encouraged us not to be too rigid with our view. Yet, interesting themes and insights do not just appear. Rather, we are responsible for 'emerging' them (Becker 2005). Being alert to our 'double location' (Strathern 1999, 1)—simultaneously in the courtroom and in the study—is part of what makes us ethnographers. For Ewick and Silbey, self-proclaimed 'deeply interpretive social constructionists'(Halliday and Schmidt 2009, 217), theoretical concepts are what give ethnographic data meaning and significance. I used what might be described as an abductive, quasi-grounded, or 'recursive spiral' (Grbich 2007, 20–22) approach to theme development whereby I was constantly going between theory and previous literature, research questions, time in the field, and examination and interpretation of my data. I wrote regular summaries while writing up notes and transcribing interviews, and continually mapped out thematic headings and links.

In the courtroom, I endeavoured to take a 'holistic' approach to notetaking (Good 2007, 43), whereby one aims to capture as much from different aspects of the scene as possible. I tried frantically to scribble as much as I could each day—about people present, voices, clothes, gestures, emotions, as well as the physical surroundings, furniture, lighting, temperature, and noise. I also tried to convey in my notes a sense of the atmosphere or feeling in the room—tensions, sadness and joy that hung in the air, hesitations, and devastations (for key work on emotions in courtrooms see Flower (2020, 2021); on 'sensory ethnography' see Pink (2015). I used sketches, maps, and annotations along with text. I deployed a layering technique whereby I would capture as much as I could in the immediate moment, and then layer on more notes while eating lunch, or on the journey home. Then I would add more reflections while typing up the notes. And, on top of that I would write broader reflections each week.

When working in a team, we discussed notetaking techniques and, through reflecting on our own, as well as each other's, notes, we added yet more layers. We visited each other's sites to get a feel for different locations. Still, we recognised that, across our team, it was possible and even likely that we would produce different accounts of the same situation based on our varying worlds of sensation and perception (Ingold 2000).

So, again, we face a balancing act. In one sense, ethnography invites us to collect as detailed and rich a record as possible. At the same time, we must accept that it will always be deficient. Moreover, there are always limits: 'writing always means betraying' (Fassin 2013, 32). Our interpretations and written reconstructions will always be partial, and obscure or overlook some features of the situation. We can nevertheless strive to give as much context to records as possible (see Faria et al. 2020 on creating embodied transcripts). This enables an ethnographic approach that guards, as far as possible, against focusing on 'the discrete at the expense of continua, things at the expense of processes, recognition at the expense of encounter, results at the expense of tendencies' (Massey 2005, 20).

Sometimes no words or pictures can capture the meanings we seek to convey. Going beyond the visual, thinking creatively of ways to present ethnography that evoke feeling and emphasise sensation of the non-verbal is perhaps an area for future courtroom ethnographers to explore. Maybe advancing technology will develop new possibilities for seizing and communicating ethnographic data. For example, moving beyond text, and thinking about visual and sonic reconstructions. But this is not a call for more sophisticated ways of replicating or reproducing by removing the researcher. A crucial element of ethnography remains the delicate and time-consuming process of pulling apart and piecing back together by the researcher—extraction, abstraction, and re-crafting. The task of representing the view is an intensely personal one, and again the ethnographer stands with one foot firmly inside the frame.

Closing Remarks

Ethnography draws us to remark upon mundane details of the everyday, and it is these things that may provide the basis for building rich, theoretical stories about our chosen setting. As Latour (2010) says, 'minor brushstrokes' allow us to redefine the law. How to approach the process of selection, distillation, and presentation of ethnographic data ultimately depends on the desires and demands of each researcher and research project (including requirements of funders and institutions). There is no right or wrong ethnographic perspective. Like adjusting a microscope lens, it can take time, trial, and error to find a satisfactory and legible focus. There are methodological choices to be made along the way, and some aspects of view-framing will remain, to a greater or lesser extent, outside the control of the researcher. Moreover, the nature of ethnography is such that we may well shift our focus throughout the research process. It is a continual process of 'turning the complex noise of observable reality into the pursuit of sociological cases' (Deener 2018, 296) and even though we may impose some spatial, temporal, and theoretical boundaries, these are capable of expansion and contraction. Indeed, we might say the beauty of ethnography is that you are 'not enslaved by a theoretical straitjacket' (Flood 2005, 35). And yet, this freedom and flexibility does not relieve the researcher of the need for methodological honesty and rigour.

Drawing on theory to frame the view is what can turn a bare witness report or observational note into ethnography, or a sociologically relevant case study. But, returning to the figure of Maria Reiche invoked at the start of the chapter, theory should not stand at a distance from the scene taking place. Frichot rejects 'the figure of the theorist, who arrives as an ambassador to a strange, far-off land and bears witness to events from a safe distance, returning again to her safe haven with an authoritative report in hand' (Frichot 2019, 199). Instead she draws on feminist post-human methodologies of Donna Haraway and Jane Bennett to call us down into the gutter, into the slime, to embrace messy, non-linear entanglements of concepts and things. The significance of this to courtroom ethnography can be interpreted as a call to embrace the complexities and twisted dynamics of courtroom activity, and turn towards the contradictions and indeterminacies. Investigate and speculate as to the different forces at play in courtroom environments. But do so with methodological clarity, and with an awareness of the socio-political commitments and implications of the research.

Tips for Practical Guidance

(1) Be open and reflexive about your starting point (discipline, background, theoretical and ethical commitments, what sparked your intervention).
(2) Working in multidisciplinary teams is an efficient way to construct rich, comparative ethnographies. Collaboration between members can enhance data quality and reduce loneliness in the field.
(3) Make notes/sketches while in the room, but also allow time to keep layering context and adding reflections afterwards.
(4) Do not be afraid to shift focus, throw out stuff, and recognise new frames along the way.
(5) Framing the view is about setting limits. Meander. Explore. But figure out the contours of your project (which could be practical: funding, balancing other work or caring responsibilities, ability to travel, etc.) to make it manageable.

References

Anders, Gerhard. 2015. Law at its limits: Interdisciplinarity between law and anthropology. *The Journal of Legal Pluralism and Unofficial Law* 47 (3): 411–422.

Anderson, Jessica, Jeannine Hollaus, Annelisa Lindsay, and Colin Williamson. 2014. *The culture of disbelief: An ethnographic approach to understanding an under-theorised concept in the UK asylum system.* 102. Refugee Studies Working Paper Series. University of Oxford.

Becker, Howard. 2005. Making it up as you go along: How I wrote art worlds. https://www.howardsbecker.com/articles/writingaw.html. Accessed November 8th, 2023.

Bourdieu, Pierre. 1987. The force of law: Toward a sociology of the juridical field. *Hastings Law Journal* 38: 814–853.

Campbell, John. 2017. *Bureaucracy, law and dystopia in the United Kingdom's asylum system*. London: Routledge.

Canning, Victoria. 2017. *Gendered harm and structural violence in the British asylum system*. London: Routledge.

Carlen, Pat. 1976. *Magistrates' justice*. Martin Robertson.

Conley, John M., and William M. O'Barr. 1990. *Rules versus relationships: The ethnography of legal discourse*. Chicago: University of Chicago Press.

Coutin, Susan Bibler, and Véronique Fortin. 2015. Legal ethnographies and ethnographic law. In *The handbook of law and society*, 71–84. Hoboken: Wiley.

Darian-Smith, Eve. 2017. *Ethnography and law*. Milton Park: Routledge.

Deener, Andrew. 2018. The architecture of ethnographic Knowledge: Narrowing down data and contexts in search of sociological cases. *Sociological Perspectives* 61 (2): 295–313.

Duch, Henriette, and Annette Rasmussen. 2021. Familiarity and distance in ethnographic fieldwork: Field positions and relations in adult education. *Ethnography and Education* 16 (1): 77–91.

Eisenstein, James, and Herbert Jacob. 1977. *Felony justice: An organizational analysis of criminal courts*. Boston: Little, Brown.

Ewick, Patricia, and Susan S. Silbey. 1998. *The common place of law: Stories from everyday life*. Chicago: University of Chicago Press.

Faria, Caroline, Sarah Klosterkamp, Rebecca Maria Torres, and Jayme Walenta. 2020. Embodied exhibits: Toward a feminist geographic courtroom ethnography. *Annals of the American Association of Geographers* 110 (4): 1095–1113.

Fassin, Didier. 2013. *Enforcing order: An ethnography of urban policing*. Cambridge: Wiley Polity.

Flood, John. 2011. Adversarial case-making: An ethnography of English Crown Court procedure by Thomas Scheffer. *Journal of Law and Society* 38 (2): 336–339.

Flood, John. 2005. Socio-legal ethnography. In *Theory and method in socio-legal research*, 33–48. Oxford: Hart.

Flower, Lisa. 2020. *Interactional justice: The role of emotions in the performance of loyalty*. Milton Park: Routledge.

Flower, Lisa. 2021. Rumbling stomachs and silent crying: Mapping and reflecting emotion in the sensory landscape of the courthouse. In *Sensory penalities: Exploring the senses in spaces of punishment and social control*, 159–174. Emerald Publishing.

Frichot, Helene. 2019. *Creative ecologies: Theorizing the practice of architecture*. London: Bloomsbury.

Gibb, Robert. 2019. Communicative practices and contexts of interaction in the refugee status determination process in France. In *Asylum determination in Europe: Ethnographic perspectives*, 155–74. Cham: Palgrave Macmillan.

Gill, Nick, and Anthony Good, eds. 2019. *Asylum determination in Europe: Ethnographic perspectives*. Cham: Palgrave Macmillan.

Gill, Nick, Nicole Hoellerer, Jennifer Allsopp, Andrew Burridge, Dan Fisher, Melanie Griffiths, Jessica Hambly, Natalia Paszkiewicz, Rebecca Rotter, and Lorenzo Vianelli. 2022. Rethinking commonality in refugee status determination in Europe: Legal geographies of asylum appeals. *Political Geography* 98 (October): 102686.

Gill, Nick, Rebecca Rotter, Andrew Burridge, and Jennifer Allsopp. 2018. The limits of procedural discretion: Unequal treatment and vulnerability in Britain's asylum appeals. *Social and Legal Studies* 27 (1): 49–78.

Goffman, Erving. 1963. *Behavior in public places: Notes on the Social organization of gatherings*. Florence: Free Press.

Goffman, Erving. 1974. *Frame analysis: An essay on the organization of experience*. Cambridge: Harvard University Press.

Good, Anthony. 2007. *Anthropology and expertise in the asylum courts*. Glasshouse.

Gould, Jon and and Scott Barclay. 2012. Mind the gap: The place of gap studies in sociolegal scholarship. *Annual Review of Law and Social Science* 8 (1): 323–335.

Graeber, David. 2009. *Direct action: An ethnography*. Chico: AK Press.

Grbich, Carol. 2007. *Qualitative data analysis: An introduction*. London: Sage.

Halliday, Simon, and Patrick D. Schmidt. 2009. *Conducting law and society research: Reflections on methods and practices*. Cambridge: Cambridge University Press.

Hambly, Jessica. 2019. Interactions and identities in UK asylum appeals: Lawyers and law in a Quasi-Legal setting. In *Asylum determination in Europe: Ethnographic perspectives*. Cham: Palgrave Macmillan.

Hambly, Jessica, and Nick Gill. 2020. Law and speed: Asylum appeals and the techniques and consequences of legal quickening. *Journal of Law and Society* 47 (1): 3–28.

Hambly, Jessica, Nick Gill, and Lorenzo Vianelli. 2020. Using multi-member panels to tackle RSD complexities. *Forced Migration Review* 65. Online accessible: https://www.fmreview.org/recognising-refugees/hambly-gill-vianelli. Last Access: November 8th, 2023.

Haraway, Donna. 1988. Situated knowledges: The science question in feminism and the privilege of partial perspective. *Feminist Studies* 14 (3): 575–599.

Hawkins, Keith. 2002. *Law as last resort*. Oxford: Oxford University Press.

Henderson, Emma, and Kirsty Duncanson. 2018. The space of justice: Courtrooms, innovation and practice. *Griffith Law Review* 27 (2): 173–175.

Ingold, Tim. 2000. *The perception of the environment: Essays on livelihood*. Dwelling and Skill: Routledge.

Johannesson, Livia. 2022. Just another benefit? Administrative judges' constructions of sameness and difference in asylum adjudications. *Citizenship Studies* 26 (7): 910–926.

Klosterkamp, Sarah. 2023. Affectual intensities: Toward a politics of listening in court ethnography. *Gender, Place & Culture. A Journal of Feminist Geography,* 30 (11): 1529–1551.

Laacher, Smain. 2018. *Croire a l'incroyable: Un Sociologue a La Cour Nationale Du Droit d'asile*. Paris: Gallimard.

Latour, Bruno. 2010. *The making of law*. Bodmin: MPG Books.

Liboiron, Max. 2021. *Firsting in research*. Discard Studies. January 18.

Liu, Rui-Fan. 2022. Hybrid ethnography: Access, positioning, and data assembly. *Ethnography*. https://doi.org/10.1177/14661381221145451

Mack, Kathy, and Sharyn Roach Anleu. 2010. Performing impartiality: Judicial demeanor and legitimacy. *Law & Social Inquiry* 35 (1): 137–173.

Massey, Doreen. 2005. *For space*. London: Sage.

McDermont, Morag, and John Clarke. 2017. Introduction: Working the boundaries of law. *Oñati Socio-Legal Series* 7 (7): 1383–1396.

Merry, Sally Engle. 1990. *Getting justice and getting even: Legal consciousness among working-class Americans*. Chicago: University of Chicago Press.

Moore, Sally Falk. 1973. Law and social change: The semi-autonomous social field as an appropriate subject of study. *Law and Society Review* 7 (4): 719–746.

Moorhead, Richard, and Dave Cowan. 2007. Judgecraft: An introduction. *Social & Legal Studies* 16: 315–320.

Mulcahy, Linda. 2007. Architects of justice: The politics of courtroom design. *Social & Legal Studies* 16 (3): 383–403.

Naber, Nadine. 2014. Sondra Hale's ethnographic accountability. *Journal of Middle East Women's Studies* 10 (1): 128–132.

Pink, Sarah. 2015. *Doing sensory ethnography*. London: Sage.

Rock, Paul Elliott. 1993. *The social world of an English Crown Court: Witness and professionals in the Crown Court Centre at Wood Green*. Oxford: Clarendon Press.

Scheffer, Thomas. 2010. *Adversarial case-making: An ethnography of English Crown Court Procedure*. Leiden: Brill.

Strathern, Marilyn. 1999. Property, substance, and effect: Anthropological essays on persons and things. In Classics in ethnographic theory, ed. Eric Hirsch. London: Athlone Press.

Thomas, Philip. 1997. Socio-legal studies: The case of disappearing fleas and bustards. In *Socio-legal studies*. Aldershot: Bloomsbury.

Thomas, Robert. 2011. *Administrative justice and asylum appeals : A study of tribunal adjudication*. Oxford: Hart.

Torres, Rebecca. 2018. A crisis of rights and responsibility: Feminist geopolitical perspectives on Latin American refugees and migrants. *Gender, Place & Culture* 25 (March): 1–24.

Travers, Max. 1997. *The reality of law: Work and talk in a firm of criminal lawyers*. Aldershot: Ashgate.

Travers, Max. 1999. The British immigration courts : A study of law and politics. Bristol: Policy Press.

Vetters, Larissa. 2022. Making sense of noncitizens' rights claims in asylum appeal hearings: Practices and sentiments of procedural justice among German administrative judges. *Citizenship Studies* 26 (7): 927–943.

Wheeler, Sally. 2020. Socio-legal studies in 2020. *Journal of Law and Society* 47 (S2): S209–S226.

Willis, Paul, and Mats Trondman. 2000. Manifesto for 'ethnography.' *Ethnography* 1 (1): 5–16.

Young, Richard. 2013. Exploring the boundaries of the criminal courtroom workgroup. *Common Law World Review* 42 (3): 203–239.

3

Negotiating Access

Sara Uhnoo, Moa Bladini, and Åsa Wettergren

Introduction

Generally, the term *negotiation*[1] refers to a discussion in which the parties attempt to reach an agreement through argumentation, bargaining and persuasion. As we will show, negotiating research access for qualitative projects is an open-ended process over which the researchers have only limited control. In this chapter, we explore the question of negotiating and

[1] The term *negotiating* implies that a "no" must not be accepted as a "no", but must instead be met with persuasion or bargaining. We want to comment on this from a research ethics point of view. As participation in research studies must be voluntary, this might be a sensitive issue. First, we do not push legal actors to participate if they are clearly negative about our research project, but rather, we are open and careful in our approaches to potential participants. Second, since our participants are legal actors, they belong to the elite, and are thus not in a vulnerable position.

S. Uhnoo (✉) · Å. Wettergren
Department of Sociology and Work Science, University of Gothenburg, Gothenburg, Sweden
e-mail: sara.uhnoo@socav.gu.se

Å. Wettergren
e-mail: asa.wettergren@socav.gu.se

M. Bladini
Department of Law, University of Gothenburg, Gothenburg, Sweden
e-mail: moa.bladini@law.gu.se

L. Flower and S. Klosterkamp (eds.), *Courtroom Ethnography*,
https://doi.org/10.1007/978-3-031-37985-7_3

gaining access in courthouse ethnography by drawing on our experiences of negotiating access to Swedish rape trials, which in Sweden normally take place behind closed doors. Based on ethnographic field notes from a project exploring the application of a new Swedish consent-based rape law, we analyse our work to gain access during our fieldwork from autumn 2020 to spring 2022. We describe the challenges and dilemmas we encountered, and we highlight access as a continuum between wholly granted and wholly denied. But first, we provide a short general overview of the method literature on gaining access in ethnographic studies, with a focus on courtroom ethnography.

Practical Considerations for Gaining Access to Criminal Courts

It is well known that negotiation of research access in ethnographic studies is not a straightforward formal procedure, nor is it a matter of a "one-off" procedure that ends when all the formal permissions or clearance documents are signed. The access process has been described as comprised of *several steps* of establishing, securing and maintaining (trustful) relationships within the field (see e.g., Bergman Blix and Wettergren 2015). Kraska et al. (2021) illustrate the process as "the access ladder"; with more time spent in the field, higher levels of trust can be established. Even for highly experienced researchers, successful access requires hard work, time, patience, stubbornness, persuasion, social skills, judiciousness, insider knowledge of the field and personal contacts. Access requires careful preparation and strategic planning, but also a great sense of flexibility. Emotions experienced during the access process can be strategically used to enhance the researcher's empathic skills during the research process, for example, to better understand barriers to access, build trust, gain self-confidence and to manoeuvre one's position in the research field (Bitsch 2018). Building trust thus entails substantial "emotional labour" (Bergman Blix and Wettergren 2015) on behalf of the researcher. This includes preparedness to adapt to dress codes and behavioural norms, and to fake self-confidence—sometimes pleasantness and complacency—particularly when researching elites.

An often-repeated assumption in the method literature about gaining access is that it "varies with the research problem, the researcher, and the researched" (Shaffir and Stebbins 1991, 30), but that it has some basic problems in common across all projects, and that there are general tips and strategies that can be learned. The literature describes examples of successful entries, but also (often more interesting) examples of restricted, reluctant, delayed or denied access (see e.g., Bitsch 2018). The literature on access challenges includes, for example, delay tactics used by officials (Lees 1996) and uninterested, manipulative or hostile elite professionals (Empson 2018).

Methodological reflections about negotiation of access to court observations is often underdeveloped (see however, e.g., Bergman Blix and Wettergren 2015; Gill et al. 2021). Most articles based on court observations lack descriptions of how access was negotiated and gained, leaving readers with the impression that the access process was quite straightforward. One possible reason may be that criminal courts are usually open to the public. As argued by Baldwin (2008, 237) "therefore no difficulties of access arise in observing them. Conducting research on the criminal courts [in the UK] need involve no more than turning up with a notebook". This general principle of openness is, however, just one end of the access to court hearings continuum. And even at this basic end, access cannot be taken for granted.

First, even if hearings are generally public, judges have the discretion to exclude spectators, including researchers, from court. Local rules and regulations on a court's degree of openness to the public differ between jurisdictions. Some courts (e.g., juvenile courts in many US states) or specific types of hearings (e.g., rape trials in Sweden and family law cases in Germany) might be held behind closed doors to protect a vulnerable party. Consequently, researchers must ask permission from the presiding judge to get into "their courtrooms". To know whether access needs to be negotiated or not, researchers need to acquire knowledge about local requirements and necessary permissions required by particular courts, or required in particular types of cases.

Second, depending on the purpose of research, researchers may need informed consent from the parties prior to hearings for research ethics reasons. This may require access negotiation not only with judges, but also with other legal actors (prosecutors, defence lawyers, the victim's legal counsels) or lay people (defendants, complainants, witnesses). Gaining access to lay people involved in a hearing may be more ethically difficult as they are generally considered to be people in a vulnerable position. However, depending on the research aim and focus, researchers can also argue that informed consent is not necessary if the observed court hearings are open to the public (see e.g., Flower 2019).

A *third* reason why access may have to be negotiated is that courthouse ethnographers sometimes want access not only to the courthouse (gained through screening procedures, etc.), the courtroom and the public spaces outside of the courtroom, but also to legal professionals' backstage informal settings, such as their offices, corridors and coffee rooms (see e.g., Faria et al. 2020; Spiegel 2021). Additionally, once inside the courtroom, the researcher probably wants to observe as many parts of the court hearing as possible, for example, the deliberations, which can be a challenging task for many different reasons (see also, e.g., Chapters 2 and 7).

A *fourth* point, closely related to the third: a *multi-method approach* combining ethnographic methods (e.g., court observations, formal and informal interviews, "shadowing"[2] and document analysis) makes the process of access even more complicated. Courthouse ethnographers may want to conduct *formal interviews* with legal actors and/or interview defendants, complainants and witnesses (see e.g., Fielding 2013). Since legal actors can be characterised as elite professionals (with power, authority and status), gaining access to them can be challenging (Baldwin 2008; Bergman Blix and Wettergren 2015; Empson 2018). Courthouse ethnographers may also strive to access legal *documents* pertaining to the observed cases. While some official documents are relatively easy to retrieve (e.g., written judgements because they are public), provisions on secrecy might restrict access to other types of documents (e.g., preliminary criminal investigations). Getting access to these documents will require extra work, insider knowledge and the establishment of trust (Faria et al. 2020; Walenta 2020).

To sum up, aspects such as court hearings behind closed doors, ethics considerations and the wish to gain deeper access—for instance, in-depth interviews and shadowing of everyday court work—may result in complicated and time-consuming access negotiations. Moreover, the process of gaining access becomes more complicated in: (1) multi-sited studies because researchers must learn local rules and customs in more than one legal setting; and (2) in studies in which researchers must negotiate access across several levels and bodies of legal decision-making or build trust with many legal actors across different organisational hierarchies.

Gaining Ethnographic Access to Closed-Door Rape Trials

This section examines challenges to fieldwork methodology and possibilities related to gaining access to Swedish rape trial court proceedings. While some courthouse ethnographies are limited to a single trial (Walenta 2020), or a

---

[2] "Shadowing" as a method means following research participants through the field, in and out of court, at lunch and coffee breaks (see Bergman Blix and Wettergren 2015; Darbyshire 2011; Roach Anleu et al. 2016).

single courthouse or courtroom (see e.g., Booth 2012), our study was a multi-sited study (see also, e.g., Darbyshire 2011; Flower 2019; Bergman Blix and Wettergren 2018; Rouch Anleu et al. 2016). We attempted to track the trajectory of rape cases through different legal instances, and to include several courts and all legal professions involved.[3]

Ethnographic observations of trials are an underused method in rape research (see however, Bitsch 2018; Burman et al. 2007; Daly 2022; Lees 1996; Smith and Skinner 2012, 2017; Smith 2018; Temkin et al. 2018; Hvala and Mulla 2018), and to our knowledge, observations of deliberations in rape hearings have not previously been conducted. As a rule, Swedish rape trials are conducted behind closed doors to protect the complainant, who is always present as a party in the Swedish legal system. Information identifying the complainant in rape cases is also classified.[4]

However, the Swedish Court may permit other persons to attend such hearings if there is special reason for doing so. In terms of gaining access to closed-door rape trials, our project had good conditions in which to succeed. Wettergren and Bladini had prior experience of negotiating access in studies with a similar methodological approach (Bergman Blix and Wettergren 2015), and they had developed a wide contact network in the Swedish judiciary. Moreover, as a senior lecturer in law, Bladini was acquainted with many legal actors. Certainly, social and professional networks, a good reputation from previous research in the field and knowledge of the legal system, including social codes and the language of the court, are facilitators in the process of gaining access. Above all, established networks mean that trusting relationships are already in place, or easier to build, as trust can be transferable within networks (e.g., Ntamazeze 2016). When elites are approached, academic titles and achievements are helpful; all three researchers were established in academia and had previous knowledge of similar projects. When negotiating access, the presentation of self as a sociable, academically professional and generally trustworthy person can be more important than the purpose, contents and rigour of the study (Bergman Blix and Wettergren 2015).

[3] In the project *Rape or Consent? Effects of the new rape law on legal reasoning and thinking* (RJ P19-0515:1), three types of qualitative data were collected; field notes from *observations* of 20 court hearings (6 in Districts Court, 13 in Appeals Court, 1 remand hearing), including 5 deliberations; *written judgements*; and tape-recorded and transcribed *interviews* with 62 legal actors (23 judges, 15 prosecutors, 24 defence lawyers/victims' counsels).

[4] Even if the Swedish code of judicial procedure declares that "court hearings shall be open to the public" (5 chapter. 1 §), exceptions to this general rule prevail, e.g., if "it deems it to be of extraordinary importance that the information is not disclosed" as regulated in the Secrecy Act. It should be noted that the situation is different in, e.g., Denmark, Norway and the UK, where rape trials are usually open to the public.

Despite our promising point of departure, the research team's access to rape trials behind closed doors was not uncomplicated, nor was it straightforward. At the time of our investigation, in the aftermath of #MeToo, the new consent-based rape legislation was ideologically charged and controversial, and it was widely debated in the media and amongst legal actors. As the legislation was new and recently implemented, it soon became clear that many of the legal professionals (judges, prosecutors, lawyers) felt uncertain concerning the presentation and evaluation of evidence, and found it hard to predict the outcome of cases.[5] The newness of the law was, on the one hand, a reason for legal professionals to welcome the research project, hoping that it would illuminate some difficulties associated with the implementation. On the other hand, it was a reason to feel anxious about our involvement. The uncertainty about the implementation rocked legal professionals' confidence in their knowledge and experience. Judges' uncertainty created more space for discretionary judgements. Consequently, prosecutors and defence lawyers were uncertain about the outcome of each case, even if they had had similar cases before. Being followed by a researcher in such a stressful situation could be perceived by legal actors as either a resource (the researcher as discussant or external observer) or as a burden (the researcher as a potentially critical examiner). Once more, trust was key in legal actors' decisions to grant access, or not.

Strategies to Gain Access

In our study, we gained access to rape cases by using several strategies: (1) we presented the project at courts and prosecution offices in formal meetings to raise awareness and interest for the project; (2) we asked familiar, or already participating legal actors, if they knew of any upcoming rape hearings that we could observe; and (3) we looked at the courts' weekly published public lists of upcoming rape trials on their websites. The output of these strategies was uncertain, as they entailed negotiations with legal actors, and thus, outputs depended on actors' response and reactions.[6]

Before starting to collect data, we needed *formal approvals* from key institutional *gatekeepers*, that is, from the chiefs of the prosecution offices and from the courts we wanted to involve. Formal approval of a research project is crucial. If one of the central gatekeepers feels their authority is not properly

---

[5] The new Swedish rape legislation is based on voluntariness as a basic requisite for rape (see Bladini and Svedberg Andersson [2020] for more information about the legal reform).

[6] In practice, strategy 1 gave us access to 6 cases, strategy 2–7 cases and strategy 3–5 cases.

acknowledged by the researchers, they can put an end to the project immediately. In our case, we knew from previous projects which formal approvals had to be obtained, and by whom. If we managed to get formal approvals, in the next step, we proposed to present the research project to potential participants at each prosecution office and court. Initially, we invested a lot of time and reflection in planning and presenting the project to legal actors at four District Courts, three Appeals Courts and three prosecution offices. At these presentations, there were prosecutors and judges present, but also other staff categories, such as administrative staff, who could facilitate our access by giving us contact details, schedules or various documents. A crucial part of these presentations was to present the project in detail, but also to present the research ethics aspects and confidentiality regulations.[7] We also offered to sign local confidentiality agreements.

The advantage of the first two strategies (1, 2) was that both helped us to get a foot in the door, insofar as at least one legal professional in a rape case agreed to participate. Even if this was no guarantee we would be granted access to rape hearings, it was a good start. The third strategy, on the other hand, implied that we had to approach all legal professionals involved in the cases without having anyone in the case involved in the project beforehand. We searched for upcoming rape hearings through the public list and contacted the court's information desks to get the name of the presiding judge and the indictment (to get the names of the other legal professionals). Thereafter, we contacted the presiding judge to inform her or him about the project and to ask for permission to access the hearing (including closed parts). If the judge approved, often with the reservation that the complainant also had to approve (because confidentiality in rape cases aims to protect the complainant), we contacted the other legal parties to ask for their permission to access the hearing, or just to inform them about our wish to attend and observe the hearing.

[7] The research ethics guidelines (Swedish Research Council 2017) offer a stronger protection than the legal regulations on confidentiality, which is an important aspect to highlight because this aspect is crucial in building trust.

The Judges' Authority to Control Access

Independent of access strategy, before a court hearing, we contacted all involved legal actors. Given their ability to exercise discretion, the law judges were the most important gatekeepers in our study.[8] It is well known that elite groups like judges "can be particularly difficult to access because they have the power and knowledge to obstruct access in subtle ways, and perhaps have more reasons than others not to want to be exposed" (O'Reilly 2009, 9). Judges are used to being in charge, making quick and difficult decisions, and they are rhetorically skilled. They do not have to justify their decisions to deny access. We never knew beforehand how the presiding judge would reason, and until the very last minute, the judge could change her or his mind. It was highly valuable to act as a research team; we could offer each other support, we could collaborate and we could discuss challenges and dilemmas in the process of negotiating access (see Roach Anleu et al. 2016).

Before every court hearing, we contacted the victim's counsel and the defence lawyer to ask them to pass on information about the research to their clients. The following extract from our field notes illustrates reflections on strategical moves and potential pitfalls in the negotiation process:

> I contacted the presiding judge a week before the hearing. She was positive but informed me that she would contact the complainant. This week, when I contacted the other actors to prepare them in case I would be allowed to participate, the prosecutor and the victim's counsel granted me access to the hearing. I got a little nervous that the judge might have perceived it as if I acted behind her back by checking with the victim's counsel instead of waiting for the judge to do it. But I emailed her about it, and she did not seem offended. The defence lawyer answered but had handed the case over to a colleague. The two defence lawyers did not respond to my email. However, my email was framed as information rather than as a question to answer. (Fieldnote, June 2022)

We always asked the complainant's permission to attend the trial. Regarding the defendant, we discussed whether we should *ask* them about our attendance *or* merely *inform* them that the complainant had no objection. We wanted to avoid giving the defence lawyers the impression that the defence could object to our presence.

---

[8] At main hearings in Swedish District Courts, the members of the courts are one law judge and three lay judges, unless otherwise prescribed. The law judge is the presiding judge with the authority to control access to the courtroom. In a Court of Appeal, the members of the court are three law judges and two lay judges. One of the law judges is the presiding judge.

The literature on research access address the question of whether people may agree to participate, but then resist in various ways by manipulating information or refusing the researcher access to the organization's backstage (Bryman 2004, 299). The extract from our field notes below is an example of reluctant access granted by one judge. In our email conversation before the court proceeding, he announced that he did not want to be interviewed and that he "would never allow us to participate in any of his deliberations". Eventually, the judge granted us access, but he was visibly irritated, ignored us and demonstrated that he did not want us in the courtroom.

> I was a little worried before the hearing. In an email correspondence with the judge about access, he replied that it is up to the complainant and the victim's counsel to decide if they feel comfortable having researchers at a hearing held behind closed doors. "That question will be raised on Wednesday". The judge begins the hearing by saying: "We have received a request here from the university". So far, he hasn't even acknowledged us with a glance. [...] He told the court that he had informed us that the complainant decides whether we can join behind closed doors because confidentiality is for her. He therefore asks the complainant directly, who replies that she approves. "And the defence had been informed?", he says facing the defence lawyer. "Yes". "How do you feel about it?", he then asks. They replied that it was okay. I got nervous because, even though he had said that it was the complainant who decided, he still opened the door for the defendant to say no. It was very clear from the way he treated us that he did not like having us in the hall. (Fieldnote, March 2021)

After negotiations with both the presiding judge and the parties, through their legal representatives, we were given access to some court hearings. We learned, however, that this was not necessarily the same as getting access to all parts of the hearing. If access to rape trials behind closed doors was a challenge, getting access to deliberations was even more tricky. The matter of trust can possibly be even more important in relation to access to the deliberations, from which researchers are normally excluded (Darbyshire 2011). In all types of cases, deliberations are strictly confidential, and judges are strongly hesitant to let anyone sit in.

Out of our 18 cases included in the project, we were allowed to attend the deliberations in 5 cases. One methodological difference between the former projects carried out by Wettergren, Bergman Blix, Törnqvist and Bladini and this project, is that we did not use the method of shadowing to any significant degree. In addition, rape cases are most often short hearings, only a day, or even only half a day. Just a few cases have lasted several days. This gave us less time to build trust in relation to the judges. The more time spent in the field with the participants, the higher the level of trust that can be established (Bergman Blix and Wettergren 2015; Kraska et al. 2021).

A final example of how our access to the court hearings turned out to be only partial was at hearings in the Appeals Courts. Relatively often, judges decided to apply "evidence collection by referral", which means that they watched the recorded evidence (the interrogations with the parties and witnesses) from the District Courts; all other people were expected to leave the room. Sometimes, we were allowed to stay, but sometimes, judges asked us to leave; they argued that the session (watching the video recordings from the District Court) was not part of the hearing.

Ethics Considerations and Dilemmas

To get access, we needed to think through how to describe the project. As pointed out by Noaks and Winrup (2004, 72), "researchers must adopt [the role] of salesperson, trying to convince those who are in position to help of the importance of their research". Framing the project in a strategic way to gain access might involve balancing between different interests (access and transparency) and involves research ethics considerations. Our project was sometimes met with scepticism and reluctance from actors in the field. Some of them wondered what we were "actually" looking for, as if worried that we had ulterior motives. Either they explicitly asked for clarifications, or we sensed by their hesitance that we needed to frame the project differently. We learnt to be sensitive to aspects of the project that could be perceived as "problematic". For example, the "feminist legal perspective" often raised questions about how this perspective was intended to be used (see Bitsch 2018; Törnqvist 2017). If questions were raised, we clarified that the feminist perspective was a robust scientific perspective that allowed for critical reflexivity regarding taken-for-granted judicial ideals like objectivity, autonomy and freedom of choice. We also underlined that we were not interested in assessing the juridical quality of an individual's legal decision-making, but rather, we were interested in how decisions were the result of professional collaboration and negotiation, particularly in rape cases. Sometimes, legal actors already participating helped us convince their colleagues. Some gatekeeping judges, when convinced to allow us access to the court, suggested strategies to us to facilitate access. Their suggestions covered how we should present the project and "unpack" perspectives and central concepts, our purpose and research questions.

However, framing the project in a strategic way involves research ethics considerations. One should never be dishonest or withhold any facts, but awareness of sensitive matters, empathy and intuitive feeling are helpful in the process of gaining access. No independent researcher can promise results that are only kind and accommodating to all. Research results are open-ended and impossible to know beforehand, and explaining to participants how research may be critical but still helpful in the field of study is difficult. On the one hand, the critical perspectives of the project's theoretical framing may have to be carefully presented, at least until the researcher trusts the participants enough to share these. In our case, the feminist perspective had to be downplayed as sceptical legal professionals sometimes got stuck on it and lost sight of the project as a whole. On the other hand, the gains from participating, and in what ways participation might benefit individuals or professionals, should not be over-emphasised.

How subtle signals of resistance or disinterest in participating given by legal actors should be interpreted is also an ethical question, as is how much a researcher can continue to insist on someone's participation before crossing an ethical line. In some cases, defence lawyers and victim's counsels agreed to be interviewed when asked face-to-face in connection with the trial, but they did not respond to emails about scheduling an interview. In these cases, how many times is it ethically acceptable to repeat the request?[9]

Closing Remarks

In this chapter, we have reflected on challenges, strategies and lessons learned in the complicated process of negotiating access to rape trials in Sweden. We have dealt with themes such as managing barriers to access; the constantly renegotiated and fragile nature of access; dependency on law judges as elite gatekeepers with the power and knowledge of how, in subtle ways, to hamper access to "their courtroom"; and degrees or layers of access, e.g., to different parts of the judicial process, to different legal actors and to different types of legal documents.

To gain formal approval is crucial, and to proceed in a correct manner is an important prerequisite for approval. If one of the central gatekeepers, such

[9] A top tip is to be prepared with your calendar when approaching potential participants outside the courtroom; try to schedule a date for the interview directly, especially with the lawyers. Our experience was that, compared with privately employed lawyers, prosecutors employed in the public sector and judges answered our emails more frequently.

as a president of the court, feels that their authority is not properly acknowledged by the researchers, they can put an end to the project immediately. At the same time, an approval from a gatekeeper is not enough to gain access to trials behind closed doors, nor to all the legal actors. Judges are independent and have considerable discretionary power, so even if the project is formally approved, each court case and its people need to be approached in a similar manner, and the project may need to be explained again and again. Different people, days, situations and moods may actualize (re)negotiations of access at any time.

Practical Guidance

(1) Take issues of access seriously at an early stage of the research process and prepare by recognising and adapting to the various obstacles that may come up during the negotiation process.
(2) Reflect upon the continuum of access in your specific study before and during the research process, and do not undervalue partial access.
(3) Use several access strategies, for example, formal presentations, asking legal participants directly and looking at public court lists for upcoming hearings.
(4) Be prepared to be denied access and do not give up; be firm and persistent (see e.g., Noaks and Winrup [2004] for strategies to use if denied access).
(5) Find out which formal approvals you need (in which instances, from which people and for what purpose) and think strategically about how to approach important gatekeepers such as the presiding judges or the complainants.
(6) Think carefully about how the project is to be presented, and learn from and adapt to reactions from the field (see e.g., Bergman Blix and Wettergren 2015).
(7) Use methods that facilitate trust, for example, shadowing of legal actors and initial interviews.
(8) Continually reflect upon research ethics issues (see also Chapter 4). For example, how do you approach sceptical and resistant actors? Where does your positionality come into play? How does it hinder, circumvent or enable certain research projects and inquiries?

References

Baldwin, John. 2008. Research on the criminal courts. In *Doing research on crime and justice*, ed. R.D. King and E. Wincup, 375–398. Oxford: Oxford University Press.

Bergman Blix, Stina, and Åsa Wettergren. 2015. The emotional labour of gaining and maintaining access to the field. *Qualitative Research* 15 (6): 688–704.

Bergman Blix, Stina, and Åsa Wettergren. 2018. *Professional emotions in court. A sociological perspective*. London: Routledge.

Bitsch, Anne. 2018. The micro-politics of emotions in legal space: An autoethnography about sexual violence and displacement in Norway. *Gender, Place & Culture* 25 (10): 1514–1532.

Bladini, Moa, and Wanna Svedberg Andersson. 2020. Swedish rape legislation from use of force to voluntariness-critical reflections from an everyday life perspective. *Bergen Journal of Criminal Law & Criminal Justice* 8 (2): 95–125.

Bryman, Alan. 2004. *Social research methods*. Oxford: Oxford University Press.

Burman, Michele, Lynn Jamieson, Jan Nicholson, and Oona Brooks. 2007. *Impact of aspects of the law of evidence in sexual offence trials: An evaluation study*. Scottish Government.

Booth, Tracey. 2012. 'Cooling out' victims of crime: Managing victim participation in the sentencing in a superior sentencing court. *Australian & New Zealand Journal of Criminology* 45 (2): 214–230.

Daly, Ellen. 2022. Making new meanings: The entextualisation of digital communications evidence in English sexual offences trials. *Crime Media Culture* 18 (4): 578–596.

Darbyshire, Penny. 2011. *Sitting in judgment: The working lives of judges*. London: Hart Publishing, Bloomsbury Collections.

Hvala, Heather R., and Sameena Mulla. 2018. "That's how she talks": Animating text message evidence in the sexual assault trial. *Law & Society Review* 52 (2): 401–435.

Empson, Laura. 2018. Elite interviewing in professional organizations. *Journal of Professions and Organization* 5: 58–69.

Faria, Caroline, Sarah Klosterkamp, Rebecca Maria Torres, and Jayme Walenta. 2020. Embodied exhibits: Toward a feminist geographic courtroom ethnography. *Annals of the American Association of Geographers* 110 (4): 1095–1113.

Fielding, Nigel G. 2013. Lay people in court: The experience of defendants, eyewitnesses and victims. *The British Journal of Sociology* 64 (2): 287–307.

Flower, Lisa. 2019. *Interactional justice: The role of emotions in the performance of loyalty*. Oxford: Routledge.

Gill, N., J. Allsopp, A. Burridge, D. Fisher, M. Griffiths, N. Paszkiewicz, and R. Rotter. 2021. The tribunal atmosphere: On qualitative barriers to access to justice. *Geoforum* 119: 61–71.

Kraska, Peter B., Brent, John J., and W. Lawrence Newman. 2021. *Criminal justice and criminology research methods*. Oxford: Routledge.

Lees, Sue. 1996. *Carnal knowledge. Rape on trial*. London: Hamish Hamilton.

Noaks, Lesley, and Emma Wincup. 2004. *Criminological research: Understanding qualitative methods*. London: Sage.

Ntamazeze, Janvière. 2016. *Trust and capabilities. Experiences from Rwanda's informal financial institutions*, PhD Thesis, University of Gothenburg, School of Global Studies.

O' Reilly, Karen. 2009. *Key concepts in ethnography*. London: Sage.

Roach Anleu, Sharyn, Stina Bergman Blix, Kathy Mack, Åsa Wettergren. 2016. Observing judicial work and emotions: Using two researchers. *Qualitative Research* 164: 375–391.

Shaffir, B. William, and Robert A. Stebbins. 1991. Getting in. In *Experience fieldwork. An inside view of qualitative research*, ed. B.W. Shaffir and R.A. Stebbins. London: Sage.

SFS 1980:100. The Swedish code of judicial procedure.

Smith, Olivia, and Tina Skinner. 2012. Observing court responses to victims of rape and sexual assault. *Feminist Criminology* 7 (4): 298–326.

Smith, Olivia, and Tina Skinner. 2017. How rape myths are used and challenged in rape and sexual assault trials. *Social & Legal Studies* 26 (4): 441–466.

Smith, Olivia. 2018. *Rape trials in England and Wales: Observing justice and rethinking rape myths*. Cham: Palgrave Macmillan.

Spiegel, Samuel J. 2021. Climate injustice, criminalisation of land protection and anti-colonial solidarity: Courtroom ethnography in an age of fossil fuel violence. *Political Geography* 84: 102298.

Swedish Research Council. 2017. *Good research practice*. Stockholm: Swedish Research Council.

Temkin, Jennifer, Jacqueline M. Gray, and Jastine Barrett. 2018. Different functions of rape myth use in court: Findings from a trial observation study. *Feminist Criminology* 13 (2): 205–226.

Törnqvist, Nina. 2017. *Att göra rätt: En studie om professionell respektabilitet, emotioner och narrativa linjer bland relationsvåldsspecialiserade åklagare*. Stockholm: Stockholms universitet.

Walenta, Jayme. 2020. Courtroom ethnography: Researching the intersection of law, space, and everyday practices. *The Professional Geographer* 72 (1): 131–138.

4

Positionality and Research Ethics

Sarah Klosterkamp and Tasniem Anwar

Introduction

In this chapter, we explicitly discuss how courtroom ethnography is a unique research method where research ethics are important yet underdiscussed. For us, such a reflection is inevitably aligned to questions of positionality, because some people in the court are particularly privileged due to their social position, while others are particularly vulnerable along the dimensions of socialisation, hetero- and cis-normativity, racialisation, disability, socio-economic inequalities or migration status. We, as researchers, are undoubtedly part of these power-disbalances present in the field. At the same time, and although there is a very rich literature reflecting questions of positionality and research ethics (Billo and Hiemstra 2013; Ellis 2016; England 1994; Faria and Mollett 2014; Fernando 2014; Ybema et al. 2009; Vorbrugg et al. 2021), we rarely read personal reflections of fieldwork in settings like the courthouse, institutions grounded in police information and carceral logics (however: Bitsch 2018; Fassin 2017; Flower 2021; Klosterkamp 2023). Yet, uplifting and

S. Klosterkamp (✉)
University of Bonn, Bonn, Germany
e-mail: s.klosterkamp@uni-bonn.de

T. Anwar
Vrije University of Amsterdam, Amsterdam, The Netherlands
e-mail: t.anwar2@vu.nl

L. Flower and S. Klosterkamp (eds.), *Courtroom Ethnography*,
https://doi.org/10.1007/978-3-031-37985-7_4

highlighting these challenges one may face when doing institutional ethnographies has a lot to offer as these moments are most often the starting point for individual doubts and ethical concerns when doing courtroom ethnographies, especially for junior scholars. As such, this chapter is dedicated to shedding light on the challenges of positioning oneself and the field, by asking: How do we manage such power differences when doing courtroom ethnographies, and how can we recognise, mark and unlearn colonial and privileging mechanisms in our thinking, research and everyday practices (Faria and Mollett 2014)? How do we handle the issues of access and information presented to us in these court cases in a way, which feels ethically right and without 'doing harm' (Ellis 2016; Fernando 2014)?

By following the lead of Vorbrugg et al. (2021) we consider courtroom ethnography as a method that is neither fully a study of the powerful nor a study of the marginalised. As such, courtroom ethnography requires a specific engagement with research ethics and questions of positionality, which is elaborated throughout the first section of this chapter. In the following, we introduce a framework of 'Politics of Fieldwork', where we elaborate the questions empirically and grounded in our own fieldwork experience, which derive from the method of courtroom ethnography and which focus on terrorism-financing trials in the Netherlands (Anwar) and state-protection proceedings in Germany (Klosterkamp). In doing so, we particularly draw on the concepts of positionality, situatedness and embodiment to grasp and consider social differences and hierarchies, and develop these concepts into research ethics. We propose that recognising the power imbalances that come with ethnographic observations—particularly within state-led, police-rendered and institutionalised settings like courtrooms—is important because they entail certain vulnerabilities aligned to this specific mode of studying up and/or studying down power (Nader 1972). In the end, we outline some concrete suggestions for bringing 'Politics of Fieldwork' into practice when conducting courtroom observations.

Studying Up or Down? Courtroom Ethnography and Reflections on Power

Ethnographic studies on powerful institutions such as the judiciary courtroom (Anwar 2022; Faria et al. 2020; Klosterkamp 2021), prisons and carceral spaces (Drake et al. 2015; Liebling et al. 2021) and the police (Herbert 2021) are quite common in the social sciences. By 'studying up', we shift our research focus to actors and institutions of power, rather than marginalised communities alone. Such approaches help us to better understand how law operates in practice and how legal decisions affect marginalised or privileged subjectivities in the courtroom. Here, as Vorbrugg et al. (2021) suggest, 'Researchers can use their privileged position to research not the impoverished but the profiteers, not the controlled but the police, not the rejected but the decision-makers' (p. 86).

When researching powerful institutions, we enter different power relations. Sometimes, researchers find themselves in comparatively precarious situations, fearing closed doors or even lawsuits, especially when researching legal proceedings within and beyond the courthouse. The work of law enforcement agencies is often surrounded by secrecy, sometimes with little motivation on the side of practitioners to share details about their work. Negotiating access (see also Chapter 2) is therefore a complex process, concerning ethical dilemmas on anonymisation, signing a non-disclosure agreement, withdrawal of consent or even extensive forms of control over one's writing (Ellis 2016; Fernando 2014). As researchers are very much interested in getting access to information and publishing our findings afterwards, we are often more aware of the fundamental risks in such research projects, not least because they affect us. Have we done everything 'right'? How will institutional representatives react if they don't 'like' what we write? Would they mobilise their institutional power against us? Would we be prepared for a confrontation? Many of our colleagues studying up powerful institutions have had sleepless nights over such questions (Vorbrugg et al. 2021, p. 86; Ybema et al. 2009).

While it is true that we focus on the judge, the prosecution and even the law itself as an object of study, the defendants in the cases we have studied all belonged to marginalised communities. As explained above, their stories are part of the courtroom interactions we observe and analyse. As researchers, we need to foster an awareness that despite the institutionalised and legal setting, we are still researching people's lives, families, desires and inner thoughts. As such, courtroom ethnographies require very particular research ethics that do not fit a simple approach of 'studying up' nor the more traditional anthropological research ethics for ethnographies of the marginalised. Therefore, in the following paragraph, we draw from feminist and post-colonial studies to develop a conceptual approach to conducting courtroom ethnographies with attention to the 'Politics of Fieldwork' that comes into play when doing so.

Key Concepts for Research Ethics in Courtroom Ethnographies

A growing body of literature surrounds and deals with the specific enjoyment and the burdensome moments of doing fieldwork (Billo and Hiemstra 2013; Ellis 2016; England 1994; Faria and Mollett 2014; Fernando 2014; Klosterkamp 2023; Vorbrugg et al. 2021). Hence, debates around feminist fieldwork practice offer important guidance when dealing with complex social situations and political and ethical claims and contributions. By following the lead of Vorbrugg et al., we are concerned here with research that should be power-sensitive in a double sense: suitable for naming, analysing and critiquing power and domination relations and subsequently linked to a practice that considers power relations even within social fieldwork situations and academic knowledge production (Vorbrugg et al. 2021, p. 79). In this context, the term 'Politics of Fieldwork' as a concept rather than a clear agenda has been found much useful as it does not denote a uniform or closed position but refers to fundamental concepts and principles (Vorbrugg et al. 2021, p. 79), of which we will outline some of the most important ones below: (1) reflexivity, (2) positionality and (3) embodiment.

Reflexivity

The principle of *reflexivity* is considered a basic element and prerequisite of feminist research practice. It assumes that researchers do not uncover facts but develop and offer interpretations, thus actively co-constructing knowledge. Recognising the fugitivity of these interpretations requires explicit attention to how they come about (Billo and Hiemstra 2013; Faria and Mollett 2014). If knowledge is constructed in a context- and position-dependent way, then the context and conditions of knowledge production are also of interest (Fernando 2014). In research, reflexivity also requires us to examine how our social identity, social positioning and personal involvement in research processes affect and shape the results (England 1994; Faria and Mollet 2014; Kobayashi 2003). Thus, reflexivity serves to situate one's perspective and the knowledge generated and determines and limits the claim to validity of this knowledge. It also leads us to ask under what circumstances is it (il)legitimate to speak and write about or for the researched, especially if they belong to marginalised groups (Ellis 2016; Mohanty 1984).

In the context of courtroom ethnographies, this ability to reflect critically is essential. Not only because the researcher learns about intimate details of the persons in court but also because it is during the court proceedings that the question of law, evidence and political stakes are negotiated. The court proceedings reflect the moment where the (legal) dust has not settled yet, and the courts' deliberations and decisions are still pending. Observing, analysing and writing about these moments of 'law in action' (Travers and Manzo 1997) requires a great sense of reflexivity and acknowledgement of the social and political context in which legal decisions are made. However, (self-)reflexivity is not a universal answer for dealing with contradictions: it can neither create complete transparency in the research process and its representation (Billo and Hiemstra 2013; England 1994) nor completely resolve political-ethical tensions (Ellis 2016; Fernando 2014) or power asymmetries (Faria and Mollett 2014; Klosterkamp 2023).

Positionality

The concept of *positionality(ies)* is significant in terms of its epistemological foundations and implications for research practice. Our social position and our thoughts and actions are shaped by social axes of difference, power and oppression, such as gender, class, racialisation, sexual orientation and identity, nationality or migration status, disability and many others. This contextual shaping of our own position has been pointed out above all by repeatedly marginalised researchers from black, post- and decolonial feminist theories, feminist racism research and queer-of-colour theories (Muñoz 1999). Kimberlé Crenshaw (1991), for example, elaborated on the concept of intersectionality, which can be used to show how social dimensions of power and oppression interact in a complex way and reinforce each other. Therefore, positionalities cannot be considered separately or simply added up (Faria and Mollett 2014). Positionalities are neither rigid nor arbitrary, but intersectionally entangled, context-dependent and embedded in epistemic and economic power relations and structures. Positionalities thus frame and render how we view, observe and analyse the world (Kobayashi 2003). Donna Haraway (1988) coined the term *situated knowledge* to emphasise that there is no objective scientific worldview but that the knowledge we produce and interact with is always situated and embodied in space and time and imbued by our experiences.

Positionality is highly relevant for courtroom ethnographers. There is often a notion that sitting in the public gallery of the courtroom might seem as if our presence is irrelevant since we are not actively participating in any of the legal practices. Feminist research ethics, however, remind us that this is not true—by being present, we have already become part of and impacted the legal proceedings (Klosterkamp 2023). Rather than being neutral observers, we actively listen, observe, take notes and reproduce knowledge about the cases that we study (Billo and Hiemstra 2013; Ellis 2016). Furthermore, as we will illustrate below, our presence is noted by the court, the defendants and the legal practitioners. In this context, we are not faceless observers, but our positionality as researchers, our gender, ethnicity, religion and other facets of our identity become relevant and part of the ethnographic practice (Koch 2019).

Embodiment

Understanding knowledge as integrated and situated in social structures and processes also includes bodily experience. Bodies are not assumed to be given and *natural* but shaped by power relations. Bodies are not only there but get read, interpreted and judged upon stereotypes and narratives, shaping and rendering the body's perception as *wanted* or *unwanted* and *able* or *unable*. These hegemonic readings are always socially produced anew and hierarchised or standardised along differences (Ahmed 2012). The *embodiment* approach, according to which knowledge is always embodied and inscribed in bodies, is therefore central to power-critical knowledge production and research practice. Our bodies and those of others play a double role. On the one hand, they serve us as a medium of knowledge; conversely, they manifest barriers to access and perception spatially and along heterosexist and cis-normative, racist and socio-economic demarcations. As researchers, this means that questions of our physical ability or disability also significantly influence how, where and in what form we gain access to knowledge and (can) process it accordingly (Chouinard 1997). At the same time, and since the production of knowledge itself takes place through and with certain bodies, mechanisms of attraction and rejection, and individually experienced but socially charged emotions such as fear, rejection and shame cannot be detached from the conditions of production and reproduction of certain orders of knowledge (Vorbrugg et al. 2021, p. 80; see also: Hyndman 2001).

As we will elaborate in this chapter, there are many different layers of how our bodies *do* courtroom ethnography. Researching courtroom proceedings requires stamina, as often cases are delayed, prolonged or even cancelled at the last moment (see also Chapter 2). Researchers travel to the courtroom, not knowing if they can enter or sit for hours waiting for the case to commence. Our appearances as white, Muslim, female, educated, innocent or suspicious are noted by legal practitioners, guards, family members and friends of the defendants and affect our abilities to access information and respondents from them. We propose that all these moments of being in the field are embodied instances of doing research, not empty moments of waiting but moments full of interaction, affect and emotion. Fundamental to power-critical and collaborative research practice is, therefore, responsible engagement with research participants, honest listening and an openly negotiation of interests and concerns with anyone involved or present, when being in the field (Klosterkamp 2023; Vorbrugg et al. 2021, p. 82).

In the following paragraphs, we offer a few glimpses of what to expect and how to deal with unforeseen challenges and questions of positionality, reflexivity, embodiment and ethics. Both examples depart from and are grounded in our own courtroom ethnographies on terrorism-financing trials in Germany and the Netherlands. In the conclusion, we move beyond the specific empirical example and provide broader practical guidelines for researchers undertaking courtroom ethnography.

Stories from the Courthouse

Fieldwork example 1: Negotiating access as a Muslim woman and researcher, working on terrorism-financing trials in the Netherlands:

> In common understanding, court proceedings are transparent and open to the public. Compared to other counter-terrorism measures, such as blacklisting or increased surveillance, it seemed that studying counter-terrorism trials would be less secretive, more accessible and better documented. While trials are indeed open to the public, they are also very unpredictable. Even if there is an overview by the court of the sittings, not all trials are listed or made public. Hence, getting information about the details of a trial is very difficult for an outsider. It requires connections with legal professionals and journalists with access to more information and a persistent strategy to 'get in'. As such, courtroom ethnography does not only take place in the courtroom but requires multiple connections with the field and its actors (see also Chapter 3). Being connected in the field is a good strategy to get access to court cases, yet it also brings up new ethical concerns about positionality and anonymity. In 2019, at the court in Rotterdam where Anwar was visiting a terrorism trial, one employee of a law enforcement organisation recognised her and approached her. The employee jokingly called her 'the girl with the book'. While at that moment, it was frustrating being read not as a researcher but through a gendered lens, she was more concerned with continuing the conversation to get access to this secretive law enforcement organisation. It, therefore, opened a space for conversation and negotiation of access more broadly in countering terrorism. At the same time, such strategies require the researcher's

reflexivity. After that day in the Rotterdam court, Anwar wrote in her field-notes, 'What does it mean when others see me speaking or knowing them, and how will it affect access to other stories? At some point, I might know everyone in the courtroom. Can I still write about all of them?' Doing court-room ethnography, therefore, requires a delicate balance between knowing the actors in the field and maintaining enough distance to formulate adequate analyses and critiques. Hence, how we carry ourselves as researchers impacts our courtroom ethnography possibilities and methods.

Aside from the necessity of *reflexivity*, Anwar's *positionality*, and particularly her appearance as a Muslim woman, played a crucial role. Often people assumed that she belonged to the entourage of the defendant. Indeed, in almost all trials she visited, the defendants were Muslims, the only people in the court-room who 'looked' like her. This lack of diversity in the courtroom reflects a broader political context in which counterterrorism practices are focused on the suspicious 'Other'—racialised and Muslim communities. On another occasion, during a practitioner's meeting on countering and prosecuting terrorism financing, a participant approached her to inquire, 'How do you experience all these discussions *as a Muslim?*' While it is relevant to reflect on our positionality when conducting research, this question reveals even more about the questioner's assumptions and stereotypes, as such a question is rarely posed to white researchers studying terrorism. 'How do you experience countering terrorism as a *white person?*' is not a common way to start a conversation. In some instances, being a Muslim researcher raises suspicion; however, on other occasions, it allowed research conversations. The researcher's positionality is always relational yet requires a very particular form of (emotional) labour if researchers are not white, male, able-bodied or otherwise privileged identities. This implies how our courtroom observations are not apolitical instances but are related to broader societal and political hierarchies and inequalities. (cf. for more details: Anwar 2022)

Fieldwork Example 2: Dealing with contradictions and conflicting goals as a white, first-generation academic in anti-terrorism trials and within uprising right-wing tensions in Germany:

Law and justice are not necessarily always close to each other but are usually strongly dependent on the observer's perspective. This is all the more true for state-led proceedings in which a federal republic like Germany is to be defended against terrorism strikes and/or actions of participation of the country's own citizens have been undertaken abroad. In the past few years, Klosterkamp has entered the spectator areas of state-protection trials and examined how German and Syrian citizens become the target of police investigations, surveillance and prosecution when the organisations they support are classified as 'terrorist' by the state. In doing so, she experienced that being read as a white, enabled woman with a German passport can lead to very challenging moments of (de-)privilege and expectations of third parties, for which there is no universal solution. The longer she attended these proceedings, the more she was approached by various other people who showed an interest in her work. On the one hand, through encounters with family, friends or lawyers of the accused, she gained insight into the various ways in which police knowledge was incorporated, and she found herself clarifying questions and reconciling interpretations through her various engagements in these proceedings. On the other hand, there were also repeated encounters with journalists or law enforcement officers investigating these proceedings, even right-wing-affiliated local groups, with whom she strictly rejected such an exchange of information.

These encounters addressed Klosterkamp's *positionality* as (a) a German citizen; (b) an empowered woman, presumably against the oppression of other (especially Muslim) women; or (c) a junior researcher, presumably willing to share a lot of her valuable fieldnotes and insights because this is what researchers are supposed to do – serve the public by sharing their state-funded knowledge. While her openness for the former (the family, friends and lawyers of the accused) may have resulted in her empathetic, reserved and helpful manner proved to pave the way for the provision of many non-public file components and additional information in the context of joint lunches and train journeys, the latter (journalists, police personnel and right-wing affiliated civil groups) addressed her as an academic knowledge producer whose analysis was to serve a broader public predefined by them.

Refusing these attempts was important to Klosterkamp, but it is not always easy. Her main reason for refusing such cooperation was that most certainly, it might have resulted in unwanted media reports of those who trusted her in the first place and may have even resulted in violent repression or a dangerous distortion of the circumstances (of the crime). Nevertheless, the families and lawyers who watched her denying these approaches in their courtroom waiting areas highlighted in most cases that it would have been okay if she had shared some details, at least with journalists, because in this way, their family's coverage might have been more accurate than it had been done so far. Another family told her, 'People, in general, behave much better when they are being watched'. But they didn't anticipate the strong tension, often accruing, after some more distinct media coverages went public. In the end, it was often challenging for Klosterkamp to find the appropriate level of expressiveness for each form of speaking/writing about these trials without harming others but also not minimising the violent acts at stake (e.g., beheadings, manslaughter, human trafficking, etc.), especially if there are different experience levels involved. She noted in her field book, 'How to protect individual data if those, who are about to be depicted, don't want to be hidden?'.

Aside from *reflexivity* and *accountability*, exploring and foreseeing legal consequences and finding ways for telling the underlying court cases' stories of state security in a way that would not produce new vulnerabilities of individual persons or expose people (further) against their will, were then Klosterkamp's ongoing struggle in dealing with contradictions and conflicting goals within these difficult (unchosen) positionings. For her, thoughtful anonymisation and attention to the different vulnerabilities at play are key to circumventing different power dynamics within studying-up power approaches and by encountering marginalised groups at the same time. (cf. for more details: Klosterkamp 2021, 2023)

These short reflections show that courtroom ethnography entails more than our observations during court cases. It encompasses the interactions with multiple actors in the field, the efforts to know when cases take place and the visibility of sitting in court. They also demonstrate how our positionality requires constant reflection—not only on how we as researchers are trained and how we collect, understand and analyse our data but also on the social and political structures in which we operate. Our appearances impact the conversations that we have, how our interlocutors approach us and the type of access given to us.

Closing Remarks

Courtroom ethnography is particularly challenging as the research participants often consist of various actors intertwined in multiple power relations: defendants, judges, prosecutors, police officers, lawyers and many other related institutions and individuals. The different constellations of actors within the court make courtroom ethnography a complex methodology that requires attention to the Politics of Fieldwork. Without universal advice that every researcher can follow, we can still prepare ourselves in advance about relevant legal bases and how to navigate this specific research space. In this conclusion, we zoom out from our vignettes and broaden our practical suggestions for research ethics and tie these to conceptual building blocks on positionality, reflexivity and embodiment.

In many cases, the established research codes of the universities, professional societies or field research guidelines are sufficient. For example, the 'informed consent' of research participants is a principle that must always be upheld for reasons of research ethics, but it also protects us from unpleasant disputes by clarifying the principles of data use in advance (Vorbrugg et al. 2021). In the case of courtroom observations during public trials, where informed consent is not explicitly given by all actors in the room, we propose that the researcher should still follow similar guidelines that protect the personal information of the defendant and other legal practitioners. Personal details irrelevant to the legal analysis should be deleted, and the researcher should be aware of the responsibility to protect vulnerable data. Furthermore, it should be made explicit in publications when data is collected from interviews done with informed consent or from the court observations of the researcher. Here, the principle of anonymisation and careful handling of personal information protects the research participants and the researchers. The legal services of universities or ethics committees may also be able to provide helpful information and advice to better mitigate the risks of publishing sensitive information. Additionally, the advice of experienced colleagues is irreplaceable.

As discussed above, access and presence in the courtroom is not neutral choice but requires the researcher's *reflexivity*. Negotiating research access as openly as possible and thus also cooperating with representatives of powerful institutions can be demanding and challenging. However, it is necessary and does not contradict a critical perspective. A reflective process of negotiation of access and research opportunities is a fundamental research principle. For those actors with whom we do not want to negotiate for good reasons, we would have to research differently (see recommended reading). It is essential for us as courtroom ethnographers, to adopt a reflexive attitude towards negotiating access: By which institution was the access granted and under which conditions? How do the access and presence in the courthouse allow the researcher to conduct their research? What kind of legal practices or questions are visible and observable, and what practices are (made) absent or invisible? Reflection on such questions is vital to emphasise how courtroom ethnography is as a *situated and embodied* practice, limited to a particular legal context, time and space.

Publishing research results is certainly the most critical moment in research with powerful actors—from both sides, the observed and the observers. Once our texts are published, we have little control over how they circulate, who reads them and how they are understood (Abu-Lughod 1991; Fernando 2014). Still, we should not be discouraged in maintaining a critical position vis-à-vis the actors we study. We offer two ways to think and reflect about writing and publishing critically. First, there are no uninvolved or innocent standpoints of critique (Ahmed 2012). Therefore, we should not take our own critical viewpoints more seriously than surprising insights in the research process (Billo and Hiemstra 2013). Involved engagements with the representatives of critical institutions or practices can also provide opportunities to learn and develop our positions. In this development, it is helpful to place our courtroom observations into broader political and societal debates (Anwar

2022; Fernando 2014). Second, a reflexive approach to learning, listening and developing is key for establishing an ethical research framework (Vorbrugg et al. 2021). Therefore, writing up and publishing results should always be done with an explicit reference to the researcher's positionality and how this affected the researcher's access, findings and analysis.

Finally, our courtroom ethnographies are an embodied but not isolated experience—we observe, listen to and record legal practices—and as such, our training and identity fundamentally impact the knowledge we produce. Therefore, we encourage early scholars to pay attention to the different layers of courtroom ethnographies and develop some reflexive strategies and preparations before and during emerging with the field of choice. Some tips for such an approach are compiled in the Checklist (see below).

Tips for Practical Guidance

1. Have I clarified which compromises are acceptable to me and which are not? For example, would I conduct research in an institution that requires me to sign a non-disclosure agreement, or would this be incompatible with central research interests or political principles?
2. How do I want to position myself in the institution I work with in the field? Do I want to remain distant, or do I also want to 'give something back'? Can or should institutions profit from my results? Do I want to put any criticism up for discussion internally and/or make it public? Conscious decisions on such questions and careful consideration can help me in the concrete negotiation of approaches, unexpected turns and the publication of results.
3. Especially when conducting research with powerful institutions, such as courts and law enforcement agencies, it can be useful and helpful also to check the support options, research rules and risk management requirements of your university or research institution. Do I know these? Who can I turn to if problems arise?
4. The secure management and storage of research data are crucial for the researcher and the research participants. Secure management and storage is particularly relevant for sensitive information presented during court cases that could result in legal sanctions or other forms of violence. Researchers should check in their jurisdictions the legal frameworks for citing from court cases. Furthermore, they should consider how to store, archive and encrypt the data obtained. Who has access to it, and under what conditions? Can it be made available to 'third parties' after making appropriate arrangements, or should this be categorically ruled out?

References

Abu-Lughod, Lila. 1991. Writing against culture. In *Recapturing anthropology: Working in the present*, ed. Richard G. Fox, 137–162. Santa Fe: School of American Research Press.

Ahmed, Sara. 2012. On being included: Racism and diversity in institutional life. Durham and London: Duke University Press.

Anwar, Tasniem. 2022. Time will tell: Defining violence in terrorism court cases. *Security Dialogue* 53 (2): 130–147.

Billo, Emily, and Nancy Hiemstra. 2013. Mediating messiness: Expanding ideas of flexibility, reflexivity, and embodiment in fieldwork. *Gender, Place and Culture* 20 (3): 313–328.

Bitsch, Anne. 2018. The micro-politics of emotions in legal space: An autoethnography about sexual violence and displacement in Norway. *Gender Place and Culture: A Journal of Feminist Geography* 25 (10): 1514–1532.

Chouinard, Vera. 1997. Making space for disabling difference: Challenges to geographies. *Environment and Planning D: Society and Space* 15: 379–390.

Crenshaw, Kimberle. 1991. Mapping the margins: Intersectionality, identity politics, and violence against women of color. *Stanford Law Review* 43 (6): 1241–1299.

Drake, Deborah H., Rod Earle, and Jennifer Sloan, eds. 2015. *The Palgrave handbook of prison ethnography*. London: Palgrave Macmillan.

Ellis, Carolyn. 2016. Telling secrets, revealing lives. *Qualitative Inquiry* 13 (1): 3–29.

England, Kim V.L. 1994. Getting personal: Reflexivity, positionality, and feminist research. *The Professional Geographer* 46 (1): 80–89.

Faria, Caroline, and Sharlene Mollett. 2014. Critical feminist reflexivity and the politics of whiteness in the 'field.' *Gender, Place and Culture* 23 (1): 79–93.

Faria, Caroline, Klosterkamp Sarah, Torres, R. Maria, and Jayme Walenta. 2020. Embodied Exhibits: Toward a Feminist Geographic Courtroom Ethnography. *Annals of the American Association of Geographers* 110 (4): 1095–1113.

Fassin, Didier, ed. 2017. *Writing the world of policing. The difference ethnography makes*. Chicago: The University of Chicago Press.

Fernando, Mayanthi L. 2014. Ethnography and the politics of silence. *Cultural Dynamics* 26 (2): 235–244.

Flower, Lisa. 2021. Rumbling stomachs and silent crying: Mapping and reflecting emotion in the sensory landscape of the courthouse. In *Sensorial penalties*, ed. Kate Herrity, E. Bethany Schmidt, and Jason Warr, 159–174. Bingley: Emerald Publishing.

Haraway, Donna. 1988. Situated knowledges: The science question in feminism and the privilege of partial perspective. *Feminist Studies* 14 (3): 575–599.

Herbert, Steve. 2021. Accountability: Ethnographic engagement and the ethics of the police. In *Writing the world of policing: The difference ethnography makes*, ed. Didier Fassin, 23–41. Chicago: University of Chicago Press.

Hyndman, Jennifer. 2001. The field as here and now, not there and then. *The Geographical Review* 91 (1–2): 262–272.

Klosterkamp, Sarah. 2021. Security, mobility, and the body—Syrian insurgent groups' infrastructures and their geopolitical contestations through/by/in legal institutions. *Political Geography* 84, 102301. https://doi.org/10.1016/j.polgeo.2020.102301.

Klosterkamp, Sarah. 2023. Affectual intensities: Toward a politics of listening in court ethnography. *Gender, Place & Culture. A Journal of Feminist Geography, 30 (11)*: 1529–1551.

Kobayashi, Audrey. 2003. GPC ten years on: Is self-reflexivity enough? *Gender, Place & Culture* 10 (4): 345–349.

Koch, Natalie. 2019. Deep listening: Practicing intellectual humility in geographic fieldwork. *Geographical Review* 110 (1–2): 52–64.

Liebling, Alison, Bethany E. Schmidt, Kristel Beyens, Miranda Boone, Berit Johnsen, Mieke Kox, Tore Rokkan, and An-Sofie V. Beyens. 2021. Doing team ethnography in a transnational prison. *International Criminology* 1: 123–134.

Mohanty, Chandra T. 1984. Under Western eyes: Feminist scholarship and colonial discourses. *Boundary* 2 (12): 333–358.

Munoz, José E. 1999. *Disidentifications: Queers of color and the performance of politics*. Minnesota: University of Minnesota Press.

Nader, Laura. 1972. Up the anthropologist: Perspectives gained from studying up. In *Reinventing Anthropology*, ed. Hymes Dell, 284–311. New York: Pantheon Books.

Travers, Max, and John F. Manzo. 1997. *Law in action: Ethnomethodological and conversation analytic approaches to law*. London: Dartmouth Press.

Vorbrugg, Alexander, Sarah Klosterkamp, and Vanessa E. Thompson. 2021. Feldforschung als soziale Praxis. Ansätze für ein verantwortungsvolles und feministisch inspiriertes Forschen, In: Autor*innenkollektiv Geography und Geschlecht (Eds), *Handbuch Feministische Geographien. Arbeitsweisen und Konzepte*: 76–96. Opladen: Barbara Budrich.

Ybema, Sierk, Dvora Yanow, Harry Wels, and Frans Kamsteeg. 2009. *Organizational ethnography*. London: Sage.

5

Challenging the Authority of Sight

Alex Jeffrey

Introduction

What is knowable through the act of seeing court processes and consequently what is the scholarly value of court observation? This chapter seeks to address these questions. Court watching and court observations have become mainstays of critical academic studies of law, where the act of observation reveals to the scholar potentially unrecognised influences and outcomes of the arrangement of trial processes. Part of a wider 'practice turn' in legal studies (Brickell et al. 2021) while also reflecting the increasing role of ethnographic inquiry in understanding the operation of law (Flower 2021), observing court processes has illuminated how trials can marginalise, entrench bias and reproduce hierarchies of power. This method has been a key element of my own research into trial processes in the wake of mass atrocities, I have also used this method in my teaching of undergraduate legal geography, where students observe Cambridge Crown Court trials and explore the role of legal spaces in shaping practices and perceptions of justice (see Chapter 7). Observation brings to the fore the interplay of bodies, materials and atmospheres as significant agencies in the making of law (Faria et al. 2020). Consequently, it is a method

A. Jeffrey (✉)
University of Cambridge, Cambridge, UK
e-mail: asj38@cam.ac.uk

L. Flower and S. Klosterkamp (eds.), *Courtroom Ethnography*,
https://doi.org/10.1007/978-3-031-37985-7_5

that immediately challenges doctrinal approaches to law that emphasise the common procedures and rules that govern the judicial practices.

This chapter proceeds from a position of valuing court observation as a scholarly and activist praxis, while also seeking to probe the limits and pitfalls of using it as a standalone qualitative method. From the very outset this is a situated account: I have been studying court processes for around fifteen years and this grants an opportunity to look back at the assumptions that have framed some of my work in this field. I think in my own case I inflated the power of court observation as a method for grasping the nature, meaning and purpose of trial processes. Influenced by feminist perspectives that orientate attention to the situated and partial nature of both law and social scientific enquiry, in this chapter I want to narrate these failings while looking to contribute to debates as to how place, space and embodiment can be better understood in the making of law (Faria et al. 2020). While access to court spaces varies and can come with challenges (see Chapters 2 and 13), in some circumstances observation is a seductive method as it seemingly requires little by way of permission to gain access (in circumstances where legal processes are publicly accessible) and can be completed without uncomfortable interactions with other court users or commentators. But with these benefits come the potential costs of overemphasising the interpretative power of the observer, overlooking the agency of court users and lending primacy to the visual realm as the principal sense through which law is made.

At first, the limits of observation are also a reflection of the limits of researcher subjectivity. Following Klosterkamp (2023), it is vital to recognise the impossibility of a researcher exiting the power relations produced through the visual characteristics of trials. It is equally challenging to satisfactorily enter the inner thoughts of other court users. Both these acknowledgements point to the requirement to appreciate the embodied nature of the court processes as necessarily alienating (reflecting the separation of bodies, differential power positions and the inability to read the inner thoughts of trial participants) while also unifying (reflecting the shared bodily experience, collective affectual responses and commonly held moral positions) (Jeffrey 2020a). Sensitivity to the embodied nature of trial processes helps to move away from a reliance on the visual realm and shifts towards a textured account of the interplay of different material agencies in the making of law (Latour 2010).

It must be noted that this discussion is set within the context of legal systems that are undergoing profound and rapid change. The increased use of technology is changing what 'visibility' means, either through the increased use of digital platforms to resolve judicial disputes prior to a physical court process or using video technology to deliver a court process for one or more participants (Flower 2021; Mulcahy et al. 2020). In what follows I try and integrate consideration of the changing modalities of visibility as the chapter discusses the limits of observation in understanding trial processes. The chapter is organised into three sections. The first considers the ambiguities of visibility in trial justice, where seeing law is both a positive attribute to facilitate engagement and shared truths, while the primacy placed on visibility also acts as a mechanism for reproducing uneven power relations (see Chapter 4). Recognising the space constraints in a chapter of this length, the second section takes one aspect of observation: that of the body in court space. Using a reflexive writing approach, I trace how one court observation I made during research in Bosnia and Herzegovina over a decade ago could be critiqued and reconsidered with a deeper engagement with the politics of visibility. This section explores the different ways in which embodiment challenges the possibilities of observation, and the subsequent need for a mixed methodological approach to understand trial processes. The final section, by way of conclusion, advocates humility when undertaking court observation, recognising the partial and situated nature of interpretive praxis and to consider the value of collaborative approaches (see also Chapter 13).

The Ambiguities of Visibility

Legal processes have an ambiguous relationship with visibility. The principle of 'justice being seen to be done', a maxim originating in the words of then Lord Chief Justice of England Lord Hewart in 1924, appears to prioritise the visibility of judicial processes in asserting their impartiality (see Meyerson 2015). While the phrase in its original usage was referring to the importance of conveying the fairness of the judicial process it is often cited, particularly in British Law and associated legal systems, as an origin point for the significance of visibility and Jeremy Bentham's calls for 'open justice' (Johnston 2018). There are (at least) two strands to the perceived virtue of visibility. The first, and perhaps most fundamental, is the conflation of visibility and truth. Open justice is a reminder of the embedded assumption in many cultures that seeing is essential in conveying and establishing a shared truth. The authority of sight (*autopsia*) is a fundamental part of enlightenment philosophical traditions, where seeing was established as a 'higher order' sense in relation to 'lower order' senses, such as smell or touch (Dias 2004). The implications of this occularcentrism are felt both in the making of law and the enactment of social science (see Chapter 8). Both are concerned with the weighing of evidence, a word that is itself derived from the Latin verb *videre*, to see (Bloch 2008). In doing so a fundamental connection is formed between truth and sight, captured in phrases such as 'seeing is believing'.

The second—and connected—virtue granted to legal visibility is the connection made between visibility and accountability. Not simply a mechanism for conveying truth, the notion of open justice also suggests that seeing a legal process entails a form of participation in the making of law. This is perhaps best captured in the discursive value placed on transparency as an objective, that to see is to be able to feel connection to a legal process and somehow hold this to account. The primacy of transparency as an objective is then reproduced materially and discursively, sometimes literally using glass in the construction of new court buildings, but more often through the prioritisation of access to the justice system, either for the public and media in court space or through the increased use of video live streams to widen the audience of judicial processes (Moore et al. 2021). Underpinning these enactments of visibility is an assumption—sometimes explicit but more often implicit—that seeing legal processes contributes to a sense of democratic accountability for those making law while also engendering a sense of the overarching fairness of the judicial process. It is within this framework that we can see the activist work of 'courtwatching' as a practice that through the act of seeing seeks to challenge miscarriages of justice (Gill and Hynes 2021).

But there are counter narratives of visibility that sit alongside the virtues of truth and accountability. Within these frameworks seeing a legal process does not equate with participating in its deliberation or shaping its outcome. Any engagement with the politics of performance primes us to expect fundamental inequities between those who organise and perform a ritual and those who are cast as its audience, even where, in conditions such a trial, the lines between such designations may appear blurred and indistinct (Flower and Ahlefeldt 2021). The visual register, then, has been a central mechanism through which the authority of law has been conveyed. The spectacular nature of court buildings within urban settings, the prominence of symbols of the state and the raised status of the judicial bench are—amongst many others—devices that seek to use the aesthetic arrangement of materials to convey the authority of particular sites, actors and materials within the arrangement of law (Mulcahy 2010; Mulcahy and Rowden 2019). The court room is suffused with status and threat cues, whether the defendant in a securitised dock, the witness in a stand or the judge sitting on an elevated bench (Rossner et al. 2017). Visibility, then, is infused with power and choreographed to produce certain cognitive and affective responses to law.

There is a further aspect to the ambiguities of visibility in legal processes. The aspiration towards transparency and the authority of the visual realm sits in tension with alternative normative accounts of the visibility of law. By tracing the emergence of actual existing sites of law, legal scholars have illuminated the meticulous ways in which legal processes have cultivated a sense of invisibility and separation from wider publics, not simply on the basis of trying to hide legal processes from public scrutiny but equating such invisibility as essential in protecting judicial independence (Dezalay and Garth 1996). As an example of this virtuous separation, eighteenth-century assize courts in England were some of the first to be constructed as dedicated sites of legal deliberation, purposefully set apart from the activities of government and administration (Mulcahy 2010). This principle of legal closure maintains that legal rationality exists in isolation from wider socio-economic forces that could unduly influence the outcome of judicial processes; separation and invisibility provide the basis for the maintenance of consistency and therefore accountability in the making of law. Examples persist of such hidden aspects of law, even within legal systems that promote the values of open justice. The operation of international arbitral courts is an example where the closure of law is promoted as a strength in protecting the consistency and commercial value of legal processes.

These accounts of visibility, either as an asset, source of authority or as a potential weakness of the legal process, promote alternative accounts of justice and power. The emphasis on transparency recalls a Rawlsian interpretation of justice as a publicly acknowledge fairness, where a balance is struck between law makers and those subject to their rule (Sen 2006). But in the work on visibility and authority the visual realm becomes a site that can shape the outcome of legal processes through aesthetic decisions and spatial arrangements. Legal closure, in contrast, identifies the core value of legal expertise and non-interference as the basis of just decision making, where public attitudes are secondary to due process. To examine the interplay of these different approaches to visibility the chapter will consider the observation of the bodies in court space.

Observation and Embodiment

The role of bodies has become a focal point for feminist and critical studies of trial justice (Klosterkamp 2023; Mertus 2004). An embodied perspective recognises the necessarily partial and situated nature of engagement in trial activities, while paying attention to the reproduction of intersectional discrimination on the basis of race, sexuality, sexual identification or class (Jeffrey 2020a). The significance of embodiment both endorses court observation while also emphasising its limits. Paying attention to the unfolding of trials allows the court observer to trace issues of comportment, dress, emotion, position and enunciation as factors that shape the trial process (Blix and Wettergren 2018; Flower 2021). It allows the careful tracing of interactions that would be lost within a verbatim record and may be so subtle as to only be captured by direct observation of the event. I remember one such moment occurred in the public gallery of the War Crimes chamber of the Court of Bosnia and Herzegovina when, during the moment of a sentencing decision, a member of a victim association suddenly lost their footing and slumped into a friend (Jeffrey 2020b; Jeffrey and Jakala 2014). This gesture potentially revealed an underlying—and oft-spoken—distress at the retributive judicial process and in particular the short sentences given to those who had collaborated in planning or executing war crimes.

There are four aspects of this account of embodiment that point to the limits of observation. The first is the overdetermining of the body (as with visuality more broadly as discussed above) as a locus of truth. There is a growing field of critical scholarship examining how evidential traces of bodily a harm is elevated above other forms of testimony, in particular oral testimony. Fassin and d'Halluin's (2005) exploration of the medical certificates required by French asylum seekers provides a warning against the conflation of the body with truth. Reflecting anthropological studies of the assessment of torture, their account identities how medical observation—and its materialisation in the medical certificate—becomes the primary route through which asylum-seeker status may be conferred by the French state. In doing so the 'subjective' imagination of oral testimony is countered with the 'objective' traces left through bodily harm. Perhaps my observation of the member of the victim association in the public gallery reproduces this imagination of an objective gaze on a bodily truth? The unsteadiness on their feet could come from many different causes, and the centrality of observation invites projection of explanations to 'fit' a wider normative thesis relating to the operation of law. The research was set within twelve months of fieldwork interviewing victim associations and other groups that supported transitional justice processes in Bosnia and Herzegovina. It was often through repeat interviews and time spent with such organisations that attitudes towards the legal process came to the fore. These sentiments, complex, often contradictory or shifting, countered the straightforward narrative that could be drawn from the physical gesture in court space.

The second methodological issue concerning bodily observation relates to the limits of cognition in sites of trauma. The bodily gesture of the member of the victim association recalls the observation by Hannah Arendt in her account of the 1961 trial of Adolf Eichmann when witness Yehiel De-Nur fainted when giving testimony concerning the Holocaust (Arendt 2006). This has been interpreted in the years since as evidence of bodily limits of giving testimony, often set within a wider literary account of linguistic inadequacy in the face of trauma (Caruth 2017; Felman 2002). While this partially serves to endorse court observation—since bodily enactment may stand in place of spoken testimony—it also warns again the possibility of simple interpretations of behaviour in traumatic moments. Bodily practices are not straightforward alternatives to spoken testimony, rather the impact of trauma is felt on both bodily practices *and* acts of testimony. One representative from a different victim association in Bosnia and Herzegovina articulates how the act of giving testimony cultivated a sense of being 'lost':

> I have testified numerous times [they were] showing me photos of the entire military squad, you can imagine how big shock it was for me. One gets lost. [...] I didn't know where I was. I do not remember where I was, what I was looking at in that moment, I was there, I was not here, I cannot describe to you that feeling. Then I said that I will no more go to the Court nor testify or give testimonies without having a doctor sitting next to me. (Interview, Victims' Association, Tuzla, 19 April 2012)

This account points to the need for moments of reflection and narration of court events, out with the observation of the trial itself. It is through the subsequent interviews that the reasons for trauma—the lack of return of material remains, the absence of compensation and the perceived futility of the trials, came to the fore (see Jeffrey 2020b).

The third issue that stems from a focus on bodily observation is the necessarily relational nature of court subjects. Affective responses are collectively constituted, not held individually (Schliehe and Jeffrey 2023). Consequently, we need to consider multiple perspectives within court space and the significance of proximity to shaping understanding of the trial process. The significance of propinquity is being increasingly considered through legal geographical work examining the use of remote video links and bodily interactions within court cases (Hynes et al. 2020; Traynor and Tomczak 2021). Such issues came to the fore in recent research I was conducting into the International Court of Justice (ICJ) case of *The Gambia Vs. Myanmar* for breaches of the 1948 UN Genocide Convention. Watching the trial sessions and coding the transcripts of the legal submissions gave a sense of the legal arguments that formed the backdrop to the contestation. The ICJ is a strictly choreographed space, and the trial sessions show little space for bodily performance. In this context, it could be felt that the formalism of the process erased the significance of bodily interaction. But interviewing the participants produced a different set of embodied observations, one that illuminated a politics of proximity that both shaped participants perceptions of the process while also intervening in the legal deliberations themselves (Sands 2022). The visit of then State Counsellor and Foreign Minister for Myanmar Aung San Suu Kyi to the ICJ in The Hague to present the case for Myanmar was one of the key moments in the 'provisional measures' hearings in December 2019. Her presence in the court space, seemingly incidental in the video recordings, shaped the perceptions of the proceedings for lawyers on both sides of the dispute:

> It was really one of the hardest things I've had to do in terms of lawyering because you know like all academics I'm used to standing up and talking all the time but here you know I had Aung San Suu Kyi sitting next to me and I had cameras and everything and the Judges and you know the Court it's a big deal to be there. (Interview with international lawyer A, 10 February 2022)

> I was literally six feet from her. It was really, really something. I took a couple of snaps on my camera just to capture that sense of the flowers in her hair and everything. (Interview with international lawyer B, 3 February 2022)

While these observations illustrate the significance of proximity they could perhaps be dismissed as expected reactions to the presence of a prominent global political figure and Nobel Prize winner in close quarters of the ICJ. But in later comments the presence of Aung San Suu Kyi shaped the legal arguments themselves. One of the lawyers representing The Gambia, who were accusing Myanmar of breaching the Genocide Convention, remarked on how the proximity to Aung San Suu Kyi prompted improvisations within the legal argument, in particular the absence in the Myanmar legal submission of reference to the Rohingya by name or a reference to the very considerable allegations of sexual violence. The lawyer relays how they came to produce a response to Myanmar's defence:

> You do a first draft, the other lawyers all read it, then the Agent [the individual bringing the case to the ICJ, in this case Abubacarr Tambadou] looks at it, and everyone makes their comments and proofs it, and I had put in the draft a line about her failing to refer to rape, failing to refer to the Rohingya by name, and [my colleague] took it out. But as I was speaking, I just went off script, and I did stop and I looked at her, and I said, "Madame Agent we

> note [you did not mention the Rohingya by name or refer to the allegations of sexual violence committed by Myanmar military forces]," and in the end [my colleague] didn't mind at all, because it just captured everything. We didn't want things to be personalised, but she turned up. (Interview with international lawyer B, 3 February 2022)

There are two aspects of this case that need to be drawn out. The first is the material observation that bodily proximity shaped the nature of the legal response. The decision to improvise, to go 'off script', stemmed from bodily presence ('she turned up'). This is particularly significant as the second set of hearings in this case were impacted by the Covid-19 pandemic and held in a hybrid format where legal contributions were provided by mix of in court presentations and video link. It should also be noted that in the intervening eighteen months between the two sets of hearings the coup in Myanmar meant a change in legal team and political representation, specifically Aung San Suu Kyi was then under house arrest. The second aspect is the methodological question of how we grasp the act of improvisation. Watching the court gave a sense of the theatricality of the moment—when the legal representative looks to one side and criticises Myanmar's argument with ardour—but this gives no indication of the improvised nature of the comment. It is through the subsequent interview and explanation that the nature of this event comes to light. Observation alone may have inserted the comment as a wider collectively written statement, as opposed to one that stemmed from the personal conviction of the legal counsel, grounded as it was in a longer personal history of challenging the genocidal acts of states.

Closing Remarks

This chapter is one of celebration: that many of the points made in the discussion are reflected in the richly illustrated, patiently researched and reflexively aware field of feminist court ethnography (Flower and Ahlefeldt 2021; Klosterkamp 2023). As this work has shown, observing trials enables the researcher to grasp elements of the material and embodied nature of court processes, in doing so challenging doctrinal approaches that prioritise the linguistic aspects of legal disputes. It is a critical method in its rejection of the court as a neutral space, illuminating instead the ways in which hierarchies of power, reflecting wider social and cultural normative frameworks, incur into court proceedings. Using a reflexive approach, the chapter has sketched the limits of observation as a standalone method. Partly this is a critical act, the prominence of 'open justice'; and narrative of transparency within certain legal systems points to the ways in which visibility is always structured and orientated in ways that are beyond either the control or cognition of those conducting court observation. As long-standing work on positionality has taught us, no researcher can claim perfect self-knowledge (Rose 1997), and the impact of restrictions and choreography of court space on our own understanding of legal process are, to a certain extent, unknowable. Partly this is a call to retain a focus on long-standing methodologies such as interviews, participant observation, focus groups or shadowing that recognise the situated agency of all court users and the intrinsic value of paying attention to their accounts of court space.

But perhaps the argument also points to a broader conclusion concerning the need for humility and uncertainty in our narrations of legal practice. The discussion of embodiment was structured around a reflexive exercise of revisiting an observation made in previous research over a decade ago. My interpretation at the time fitted an argument relating to the perceived injustice of the war crimes trials process and drew on embodied action, including my own, to provide deeper 'proof' of the dissatisfaction over the perceived leniency of sentencing decisions. But this seems to overdetermine bodily practices and falls into the conflation between bodily action and truth criticised in the work of Fassin and d'Halluin (2005). Through distant observation we may project onto bodily practices any meaning we wish, knowing that bodies cannot speak back, and the interpretation is 'true' in the absence of any conflicting explanation. This feels increasingly unsatisfactory and captures a latent positivist approach that fails to appropriately locate the act within an alternative, embodied, understanding of the event. A key step in breaking the authority of sight is to acknowledge that we do not fully understand what is being seen, the court presents a set of situated actions whose interpretations are nearly limitless. Recognising the partiality of our sight is the first step, but the second is to value the plural narratives that make up a court event, each pointing to a different lived experience of the trial process.

Tips for Practical Guidance

1. Combine court observations with other methods that can help to develop a deeper understanding of the processes and motivations that shape court spaces.
2. Consider the power of sight, both in the privileging of visual aspects of court processes (for example how certain forms of evidence are made visible) but also through the notion of court watching as a political act of holding legal processes to account.

3. Trace how the visual aspects of court spaces are utilised by court users to shape the judicial process, a reflection on the theatricality of law.
4. Remain reflexive and self-critical: think about how our assumptions concerning observation can be challenged and reworked over time and space.

References

Arendt, Hannah. 2006. *Eichmann in Jerusalem: A report on the banality of evil*. London: Penguin.

Blix, Bergman, and Asa Wettergren. 2018. *Professional emotions in court: A sociological perspective*. Taylor & Francis.

Bloch, Maurice. 2008. Truth and sight: Generalizing without universalizing. *Journal of the Royal Anthropological Institute* 14 (s1): 22–32.

Brickell, Katherine, Alex Jeffrey, and Fiona McConnell. 2021. Practising legal geography. *Area* 53 (4): 557–561.

Caruth, Cathy. 2017. The body's testimony: Dramatic witness in the Eichmann trial. *Paragraph* 40 (3): 259–278.

Dezalay, Yves, and Bryant G. Garth. 1996. *Dealing in virtue: International commercial arbitration and the construction of a transnational legal order*. Chicago: University of Chicago Press.

Dias, N. 2004. *La Mesure Des Sens: Les Anthropologies et Le Corps Humain Au XIXème Siècle*. Aubier.

Faria, Caroline, Sarah Klosterkamp, Rebecca Maria Torres, and Jayme Walenta. 2020. Embodied exhibits: Toward a feminist geographic courtroom ethnography. *Annals of the American Association of Geographers* 110 (4): 1095–1113.

Fassin, Didier, and Estelle d'Halluin. 2005. The truth from the body: Medical certificates as ultimate evidence for asylum seekers. *American Anthropologist* 107 (4): 597–608.

Felman, Shoshana. 2002. *The juridical unconscious: trials and traumas in the twentieth century*. Cambridge: Harvard University Press.

Flower, Lisa. 2021. Rumbling stomachs and silent crying: Mapping and reflecting emotion in the sensory landscape of the courthouse. In *Sensory penalties: Exploring the senses in spaces of punishment and social control*, ed. Kate Herrity, Bethany E. Schmidt, and Jason Warr, 159–174. Emerald Publishing Limited.

Flower, Lisa, and Marie-Sophie Ahlefeldt. 2021. The criminal trial as a live event: Exploring how and why live blogs change the professional practices of judges, defence lawyers and prosecutors. *Media, Culture & Society* 43 (8): 1480–1496.

Gill, Nick, and Jo Hynes. 2021. Courtwatching: Visibility, publicness, witnessing, and embodiment in legal activism. *Area* 53 (4): 569–576.

Hynes, Jo, Nick Gill, and Joe Tomlinson. 2020. In defence of the hearing? Emerging geographies of publicness, materiality, access and communication in court hearings. *Geography Compass* 14 (9): e12499.

Jeffrey, Alex. 2020a. Legal geography II: Bodies and law. *Progress in Human Geography* 44 (5): 1004–1016.

Jeffrey, Alex. 2020b. *The edge of law: Legal geographies of a war crimes court.* Cambridge: Cambridge University Press.

Jeffrey, Alex, and Michaelina Jakala. 2014. The hybrid legal geographies of a war crimes court. *Annals of the Association of American Geographers* 104 (3): 652–667.

Johnston, Jane. 2018. Three phases of courts' publicity: Reconfiguring Bentham's open justice in the twenty-first century. *International Journal of Law in Context* 14 (4): 525–538.

Klosterkamp, Sarah. 2023. Affectual intensities: Toward a politics of listening in court ethnography. *Gender, Place & Culture. A Journal of Feminist Geography,* 30 (11): 1529–1551.

Latour, Bruno. 2010. *The making of law*. Cambridge: Polity.

Mertus, Julie. 2004. Shouting from the bottom of the well the impact of international trials for wartime rape on women's agency. *International Feminist Journal of Politics* 6 (1): 110–128.

Meyerson, Denise. 2015. Why should justice be seen to be done? *Criminal Justice Ethics* 34 (1): 64–86.

Moore, Sarah, Alex Clayton, and Hector Murphy. 2021. Seeing justice done: Courtroom filming and the deceptions of transparency. *Crime, Media, Culture* 17 (1): 127–144.

Mulcahy, Linda. 2010. *Legal architecture.* Routledge.

Mulcahy, Linda, and Emma Rowden. 2019. *The democratic courthouse: A modern history of design, due process and dignity.* London: Routledge.

Mulcahy, Linda, Emma Rowden, and Wendy Teeder. 2020. *Exploring the case for virtual jury trials during the COVID-19 crisis: An evaluation of a pilot study conducted by JUSTICE*. Oxford: Oxford Centre for Socio-Legal Studies. https://justice.org.uk/our-work/justice-covid-19-response/. Last Access: November 8th, 2023.

Rose, Gillian. 1997. Situating knowledges: Positionality, reflexivities and other tactics. *Progress in Human Geography* 21 (3): 305–320.

Rossner, Meredith, David Tait, Blake McKimmie, and Rick Sarre. 2017. The dock on trial: Courtroom design and the presumption of innocence. *Journal of Law and Society* 44 (3): 317–344.

Sands, Philippe. 2022. *The last colony: A tale of exile, Justice and Britain's colonial legacy*. London: Weidenfeld & Nicolson.

Schliehe, Anna, and Alex Jeffrey. 2023. Investigating trial spaces: Thinking through legal spatiality beyond the court. *Transactions of the Institute of British Geographers* 48 (1): 9–22.

Sen, Amartya. 2006. What do we want from a theory of justice? *The Journal of Philosophy* 103 (5): 215–238.

Traynor, Catherine, and Philippa Tomczak. 2021. What next for courtroom special measures? Embodying legal geographies through "appreciative-assemblage" methodology. *Area* 53 (4): 577–585.

6

Studying Legal Courts Trans-sequentially

Thomas Scheffer

Introduction

In times of crises, courts receive extra public attention. The mass media reports on 'high security' terrorism trials, on 'too soft' or 'too harsh' verdicts regarding climate activism, or on lawsuits against 'pandemic' state regulations exemplify this trend. While courts deal with increasingly existential matters, courtroom studies undergo some kind of revival. They appear as one attractive option to study our contemporary condition under the magnifying glass of witness stand and judge's bench. Despite this shared fascination with the law-in-action, socio-legal ethnographies take what happens in court in rather opposite ways. We find approaches commonly referred to as structural or as interpretive (see Banakar and Travers 2005). How do they differ and to what effect?

(1) Structural approaches view what is going on court as an articulation of societal power or domination. They expose the occurrences in open court—despite all legal self-description—as following the common hegemonic logic. The court is, in this perspective, ultimately just an extension of the societal structure. A perfect 'structural case' is one, where the outcome is fully predictable based on basic data, such as the social status of the parties or

T. Scheffer (✉)
Department of Social Sciences, Goethe University Frankfurt, Frankfurt Am Main, Germany
e-mail: scheffer@soz.uni-frankfurt.de

L. Flower and S. Klosterkamp (eds.), *Courtroom Ethnography*,
https://doi.org/10.1007/978-3-031-37985-7_6

the social image and ideological status of the matter.[1] While deciphering the workings of power, these mostly critical studies have to wrestle with the question why ethnographic observations are necessary at all. If what is going on in court can be predicted and explained by external forces, any close inspection of the words and deeds of judges, lawyers, and the laypeople seems a waste of effort.

(2) Whereas structural approach tends towards generalisation, interpretative approaches tend towards respecification. They view whatever happens as locally co-produced. They assume a rather autonomous meaning-production in and by the court and its community of practice. Hence, following the court's dealings demands for insiders' knowledge. The contributions carry a local history, derive from what happened here before, and are coloured by mundane attitudes of the professional natives. The ethnographically observed occurrences serve as data, foremost, to learn about *this* court, *this* community, *this* style. The perfect 'interpretative case' is one, that fully translates the matter and those attached to it in its own terms and according to its own logic.[2] Interpretative studies wrestle with the question of how what is going on here and now reflects the wider society,[3] its power relations, or the legal culture.

The targeted points of these styles and logics of research seem indeed opposite or even contradicting. However, they share certain concerns. Both approaches—the one critical of domination and the one affirmative to local meaning-production—counter the narrative of an impartial law and neutral procedure. Sociality matters, either by power relations external to the inner workings of law or by the locally shared views invested into the handling of the cases. The Sociolegal Studies—whether it is legal anthropology or sociology of law—teach a similar lesson: law-in-action is more than legal rules and legal expertise; it is a praxis driven by social forces. You do not understand what is going on in court, without turning to the social life of it (see Chapter 9).

---

[1] On example would be terrorism trials. They turn the courts into 'weapons' against the common threat. Hence, terrorism trials call for the legal procedure—or just certain 'technicalities' (Suresh 2019)—to be protected against the pressing external demands. Such extreme cases render observable procedural foundations that otherwise remain unnoticed in the court's business as usual. They are crises experiments, or become, for specialised courts, normal business once again.

[2] Popular culture often depicts the court as a terrain full of traps and fallacies. 'Being in God's Hand at Sea and in the Court' is an expression of this wisdom. Being exposed to a court trial calls for 'stewards' to provide for guidance and protection.

[3] Some anthropologists use the hearings in open court as a kind of window or 'lens to society' (Berti and Tarabout 2017). The methodical strategy: The courts, as micro-publics, render accessible what would be otherwise hidden away in private.

Critical and interpretative approaches start by looking for the social in whatever legal business: Habitus, rituals, symbols, narratives, metaphors, and, preferably, bias and prejudice. Rather differently, the style of ethnographic socio-legal research I propose here counters the dualism of law and society. The research style applies certain analytical motives originally deriving from Ethnomethodologists such as Karin Knorr Cetina (1992), Michael Lynch, or Steve Woolgar in their lab studies on science-in-action. The idea was this: Instead of accusing objective science of being inclined to blind spots and disturbing sociality, they would rather focus on how a laboratory is run and how the necessary work would be unfeasible without socialities such as chitchat, decorum, or speculation. It is impossible to imagine the laboratory without people, things, and their manifold relations. Common sense, natural language, media use, routines, conventions, etc., are foundational. The same idea applies to the fabric of law, being technical and mundane at the same token.

Similarly, judicial ethnography, as I place it here, is beyond the dualism of general structure and local interpretation. We ask, in an ethnomethodological-praxeological fashion: What does it take and what methods are applied in order to guarantee in any case such a thing like a binding legal judgement? This affirmative approach provides a solid basis for asking—also critically—about the effects of these well-rehearsed, methodical legal practices. What are the kind of cases that those legal ways favour, and which ones are rather dispreferred, even downright recalcitrant? Cases of terror, for example, do cause problems, because they put to the test the principle of distance between law and politics. What is more, most jurors or lay judges may know too much about the matter in advance. Cases of rape, to cite other examples (Matoesian 1993), carry a number of peculiar problems as well (see Chapter 3). Many cases come down to a testimony versus testimony constellation. The practical methodology of the court, and it needs such a methodology, has—much like our theories or approaches—its limited scope of functioning. Its practical capacity is restricted and shall be an object of our inquiries.

My emphasis on the two tendencies of structuralist and interpretative styles of sociolegal research does not intend to make a fundamental decision about their respective meaningfulness. Rather, I mean to shed light on how we reflexively and empirically catch up with these methodologies. We shall ask how to actually observe whether court trials differ in this regard, being rather structural or interpretative. We thus assume that the above-mentioned methodologies imagine their very own ideal-types, whereas real-types present themselves as variants somewhere in between. This does not exclude 'extreme' cases such as show trials in totalitarian regimes or provisional tribunals dealing with petty crimes and entitled to vast local improvisation. Hence, I suggest turning the question of opposite logics of research into an empirical concern of court ethnographies. This empirical twist implicates that at times theoretical approaches are more materially, historically, or culturally specific than generally claimed. Legal cultures, matters, and constellations tend to push their respective courts more or less forcefully in rather one or the other direction.

In the following, I present resources and procedures for ethnographic court research that stays open for such conceptual dialogues. By resources, I mean a number of core concepts to open up the court's conflictual workings without presuming it to be merely interpretative or structural by nature. By procedures, I refer to the building up of the research process including a sequence of coding exercises. The short article closes with a diagnostic outlook on the legal courts under pressure, due to a number of vital societal questions. The latter change general atmospheres (towards polarisation) and matters (towards increasing dependency) to the direction of indispensability.

Basic Concepts for a Praxeological Court Ethnography

I suggest a micro-foundational approach that involves multiple spatio-temporal scopes. It includes the a number of basic concepts. The concepts are sensitising, insofar as they render observable what exceeds the structuralist or interpretative gaze. The concepts are, additionally, resources that members themselves use in order to organise their work, to orient themselves in the legal dealings, or to tackle their regularly occurring practical problems. The order of concepts imagines the steps to open up court hearings ethnographically.

Turn-by-Turn

Legal ethnography can study and deconstruct what goes on in court on the level of the turn-by-turn unfolding of certain activities. The latter could be a ritual of giving oath, the friendly examination by the representative, the 'cross-examination' by the opposing party (see Drew 1992), the taking of 'expert evidence' (Saks 1990), the sentencing speech by the single judge, etc. All these activities appear in open court, accessible to the audience due to their very regularities. The turn-by-turn reconstruction allows us to identify regularities, preference structures, and norms on how to do this properly. Each activity, accordingly, comes with certain practical demands and problems that the members have to deal with, while co-producing this or that legal act or meaning. Atkinson and Drew (1979) could show how (institutional) talk in court makes use of a pre-structured turn-allocation including certain acts that are reserved to specific categories of members only: asking questions, e.g., is monopolised by barristers and judge; even 'taking notes' is permitted just for certain membership categories such as clerk or reporter. What is more, 'institutional talk' cultivates a certain 'recipient design'. The professionals co-address jury and public by explaining matters in—what counts as—'simple language'.

Imports and Exports

Law-in-action does not only depend on certain props and equipment[4] provided for by and in the courtroom, as Goffman's metaphor of the 'theatre stage' would teach us, but also on a number of case-related imports. This might be the defence barrister's script guiding his or her own closing speech or the prosecution's disclosed file including all the evidence to account for in court. This might be, what is more, the judges' rulings regarding the application of certain statutes or precedence. From the point of view of the law firm or the Crown Prosecution Service (to name Common Law institutions), some of these imports have been prepared by means of 'invisible work' (Laube et al. 2020) prior to the hearing. The parties in the court hearing including the judge, on the other hand, are ongoingly working on exports: the official version of the talk in court to start with. They co-produce a constantly growing body of case materials on what will count and stand for later as the actual proceeding. Closing speeches and verdict have to be argued on and refer to those 'solidified' grounds.

Import and Export Regulations

It is important to recognise the dependency of the court hearings on preparation and delegation—and thus again on various forms of 'invisible work' (Laube et al. 2020). Not everything that gains relevance derives from the here and now of the court hearings. Some key operations are outsourced (Maynard 1984). We cannot understand the practical status of the ondensed court

[4] By props, we could think of wigs, coats, pen and paper, flags, etc.

hearing without taking into account the imports and exports including their regulations. Rules of evidence, for instance, define what kinds of knowledge are admissible. The English Crown Court, e.g., would strictly forbid 'hearsay' to enter the courtroom. The parties shall not use 'untestable' rumours and speculations, or, even worse, include those in their argumentation. Other import restrictions concern the audience in the courtroom. Forbidden are generally not just weapons of all kinds, but at times also devices to prepare competing records or political symbols that undermine the court's authority. Courtrooms, one may conclude, are regularly construed as sacred space, purified from 'dirty' deeds, words, and things.

The extent by which the procedure's inside/outside interface is operated—e.g., in terms of social relations or networks (Conley and O'Barr 1990)—allows us to infer the degree of autonomy of the court. The members' boundary work can be understood in rather discursive ways also: The judge, for instance, would ask the members of the jury not to weigh the statement by a 'police officer' more than the ones of 'ordinary witnesses'; the witness is not allowed to read out her/his statement from a script. Despite such import restrictions, the lawyers carry out their procedural tactics by utilising a number of symbolic values: She would place certain characters—the 'poor victim', the 'trustworthy expert', the 'normal guy'—at certain dramaturgical points in their case's presentation in order to make subtle use of those 'cultural' images.[5] In return, trial lawyers consider certain characters as overly delicate and problematic, such as the female victim that would be hard to cross-examining without harming the own case.

Formative Objects

The members are practically oriented towards certain objects-in-the-making. The completion usually exceeds a single social situation. The object could be a case, a defence statement, a piece of evidence, etc. Members invest a whole series of work episodes including previously completed semi-objects into the case, or, more precisely, into the case's current state here/now. The formative object (a) is formed across episodes, (b) formats contributions in line with conventions, rules, and rituals, and (c) forms a collective attached to it. The challenge for our legal ethnography is this: to understand the object's career including the interim stages with their practical demands and norms.

[5] Again, membership categorisation analysis might be helpful here for our legal ethnography. Sacks (1992: VI) analytical vocabulary such as 'category-bound activities', 'category pairs', 'modifiers', etc., can inform our reconstruction of the tactical dramaturgy or of certain strategic problems or disadvantages to deal with by the lawyer.

Members need to learn how this object career works in order to further, to accomplish or to prevent the object's value.[6]

Our trans-sequential court ethnography traces objects that are not yet completed. It does not proceed on a case-to-case fashion only; it proceeds as well in terms of specific case-making methods. To explore those, we pinpoint the obligatory career stages. Here, the members infer what to do *next* in this matter at this procedural point in time: e.g., to polish a statement, to draft it, to prepare a skeleton argument, to collect ammunition for the plea-bargaining. All these work activities are oriented towards a formative object in a certain state. All of them anticipate certain time pressures: urgencies or even deadlines. The practical dealings of the legal team use these 'normal careers' and may divert from it, depending on strategies, cost calculations, or relational prospects of winning/losing. There might be early exits or excessive investments depending on the prospect of the case, the resources of those represented, or the public attention.

Once again, our affirmative reconstructions lead us towards possible translations or interruptions of social inequalities, of external statuses, of personal dispositions. Certain cases demand more input than others; certain strategies turn into options only when backed by specific external factors. Legal aid or social campaigning can alter these conditions (Bogoch 1994). Hence, some cases may dwell more on external structures; others allow for more interpretative creativity. The eventfulness or contingency of the court hearing depends on these specificities, hence does the predictability of the trial's outcome. This is one aspect of how the relevance of legal ethnographic reconstruction matters beyond the 'prejudices' of structural or interpretative approaches. It matters depending on the tendencies embedded in the legal practicalities.

Apparatuses

By apparatus, I refer to a stabilized local/grounded cluster of productive forces generally oriented towards certain referential problems (Scheffer 2020). The court, as apparatus, is oriented towards the reliable case-making and binding

[6] Imagine a text that is prepared version by version. Whereas the early versions are defined by the free space and the opportunity—and often insecurity—to fill it, later versions are demanding in terms of continuation and completion in lines of what has been set so far. The author seems free to choose at the start, but is chosen by the object later on. The author would create early versions. Here, one would ascribe agency, creativity, subjectivity to the 'creator'. Late versions, however, would dictate what the text makes do and what is no longer feasible. The ethnographer, again, shall ask when we are in the object-oriented work. It is the members, who would categorise the object accordingly: as sketch, draft version, 2nd or 3rd version, final version, ultimate version, etc. The same is true for any other formative object in line with its object career. Communities of practice establish certain object careers and related object categories in order to stabilise and negotiate legitimate expectations.

decisions. The apparatus renders certain productivities expectable and calculable. It does so by providing for (nearly) all needed to get such things done: skills, tools, symbols, technology, etc. Without everything in place, the apparatus' personnel would not get started.

The legal ethnography may study, what counts as obligatory socio-material configuration. When would a judge call off the session, when the entire trial? In open court, a first hint of the apparatus' readiness is exactly this: the adjournment of the hearing. It might be that certain figures of the cast count as irreplaceable; it might be that the division of procedural labour lacks an institution; it might be that a file, a document, or just a signature is missing. There are, as well, certain objects, symbolic or technical—such as the flag, the bible, the recording device, etc.—that need to be in place for the court hearing to start. The apparatus consists of all those socio-material components in a certain interrelation that define its integrity.

Infrastructure, Assemblage, Regime

Our micro-foundation of the workings of law has only postponed larger scales. However, it is challenging to induce the broader scheme from regular practices. The ethnographic task is to gain at least a basic understanding of the social conditions that 'all those courts' might be confronted with and the infrastructures that they depend upon. The legal court as an apparatus, doing its work regularly within the confines of a building, including its archive and filing cabinets, its theatrical stage, its appointed and summoned personnel, etc. counts on the society's support, its rule of law. To put differently, the apparatus is workable due to its place in a wider network of courts and the extra apparatuses supporting them.

The ethnography of court(s) adds another layer or scale of analysis, by asking how a court relates to other legal and extralegal institutions and by what practical means.[7] There is the judicial governance, conducted by ministries by ways of human resources, salaries, pension schemes, codes of conduct, etc. There is the self-governance of the legal profession[8] by associations, committees, and boards. Moreover, the education and university system

[7] Although there are important similarities to Actor-Network-Theory (ANT) here, we need to emphasise the basic limitation of the network metaphor. Networked are components within courts (witness stand A and judge's bench A), but not components across courts (such as witness stand A and witness stand B). Courts are networked via cases in certain ways, e.g., by formal decisions (e.g., of lower and higher courts), material circulations (e.g. of files), or communication media (e.g. law reports).

[8] Professions depend on their apparatuses. They are attached to them. Consider scientists and their labs, surgeons and their operation theatres, civil servants and their offices, pilots and their cockpits, etc.

is involved in the development of a legal and professional culture. Law schools reproduce certain legal traditions, the latter feeding into "thick comparisons" (Scheffer et al. 2010). By ways of legal traditions, customs, and media images, members share some general understanding of how to proceed here and what to expect from a criminal or civil trial, whether as witness, jury member, defendant, etc. The court's workings might foster this public understanding of law while at times disspointing it.

Trans-sequential Analytics

The concepts and scales of 'trans-sequential analysis' (Scheffer 2007, 2013) inform our use of the ethnographic data plus our understanding of achievable research results. All members' and/or apparatuses' practical trans-sequential achievements, preferably regular object-formations, can be turned into a research subject. The necessary work including its interim results are considered a methodical accomplishment that demands for resources and knowhow. The regular achievement transpire when 'following the object', as we know it from Marcus 'multi-sited ethnography' or ethnomethodological Studies of Work. But how do we analyse all the processual data[9] collected by tracing the making of statements, cases, or decisions?

Our legal ethnography aims for more than just a mapping of 'actants'[10]; it is more than the accounting for the unequal allocation of resources; we are not content with just the members' opinion on or their stories about whatever kind of legal work. By visiting court hearings and the law firms, we aim to move closer to the actual workings of law, what it demands practically and what it allows members to do. The ethnography of court treats the venue as a passage point, leaving certain marks on the subjects and objects involved in it and exposed to it. How can we analyse our data corpus right from the start in order to get an understanding of those workings?

[9] Some court hearings produce plenty of natural data, meaning data that comes about without our research. They document each procedural stage, each statement, and each admission and decision. The trial produces its own logbook—and we ought to make use of it.

[10] Latour assembled his ethnography of the 'Conseil d'état' (2002) not by listing and relating actants, but by following certain cases on their paper trails and discursive junctions. He would ask how the dealings dwell on documents and files that derive from all over the country.

Trans-Sequential Coding: Components—Composite—Composition

Court ethnography follows the principle of circular, not linear, research. Data collection, coding, and analysing go hand-in-hand and take place in various rounds. The coding and the analysis inform us what to do next in terms of—even more—field observations and document collections. We code the data corpus in its current state—including field notes, recordings, transcripts, documents, laws and legal commentaries, ethnographic interviews, etc.—by ways of a trans-sequential coding (TSC, Scheffer and Trischler 2023) in order to prevent conceptual shortcomings and to emphasise the temporalities, materialities, and practicalities of socio-legal work.

TSC operationalises the time-sensitive concepts introduced above: the turn-by-turn exchanges, the procedural course, the formation of formative objects, etc. The coding proceeds in three basic steps:

1. A first round of—rather sequential—coding covers the inter-activities that appear in a certain order, including the membership categories that go with them. This might be the opening of the hearing, giving oath, cross-examining the witness, giving advice to the jury, etc. We include sub-codes for the properties of these inter-activities: its obligatory components that render it locally available for us 'for all practicable purposes' (Garfinkel). Important here: in order to find out micro-structures of practices, we start coding two or three examplars (e.g. of drafting a statement or of a cross-examination) in one go, focusing on shared properties and patterns.
2. A second round of coding focuses on the formative object that the members work on across work episodes and situations. The formative object receives two codes: a first category for the object-to-be (such as statement, application, or deal) and a category for the object-version on each career stage (such as idea, first version, shared version, etc.). This coding depends on the extent of fieldwork and the kind of case materials we manage to collect. We sketch a provisional map of the career path including the stages and the categorisation of the object-version by the members.
3. Another round of coding focuses on the activities invested into the object-versions to push them from one level to the next, from one career stage to the other. The members develop tests, perhaps by rules of thumb or elaborated checklists, how to decide on the readiness of the object for the subsequent elevation. Before the completion of the formative object, its team carries out pre-tests, and by doing so, anticipates expectable hostile

receptions, e.g. by the opponents or the judge. This highlightss legitimate or at least regular registers of critique.[11] We would expect any procedural contribution to come with such a price, meaning with the obligation to expose it to critics before full acceptance.

These three rounds of coding provide the basis for the modelling of case-work. We find complex compositions consisting of (sequential) series of components leading towards a composite on the one hand and turnovers that transform such a composite into a component of the 'higher' sequence on the other hand. As a formula, this takes the following shape:

Component 1 + 2 + 3 => Composit/**component 1 + 2 + 3 + 4** => **Composit**^{2}

It is these kinds of formation including the turnovers that achieve the production of legal values, such as statements, argumentations, cases, or, ultimately, verdicts. These values are rarely created in single episodes. They require refinement, polishing, testing, fitting, etc., before they serve as full component on the next level. This is why following the object implies more than a 'flat ontology'; it implies more than just tracing the object trajectory. This is due to the object being treated here as a becoming. Formative objects require skilled work and skilled research to understand exactly how and to what effect they are co-produced.

Legal Case as Trinity: Matter-Norm-Verdict

What is a legal case in terms of its formation? Niklas Luhmann (1997) construed the functional systems—such as the legal system—as a series and nexus of (legal) communications or better connectable operations. The 'generalised communication media' (ibid.) of law would ristrict the respective next relevant operation to the binary choice of legal/illegal. Although this reduction seems intriguing for system theoretical recounts of societal differentiation, legal ethnographies may come up with models that are more complex. The compositions that turn connectable-storable, usable, relevant-in terms of law might be rather multi-faceted and inference-rich.

[11] Latour & Woolgar imagined this stage in the natural sciences as driven by competing 'centres of calculation' (??). Certain results, accounted for in journal articles are confronted with a number of counter-readings and -tests. This is why any result, before going into publication, needs to be solidified. The review process turns these epistemic arenas into a procedural qualification. Facts are rendered solid or hard and do therefore count as facts, once they passed it.

One finding of my ethnography on 'adversarial case-making' (Scheffer 2010) gives way to the understanding of case as such a composition. Cases are formed as the—necessary—unity or 'gestalt' of matter/rule/verdict. What does this mean? The members would (1) invest in these three components in the course of casework. While doing that (2), they are confronted with the task of integrating these three components in order to come up with a solid integrated whole: the case. Opponents can refer to each component (3) by ways of critique. A case can be criticised as not living up to the facts, as not using legal norms appropriately, or as drawing the wrong conclusions in terms of theverdict and sentence. The system of law is integrated along these lines (4), by relating cases at least in these three regards. Equivalents or divergences turn accountable in the case-system by looking at cases on somehow same matters, similar norms, or comparable verdicts.

Whereas, at the beginning of casework, each component is dealt with rather separately (just in light of a necessary, but still vague integration), we can observe how, in the later stages of the object-formation, the members need to put more effort into fitting all three components. This is, how in the course of casework, the teams of caseworkers are confronted with increasing pressures and necessities. The relative liberty of beginnings will be replaced by strict demands to 'make sense' of this, meaning in light of the case's properties already set to a good deal.

On the—limited—capacities of this legal apparatus

Court and court procedures have their productivities and capacities. They bring about verdicts with binding force and legitimisation (Luhmann 1989). The final decisions demand acceptance by all members. This, however, is not a constant accomplishment no matter what. It may vary in certain times of crises (with a decrease of institutional trust), in terms of different legal matters (such as controversial or loaded ones), or in terms of societal support (e.g. in terms of the divisions of powers). Our micro-foundation, by finding out what it takes to bring about the necessary formative objects, can show how legal power is a principally rare accomplishment that should not be taken for granted. It comes with a number of necessities, efforts, and costs. The latter is relevant not just for our socio-legal studies, but more so for the members that count on the institution to work or for political movements who wish to enforce certain laws in light of pressing problems.

Diagnosing the limited and conditioned capacities of law undermines a tendency for sociological generalisations, either in a functionalist or critical fashion. Both tend to ascribe a stable set of capacities to all the legal courts and their procedures. Focusing on certain issues helps to be more precise here: A court's workings may prove right for a range of cases and legal matters, but may struggle with certain others. They may have their preferred and their dispreferred cases, taken the former ones as the blueprint for all others. In this regard, certain courts' dependency on just *eyewitnesses* may fall short when it comes to some local crimes in certain regions or in certain milieus, where members would not take the risk of collaborating with the 'institutions'. In return, the allowance for *hearsay* may strengthen cases that are fed by discrimination or even racism. Here, the image of certain categories of members may translate directly into evidence of weight, exposing certain groups to excessive accusations by what counts all too easy as 'the normal people'.

Our empirical grounding allows us to be precise when it comes to certain tendencies and power effects inbuilt in the workings of legal apparatuses. For this, however, the affirmative effort to deconstruct the regular object-formation is pivotal. As Latour put it in the context of climate discourse, critique nowadays is passed too easily (Latour 2004). This is true for the critique of law as well. whatever critique, it shall take the variation of the apparatuses' works and legal matters into account. There are efforts and accomplishments that shall earn our respect and even support. What is more, they could serve us as teaching grounds for practical solutions that are commonly denied as unachievable. General critique, thus, can worsen the situation. The same is true for functionalist generalisations that presume a set of accomplishments, while disregarding how certain courts and jurisdictions lose their necessary support, if not generalized trust.

The legal case-teams do work on a series of hands-on problems that come with performing certain legal acts orderly and, additionally, with composing a case that will do in open court. Ultimately, the procedural competition moves the cases towards a final, socially binding decision: an inseparable unity of evidence-norm-verdict entering the legal archive of cases. The case-system resembles this kind of dynamic formation that alters the legal conditions for the case-works to come.

Closing Remarks: The Legal Courts Under Pressure

The trans-sequential deconstruction of what is going on in and around legal courts improves our understanding of the (limited) capacities of law. Not only, that we manoeuver our court ethnographies through the pitfalls of what one can refer to as structuralist or interpretative; we give room also for empirical re-specifications in light of the referential problems that the courts are dedicated to tackle. However, there is more to this diagnosis than speculating on the capacities and its limits on the ground of what any such court is supposed to deliver: Decisions with sufficient legitimisation to bind any member of society to it.

Nowadays, the courts are put to test by societal 'existential problems' (Scheffer 2021)[12] such as rapid climate change, military conflict, poverty, right-wing totalitarianism, or the dramatic loss of biodiversity. Some existential matters to deal with are dispreferred by the courts' methodical individualism, where they derive from collective ways of life and the widespread business as usual. Some causes—CO_2-emissions, excessive consumption, etc.—do not provide for 'punishable' *deviant behaviour*. If normalities turn violent and destructive, courts seem no longer serve as strongholds of problem-work. Societies may replace the delegation to legal courts by other means: moralising, stigmatisation, status degradation, political campaigning, social exclusion, etc. These functional equivalents develop and establish other tribunals, other trials, and other epistemic cultures. We might be able to study them by help of—some of the—methods and analytics that once have been developed in our legal ethnographies including the diverse data corpora of discourse work, institutional events, and process.

In times of existential problems putting societal reproduction in question, the courts are confronted with a number of excessive tests and tasks. The diagnosis of limited capacities, thus, turns even more urgent and relevant in light of a growing number of societies under pressure. It is no longer sufficient to conceptualise the workings of courts within the dualism of 'law & society'. It is insufficient, moreover, to count on stable social as well as ecological conditions for the workings of law. The contrary is the case.

Knowing this, the legal courts do their work under rising pressures. Certain infrastructures and foundations are shifting or even evaporating. Certain attacks are increasing. At the same token, some courts allow themselves to serve increasingly what appears as the societal or political hegemony.[13] We find weak(er) or strong(er) procedures (Schank et al. 2010), depending on their relational powers to perform their independence. While giving away what was formerly idealised as 'autonomy', weakened procedures complicate

[12] In the common heuristics, there are four such problems that question the very future of society as we know it: the ecological crises, poverty and inequality, the spreading organised violence including wars, and the totalitarian destruction of the public sphere including its epistemic warning functions.

[13] For our studies, such courts are confronted with a number of new tasks and challenges. How can you pass a verdict, if the result has been set right from the start? How do you act in an environment of increased pressures, including warnings, attacks, blackmailing?

the workings of courts regarding their original referential problem: the fabrication of binding decisions in any case. This means a decision that the parties and the public believes is not pre-given, but an outcome of the procedure itself and the respective in-court performances of the competing (parties') cases as partial versions of truth and legality. What happens, if this very basic belief is eroding by ways of increasingly weakened procedures?

Tips for Practical Guidance

1. Start with the core activities and how they are carried out and accounted for regularly.
2. Find out how these activities contribute to the formation of certain objects, such as statements, arguments, or the case.
3. Formative objects are formed over time, format the contributions to them, and form collectives attached to them.
4. Via the object career or status passage you can order your ethnographic data. Each status comes with certain norms and practicalities how to handle the object-version.
5. The court shall be analysed as an apparatus that—when socio-materially fully equipped—assures the fabrication of cases and verdicts.
6. Limited capacity means that the apparatus generates a certain collective agency that is, however, conditioned in terms of quantities (excessive amount of cases) and qualities (dispreferred cases).

References

Atkinson, J.M., and P. Drew. 1979. *Order in court: The organisation of verbal interaction in judicial settings*. London: Macmillan Press.

Banakar, R., and M. Travers, eds. 2005. *Theory and method in socio-legal research*. Oxford: Hart.

Berti, B., and G. Tarabout. 2017. Through the lens of the law: Court cases and social issues in India. *South Asia Multidisciplinary Academic Journal*: 17.

Bogoch, B. 1994. Power, distance and solidarity: Models of professional-client interaction in an Israeli legal aid setting. *Discourse and Society* 5 (1): 65–88.

Conley, J.M., and W.M. O'Barr. 1990. *Rules versus relationships. The ethnography of legal discourse*. Chicago and London: The University of Chicago Press.

Drew, P. 1992. Contested evidence in courtroom cross-examination: The case of a trial for rape. In *Talk at work: Interaction in institutional settings*, ed. Paul Drew and John Heritage, 470–521. Cambridge: Cambridge University Press.

Knorr Cetina, K. 1992. The couch, the cathedral, and the laboratory: On the relationship between experiment and laboratory in science. In *Science as practice and culture*, ed. A. Pickering. Chicago: University of Chicago Press.

Latour, B. 2002. *La Fabrique du droit. Une ethnographie du Conseil d'État*. Paris: La Découverte.

Latour, B. 2004. Why has critique run out of steam—From matters of fact to matters of concern. *Critical Inquiry* 30 (2): 225–248.

Laube, S., J. Schank, and T. Scheffer. 2020. Constitutive invisibility. Exploring the Invisible work of staff advisers in political position making. *Social Studies of Science (SSS)* 50 (2): 292–316.

Luhmann, N. 1989. *Legitimation durch Verfahren*. Frankfurt a.M.: Suhrkamp.

Luhmann, N. 1997. *Theory of society*. Stanford, CA: Stanford University Press.

Matoesian, G.M. 1993. *Reproducing rape: Domination through talk in the courtroom*. Chicago: University of Chicago Press.

Maynard, D.W. 1984. *Inside plea-bargaining. The language of negotiation*. New York: Plenum Press.

Sacks, H. 1992. *Lectures on conversation*, vol. I+II, ed. G. Jefferson. Oxford (UK): Blackwell.

Saks, M.J. 1990. Expert witnesses, nonexpert witnesses, and nonwitness experts. *Law and Human Behavior* 14 (4): 291–313.

Schank, J., T. Scheffer, and M. Michaeler. 2010. Procedure weak or strong. Understanding the limits of political inquiries. *European Journal for Sociology* 1: 93–128.

Scheffer, T. 2007. Event and process. An exercise in analytical ethnography. *Human Studies* 30: 167–197.

Scheffer, T. 2013. Die trans-sequentielle Analyse – und ihre formativen Objekte. In *Grenzobjekte*, ed. R. Hörster, S. Kongeter, and B. Müller, 89–116. Wiesbaden: Springer/VS.

Scheffer, T. 2010. *Adversarial case-making. An ethnography of the English Crown Court*. Leiden/Boston/Tokio: Brill.

Scheffer, T. 2020. Apparate/Apparaturen. Macht und Herrschaft angesichts der Bearbeitung existentieller Probleme. In *Macht und Herrschaft. Zur Revision zweiter soziologische Grundbegriffe*, ed. P. Gostmann and P.-U. Merz-Benz, 363–394. Wiesbaden: Springer VS.

Scheffer, T. 2021. Existentielle Probleme, soziologisch. *Zeitschrift für Theoretische Soziologie (ZTS)* 1: 3–33.

Scheffer, T., and R. Trischler. 2023. Transsequenzielles Codieren. *Sozialer Sinn* 24 (1).

Scheffer, T., K. Hannken-Illjes, and A. Kozin. 2010. *Criminal defence and procedure: Comparative ethnographies in the United Kingdom, Germany, and the United States*. Basingstoke: Palgrave Macmillan.

Suresh, M. 2019. The social life of technicalities: 'Terrorist' lives in Delhi's courts. *Contributions to Indian Sociology* 53 (1): 72–96.

7

Teaching Courtroom Ethnography

Axel Pohn-Weidinger

Introduction

In the present chapter, I describe how courthouse ethnography can be used to teach both ethnographic skills and the sociology of law. I mainly report my experience with teaching courthouse ethnography in order to offer practical guidance for scholars who intend to carry out similar teaching projects. The chapter is primarily targeted towards the average associate professor, PhD candidate, or early-career scholar who teaches within the areas of the sociology of law; criminology; criminal, civil, or welfare law; or legal anthropology and who wishes to learn more about how to engage in inquiry-based forms of teaching. At the end of the text, you should be able to take away a few easily applicable, practical tips regarding how to design a class in courthouse ethnography as well as some interesting insights into the learning processes that turn students into courthouse ethnographers. You might even consider including this text in your syllabus as it can certainly be useful for students who carry out collaborative research projects in courthouse ethnography within your class.

I initially engaged in teaching courthouse ethnography for several interrelated reasons, which serve as the pedagogical and practical pillars of the

A. Pohn-Weidinger (✉)
Department of Sociology, University of Strasbourg, Strasbourg, France
e-mail: apohnweidinger@unistra.fr

L. Flower and S. Klosterkamp (eds.), *Courtroom Ethnography*,
https://doi.org/10.1007/978-3-031-37985-7_7

teaching project that I introduce below. First, my intent was to explore new teaching methods in the sociology of law. Reading classical authors, decrypting jurisprudence (Berger 1989), and stimulating students' socio-legal imagination through writing assignments are options that are already described in literature (Kadowaki 2021). A different and interesting option involves leading students to explore and experience the places and practices where law actually happens (Callaghan 2005). Courthouses are one such place, and a privileged one at that because courts and the everyday functioning of justice represent a central area of research within the sociology of law.

Second, a class on courthouse ethnography foregoes the usual separation of the teaching of subfields of sociology from methodological training. A class that combines both should enable you to add a thematic focus on methodological exercises as well as to empirically ground discussions on socio-legal matters. Such a class is thus of potential interest both for students who wish to train their methodological skills and for those who wish to discover a subfield of sociology. Additionally, interdisciplinary potential exists in courthouse ethnography classes because these classes could easily fit into a law or anthropology programme.

Third, from a pedagogical standpoint, a course on courthouse ethnography can focus on forms of learning based on students' experiences and on their own inquiries, which can prove beneficial to their further studies and pathways. Students can experience courthouse proceedings first-hand, and you can draw on the knowledge they build in class. Moreover, the class framework can support students in the inductive processes of inquiry-based learning through the systematic gathering of data and the gradual construction of an individual research question.[1]

Finally, teaching courthouse ethnography can also help you integrate the all-too-often disjointed activities of teaching and conducting research. Scholars typically need more time for conducting research. While it is important to not leave your role as instructor for overly long periods when you are in courthouse with your students, there is still a reasonable chance that you will bring home some precious fieldnotes yourself.

Empirically, my contribution is based on teaching courthouse ethnography to sociology students in a "Conflicts, Mediation, and Social Intervention"

[1] This focus on both the construction of a socio-legal research question and the conduct of an individual research project differentiates the present article from Callaghan's (2005) brilliant work on teaching courthouse ethnography.

programme at the Faculty of Social Sciences within the University of Strasbourg (France).[2] Based on my notes and the written ethnographic accounts of two cohorts of students, I describe how students become courthouse ethnographers by focusing on the following questions: What interactions do students intuitively focus on? What questions do they (not) ask? How do students' observations evolve during the seminar? What do they learn about the justice system? What types of sociological and methodological readings are helpful to students?

Throughout this chapter, I address both how students find answers to these questions and the different techniques that I use to assist them in this experimental process. This outline should provide you—as a future courthouse ethnography teacher—with an overview of the experiences you might need to go through once your class has been scheduled. If you are a student or, in particular, a member of a student peer group that is currently carrying out a collaborative research project, this text should help you to both reflect upon and organise your first experiences as a courthouse ethnographer. The paper lays out the teaching of courthouse ethnography by walking you through the different steps of the class, which range from its conception to the elaboration of socio-legal research questions. In each step of this process, I highlight organisational elements, describe students' experiences, and provide tips concerning practical pedagogy.

Organising the Class

My class consists of twelve sessions. Students must carry out a small research project and write a term paper on a topic or a question they have investigated. I begin with a few introductory classes (i.e. at least one course on the sociology of law and the organisation of courts and another on the craft of ethnography), and we then take two trips together to the main courthouse in Strasbourg. I spend two to five hours observing co-called "emergency hearings", which are an accelerated procedure for "minor" infractions in criminal law. I take notes and observe the students. Whenever possible—mainly during waiting times, and especially when the tribunal withdraws—I discretely walk around and ask the students how they are doing while also glancing at their notebooks. Around 20 students participate in the class, which is a manageable size. If your class is larger, I would advise that you divide it into smaller groups when visiting the courthouse.

[2] The author would like to thank Eva Liebertz for editing the present text.

I advise students not to schedule leisure activities too early on the same evening because they have to gather their field notes, write them down, and upload them to a shared online folder for the next week, all of which should be done immediately after leaving the field. We discuss these notes collectively in two sessions. Students read their accounts aloud, and everyone can contribute. I usually ask students to read someone else's account and comment on it. I provide feedback, which I prepare beforehand. Next, we return to the courthouse for two more visits. The second series of observations is discussed in the same manner as the first. Usually, students must then go back to the court for at least one additional observation. The last three or four sessions aim to prepare students for writing a term paper. Each student presents their desired topic, which is discussed collectively. On the one hand, I focus on integrating different sequences of observations for the sake of answering one specific socio-legal research question. On the other hand, we discuss how to find relevant literature concerning the question on which the students want to work.

In the first class, I always ask the students to present their former training—especially regarding ethnography and the law—in order to discover what other disciplinary knowledge and perspectives they will intuitively draw on. Most students have had some methodological training, while a few have had legal education, have garnered experience in social work, or have studied psychology. Many students watch legal dramas on television, such as *Suits* or *How to Get Away with Murder* (Do not ask them about *Ally MacBeal* or *The Good Wife* unless you want to feel old!). Simple elements from these series can be used for discussion. For example, you can ask the following questions: What would be the equivalent of the pro bono system in your country? How do you become a lawyer in your country?

Additionally, explicating these outside experiences is a way of making students aware of the influence that the experiences can have on what they will see. One year, a law student noted, "*I wrote down everything I observed. Nevertheless, my law studies failed me because I had been trained to focus on factual rather than expressive elements. That's why I carefully transcribed many procedural elements.*" This student focused on procedure rather than interaction, which is quite a common orientation amongst many students both with and without a legal background. The discussion of this ethnographic account should help you introduce some very basic and fundamental questions about what sociologists actually observe and about where the difference between a sociological and a legal description of a case lies (see above).

Preparing the Field

Before beginning the class, I make an appointment with the president of the court to discuss my teaching project, which is when the dates I have scheduled with each judge are double-checked. This is not a necessary step because hearings are generally public and there is thus generally no field-access problem (on this matter, see Chapter 3); however, as sociologists of law, we should be critical of the effectiveness of such general rules as they may conflict with practical realities. Moreover, it is good to have the backing of individuals with higher hierarchical positions when court clerks become nervous about the number of people they are still willing to let into the courtroom. Additionally, if hearings are public, judges have the final say about practical organisation in "their own" courtrooms. You will be noticed, and it is therefore important that the organisation have prior knowledge of you before the beginning of the course and that it be made clear that your presence will be accepted.

The announcement of your class can have other positive effects: Once, I went to welfare law hearings with a few students. Aware of our presence, the welfare law judge asked the students at the end of the hearing whether they had any questions. He then elaborated on the specificities of welfare hearings in relation to emergency hearings—"*It's less exciting*", he said—and commented on the last case, in which a woman had become very upset about the way the court administration had treated her—"*It happens*", he said. The comment made students aware of the fact that practices of "cooling out" (Goffman 1952) litigants are common and routinised in courthouses, as is the hierarchy between areas of law within the legal professions (some of which are considered "less exciting" than others). This kind of interaction could lead to further research activities, such as interviews. A second positive effect of contacting the presidency in advance is that if you intend to conduct interviews with other court staff or to gain access to information about the organisation, you know where to begin.

Choosing Relevant Literature

The first time I held the class, I prepared a series of lectures on the major divisions of the law and the organisation of the judiciary. However, this did not work very well because the students had difficulties relating the abstract content to the immediacy of the hearings. Readings in courthouse ethnography are a better option. Be careful, though, because this literature tends to be highly specialised, with scholars focusing on specific aspects of court proceedings and drawing on literature that is largely unknown to (my) third-year sociology students. Many studies are difficult to access due to the language barrier (because sociology students in Strasbourg are not necessarily at ease with English texts). In addition, it is not easy to find literature on the precise type of hearing you will attend with your students. There are important differences in the way that hearings are conducted, in who the plaintiffs are, and between different types of procedures and areas of law, such as between criminal and welfare law. Whatever literature you choose, you will have to make it transferable in order for it to meet the objectives of your course.

For instance, *Emergency Hearings* (Christin 2008) is a book that deals with the type of procedure that I observe with students. The author investigates the mostly invisible work accomplished by state attorneys, judges, and public defence lawyers before a case goes to court. The study is very helpful for students to understand the procedural trajectory of files and the backstage work of professionals, but it does not focus on practices that are observable in the hearings themselves, which is what the course is all about. The presentation of relevant literature can thus be an opportune moment for discussing the question as to why hearings should be observed at all: What can actually be observed, and what is the socio-legal purpose of the observations?

I revert back to this question many times during the seminar. Students (mainly white and female) are generally interested in the construction of gender through the (criminal) justice system—indeed, race and social class, in particular, are less present in their accounts—and sometimes notice clues within concrete activities. Defendants who are present in emergency hearings are predominantly male, middle-aged, and non-white with a working-class background. However, it is one thing to know that the defendants are there due to their social circumstances and the way the criminal justice system reproduces social structures, but it is another thing is to observe whether and how gender, race, and/or social class matter in the practical conduct of the hearings in terms of ways of speaking, postures, expressions, images called for by the judges or other actors in the proceedings, etc. It is not easy for students to observe how categories of race, gender, or social class operate during the hearings—if the students find direct evidence at all—because finding this evidence requires paying very close attention and making a certain number of observations (and you will not find evidence in every observation). Gender is certainly the more evident dimension to observe because it is often involved in cases brought before a judge (e.g. domestic violence, drunk driving, violence during football games, drug dealing).[3] However, the fact that few women appear in emergency hearings renders systematic comparisons difficult.

The purpose behind critically discussing the literature is thus to draw students' attention to the fact that hearings are a specific type of activity that can be observed in order produce a specific type of data and knowledge, which may be different from other types of methodologies, such as interviews with state attorneys, ethnographies behind the scenes of hearings (e.g. in Latour 2010), and statistical evidence on judicial decision-making that is extracted from case files.

Observing Before Entering the Field

One solution that has worked out well involves showing students scenes from a documentary on court hearings during the initial classes. I use the film *10ième chamber: Instants d'audience* (10th C, in which Raymond Depardon presents exactly the type of procedure that I observe with my students: emergency hearings. One year, I chose a scene in which a young Black man is condemned to six months in prison after appearing for the third time in court for dealing drugs. Students' reactions to the scene were vivid: One student, visibly surprised, commented on the way the female prosecutor talked to (and interrupted) the defendant when pleading: "*She talks to the defendant like a mother to a child*". Another student added that the scene was "*a classic in the French justice system: a racialised defendant who ends up in prison, and this problem is not talked about in the hearing*". In a different vein, another student noticed that the public defender did not seem very confident. I then asked the students to be more explicit about how they had reached these conclusions in terms of what exactly they had seen. The first student stated, "*Well, the prosecutor cut the defendant off and yelled at him, and she told him that what he had done was bad and that he had already done something wrong before*". She underlined the notion that the prosecutor was using moral categories to qualify crimes and that the relationship between the defendant and the state was presented as a parent–child relationship. The second student added that most of the defendants were Black or came from the Maghreb and that this structural problem had not been mentioned at all during the hearing. Finally, the student who had observed a lack of confidence in one lawyer explained, "*Well, the hands of the public defender were moving, and he*

[3] See Chapter 14 of Lelièvre and Léonard (2012) for the French context.

once stopped and searched for his words. He was young in comparison with the [middle-aged] prosecutor, [and] he seemed inexperienced."

I then tackle students' comments individually and discuss how these types of observations could serve as the basis for further investigations and socio-legal questions. Several students are always interested in the interaction between the judge and the defendant. After making their initial observations, they write, for example, that "*the judge does not appear neutral*", that "*the president of the tribunal disrespects the accused*", and that "*the judge smiles and speaks with a slightly condescending tone, as if he were speaking to an incompetent*". This is an ideal occasion to highlight the difference between "law in action" and "law in the books" (Nelken 1984). In the cases cited above, I advise students to precisely describe how this *infantilisation* is accomplished via the following questions: Through which words, which gestures, and which sequences of interaction? Can we classify which defendants are infantilised, for what crime, by which judges? How can infantilisation be objectivised using which list of observational clues? Later in the seminar, when it comes to building a research question, this material can be used to discuss relevant literature, such as ethnomethodological texts on "degradation ceremonies" (Garfinkel 1956) or assessments of moral character in court hearings (see the contributions in Travers 1997; especially Komter 1997).

Regarding the lack of confidence of the lawyer that one student noticed, I encouraged this student to define an observational technique that would enable them to observe clues of a *lack of confidence* or self-assurance and to apply this technique systematically throughout different hearings. Such a suggestion usually leads to discussions about the systematic observation of expressions. The work of Lisa Flower is extremely relevant not only because the Goffmanian approach is applied convincingly, but also because her texts are easily accessible to students (see e.g. Flower 2020). The socio-legal question here involves the relationship between defence lawyers and their clients. Another socio-legal approach would be to ask whether different ways of pleading can be linked to lawyers' career trajectories. Students would need to conduct small interviews with lawyers, which is relatively easy to do (e.g. lawyers can be questioned when leaving the courthouse or during waiting times).

Three basic points are important to underline: First, students must be reminded that they should gather a sufficient number of observations on exactly the same type of *situated interaction* they wish to analyse, such as the plea made by the defence lawyer (see Chapter 8). These observations must be as exhaustive and accurate as possible. Second, there must be some kind of variation within the gathered data. I urge students to gather observations that will contradict their assumptions, for instance, by observing the different pleas of different lawyers on different types of cases. Finally, the students must try to find a sociologically relevant socio-legal question behind all these observations. One obvious approach would be to investigate how the right to a fair trial and a defence plays out in practice and how pro bono work is linked to lawyers' trajectories.

Finding an Angle

It is not possible to begin too early when it comes to preparing students for the fact that they will have to ask themselves what they want to observe and why. I advise my students to write down everything they see during the first hearing. In general, students tend to write down less than they should, and I view it as my role to encourage them to write more. Ethnography requires details to be noted and exchanges to be transcribed with sufficient precision and exhaustiveness. Sometimes, students only write down the reactions of the judge and neglect to include, for instance, what exactly the judge reacted to or what event the prosecutor smiled (or did not smile) at. It is critical to stress that observation can entail zooming into and out of different parts of interactions.

When following my advice, the most engaged or experienced students submit long accounts and generally note that "*it's very difficult to see everything that is going on for everyone*", that they "*write down too much*", or that "*it's impossible to focus for longer than 20 minutes*". The learning curve of these students is steep because their aching hands convince them of the necessity to choose an angle. Many students do not write down much, which may be because they have difficulty with the technique itself or because they intuitively focus on certain elements—often, the nature of the case—regarding what crime was committed, the *personality* of the defendant, and the defendant's prior contact with the criminal justice system, which do not require many notes. Finally, many students become absorbed by the flow of events that constitute a *hearing* because this flow stems from the judge's actions. Thus, their accounts may be reminiscent of stage notes for a movie in which the judge is both the director and the main protagonist—that is, students may only see the parts of the courtroom that the judge temporarily illuminates. This situation is interesting because you can witness how students participate in the courtroom activity system and how the presence of an audience plays an important role in the conduct of hearings. You can discuss these intuitive angles during the first class, during which accounts can be read aloud, and you can advise students to focus less on what happened and for what reason than on *how* actions happened in order for them to be able to grasp "how routine actions in the setting are organised and take place" (Emerson et al. 2011, 27).

In the beginning of the class, I always highlight the objective, which is for students to focus on one situated interaction, one sequence, one event, one type of actor, and one type of action and to describe this item—such as the lawyer's plea (which lasts about five minutes in emergency hearings) or reactions to the pronouncement of the judgement—in detail. However, it is not natural for students to separate themselves from what takes place in the courtroom as a whole when focusing on one small situational interaction. This is probably the greatest challenge for your class.

Another way of convincing students to adopt a certain focus for their observations is to show them the field notes of former students. I generally choose different types of accounts: a detailed one, a focused one, and a succinct one. Discussing field notes made by students who are not present is a good prelude to the discussions that are to follow without necessitating the involvement of a current student. Furthermore, publicly reading notes is always an interesting exercise in which some role-taking and role-distancing (Goffman 1961) take place as students begin to see themselves as courthouse ethnographers.

It can be a good idea to show students that you conduct fieldwork yourself and to share your own field notes with them. One year, a student wanted to focus on the police officers who were present in the courtroom. She made a series of observations but then decided to change focus because she found that "*the [police officers] just stand around*". Police personnel—such as court clerks and executory officers—are the invisible human infrastructure of the hearing and are not normally noticed by students because they lie outside the focus created by the judge. I was intrigued and began to make a couple of observations myself around the question of what happens when nothing happens.[4] I quickly discovered that police officers do a lot of things, such as crossing their arms, changing the leg they stand on, looking around, scratching their arms, and adjusting their face masks. While it would be possible to discuss whether this type of action is meaningful and falls within the jurisdiction of sociology, it is certain that police officers accomplish a specific way of waiting while also remaining visually accessible to the public. As observations accumulate, it becomes clear that police officers also control the defendant's body, for example, by asking the defendant to stand up when the judge enters,

[4] Though not an academic reference, Perec (2010) is a useful read for students on this matter.

to speak into the microphone, to raise their hands above their knees, and to sit at the end of the bench. Moreover, you will be rewarded for keeping your focus, for example, when a defendant becomes upset after hearing their sentence and is taken out of the courtroom by the police, when the police officers working in the public areas instruct the defendant's friends to stop making signs, or when these officers forcibly remove a witness's parent who has spoken too angrily to the judge. Finally, you will be able to observe role-distancing, for example, when police officers fall asleep, when they chuckle, when they gesturally comment on the case, or when they engage in visible daydreaming. These are just some of the many possible preliminary observations that have helped me convince students both (1) that when you look closely, many things actually occur even though nothing appears to happen at first and (2) that more actors participate in court hearings than only judges, defendants, lawyers, and prosecutors. If you focus on one particular element, sociologically relevant questions emerge.[5]

When the end of the course approaches and students have formulated their research questions, I advise them to look into other students' field notes (which have been uploaded to a platform that is linked to the class). Sometimes, these accounts contain elements that fellow students can use in their own dossiers, such as pleading by a different lawyer, a bystander being escorted by the police, the presence of a female defendant, or a case on a given topic that a student has finally chosen to focus on. The example of the observation of police officers in court is again instructive because physical interventions are rare yet highly significant when the goal is to build a dossier on the topic. Students might not have witnessed this type of action themselves, but if their colleagues have, they can integrate these other students' data into their own data. This process also gives students a sense of conducting collaborative research.

Being in Place

As courthouse staff will most likely notice your presence and you will want to maintain a sound working relationship with the court, you might introduce students to the role they will have to live up to. Arriving at courthouse before the doors open, putting your mobile phone on airplane mode, remaining silent throughout proceedings (and even during brief breaks), not taking photos, and not talking about the defendants if their family is seated near

[5] Consider also Flower, who revealed that lawyers who appear not to react to certain events are actually actively suppressing their emotions (Flower 2016).

you are some of the rules to obey. Lawyers can relatively easily get away with a ringing mobile phone, but judges are generally strict about noise coming from the benches. This point is relevant because a certain excitement can sometimes be felt amongst students when police bring in what appears to be the "bad guys" and prosecutors throw their best speech at them. However, this is the real world and the real drama of everyday criminal justice, not a television series that can be switched off. Students must thus take on their role seriously.

This perspective will also help students reflect on their role as observers. Courthouses are easy to access, but observers are generally noticed in some way. Once, presuming that I worked for the local newspaper, the brother of a defendant took me aside to ask me not to write about the sexual abuse charges mentioned during the hearing. He feared that making these charges public would pose a problem for his brother in prison. The brother's fear was based on his knowledge that journalists are often at the hearings (and they are sometimes mistaken for court personnel by students because they have acquired the right to sit on one of the comfortable armchairs). Anonymity in field notes is thus of paramount importance.[6] On another occasion, students were asked by a defendant's relative why they were taking notes. This might have been a scary moment for our courthouse ethnographers to overcome, but by stating that they were students, everyone was easily able to move on. However, you might prepare students for this to happen and advise them to not engage in overly visible note-taking (e.g. one of my students held her notebook in front of her face) or to hide their observation-making and writing. This is especially applicable when students try to observe defendants' relatives.

Changing Proceedings

At some point, students will become familiar with the proceedings, which could draw their attention away from relevant aspects of the social organisation of the hearings. It is thus a good idea to change the area of law and the type of proceedings that are observed. One year, I held a couple of sessions on emergency hearings and then moved to the criminal trial court. Some students wrote in their observational notes that the events of the criminal trial court reflected their understanding of justice because they had observed the thorough cross-examination of witnesses and victims, the testimony of

[6] For a thorough discussion of ethical questions in courthouse ethnography, see the other chapters of this volume, e.g. Chapter 3.

medical experts, etc. Others were surprised regarding the extent to which they had taken for granted the fact that emergency hearings are the way the justice system works. One student even wrote that she had had the impression that people were actually being defended by their lawyers and that the judge had been different in his interactions with the defendant. Such observations make for interesting discussions on different procedures within criminal justice and on the way justice is served through these procedures. Moreover, these observations can create bounce-back effects on the subsequent observations. Some students undertook a more systematic description of the emergency hearing procedure by describing the ideal–typical sequence of events that every hearing consists of, including the precise average timing of the different steps (e.g. informant consent, introduction, reading the file, the prosecution's discussion of evidence, pleas, handing down the judgement).

Another highly interesting option is to change the area of law and to observe, for instance, welfare law hearings. These hearings lead to some astonishment amongst students. Indeed, as one student wrote, "When we asked at the front desk where the welfare hearings were, the receptionist was surprised. She said, 'Usually, nobody is interested in these hearings'." The account then went on to explain that the physical disposition of the courtroom had been different, that the atmosphere had been both calmer and noisier (e.g. lawyers had talked with one another and with their clients), that no police officers had been present, that participants had mainly been female, that procedures had been longer, etc. Some features of the emergency hearings only became apparent once the students had changed their procedural frame. These differences in law, in procedure, in court ambiance, in users and companions, in legal representatives, and in the styles of judges' actions intrigued the students and led to healthy discussions. It certainly helps to develop a critical stance towards the literature in the sociology of law, in which scholars often speak of *the law* without taking into account or explicating these types of specificities in the way *procedures* work.

Concluding Remarks

My aim in the present chapter was to provide you with insights into my own teaching project around courthouse ethnography that could prove helpful for your own teaching projects. The question as to the extent to which the conclusions I have drawn based on my own process of becoming a courthouse ethnography teacher will stand the test in other contexts must be answered by future courthouse ethnography teachers themselves. What works and does not work in teaching courthouse ethnography is ultimately dependent on very many circumstantial influences, only some of which can be controlled. The ideal–typical structure of the class I describe here must certainly be adapted to the specific circumstances of your class (e.g. class size, student level, place in the curriculum, credits earned). Let me know how it played out for you.

Tips for Practical Guidance

(1) Make yourself aware of the context of your class: Have students been trained in the ethnography or sociology of law? Are they already familiar with the principles of the legal system? How many students will participate in your class? Do they know how to find relevant literature on the sociology of law? Think about how to adapt your class to these contextual elements, for instance, by adding a class on ethnography or on the legal system.
(2) Prepare a syllabus based on the different steps I have outlined above: Begin by choosing an area of law. I have mainly observed proceedings in criminal law, but less studied areas of law—such as welfare law, labour law, or administrative law—could be interesting options, as well.
(3) Visit the courthouse of the area of law you have chosen a couple of times in order to become familiar with the location and to evaluate the feasibility of a courthouse ethnography class. Then, contact the head of the courthouse.
(4) Spend at least a couple of days observing hearings and taking notes. This will help you to assist students in the development of a research question and enable you to anticipate potential difficulties in their learning process.
(5) Find easily accessible literature in the area of law you have chosen and in courthouse ethnography.
(6) Once the class has begun, make sure you have enough time after every class to take notes on students' learning processes.

References

Berger, Ronald J. 1989. Teaching the sociology of law: Alternative approaches to course organization. *Teaching Sociology* 17 (1): 49–55.

Callaghan, Elizabeth. 2005. What they learn in court: Student observations of legal proceedings. *Teaching Sociology* 33 (2): 213–220.

Christin, Angèle. 2008. *Comparutions immédiates: Enquête sur une pratique judiciaire*. La Découverte.

Emerson, Robert M., Rachel I. Fretz, and Linda L. Shaw. 2011. *Writing ethnographic fieldnotes*. University of Chicago Press.

Flower, Lisa. 2016. Doing loyalty: Defense lawyers' Subtle dramas in the courtroom. *Journal of Contemporary Ethnography* 47 (2): 226–254.

Flower, Lisa. 2020. Emotional labour, cooling the client out and lawyer face. In *Emotional labour in criminal justice and criminology*, eds. J. Phillips, J. Waters, C. Westaby, and A. Fowler. Routledge.

Garfinkel, Harold. 1956. Conditions of successful degradation ceremonies. *American Journal of Sociology* 61 (5): 420–424.

Goffman, Erving. 1952. On cooling the mark out: Some aspects of adaptation to failure. *Psychiatry* 15 (4): 451–463.

Goffman, Erving. 1961. Role distance. In *Encounters: Two studies in the sociology of interaction*, 85–152. Penguin Books.

Kadowaki, Joy. 2021. Teaching law and society in the sociology classroom: Writing assignments for engaging the sociolegal imagination. *Teaching Sociology* 49 (1): 85–95.

Komter, Martha. 1997. Remorse, redress and reform: Blame-taking in the courtroom. In *Law in action: Ethnomethodological and conversation analytic approaches to law*, ed. M. Travers. Dartmouth.

Latour, Bruno. 2010. *The making of law: An ethnography of the Conseil d'Etat*, Trans. M. Brilman and A. Pottage. Polity Press.

Lelièvre, Maxime, and Léonard, Thomas. 2012. Chapitre 17. Une femme peut-elle être jugée violente? Les représentations de genre et les conditions de leur subversion lors des procès en comparution immédiate. In *Penser la violence des femmes*, 314–329. La Découverte.

Nelken, David. 1984. Law in action or living law? Back to the beginning in sociology of law. *Legal Studies* 4 (2): 157–174.

Perec, Georges. 2010. *An attempt at exhausting a place in Paris*, Trans. M. Lowenthal. Wakefield Press.

Travers, Max (Ed.). 1997. *Law in action: Ethnomethodological and conversation analytic approaches to law*. Ashgate.

Part II

Contemporary and Critical Aspects of Courtroom Ethnography

8

Video Links and Eyework

Lisa Flower, Sarah Klosterkamp, and Emma Rowden

Introduction

Eye contact is a key component in initiating and sustaining social interaction and has traditionally demanded face-to-face presence (Goffman, 1959, 1963; Kendon 1990). However, developments in technology have led to a proliferation of interactions taking place via cameras and screens. This switch from face-to-face to hybrid or completely online hearings changes how we see and communicate with each other not only in a literal sense, but also how we see and communicate with each other in a symbolic sense, that is, how we understand, interpret, evaluate, and relate to one another. The sociologist Randall Collins (2020: 482) encapsulates this when he writes, "[b]y seeing another person's eyes and face, and the orientation of their body, you

L. Flower (✉)
Department of Sociology, Lund University, Lund, Sweden
e-mail: Lisa.flower@soc.lu.se

S. Klosterkamp
University of Bonn, Bonn, Germany
e-mail: s.klosterkamp@uni-bonn.de

E. Rowden
Oxford Brookes University, Oxford, UK
e-mail: erowden@brookes.ac.uk

L. Flower and S. Klosterkamp (eds.), *Courtroom Ethnography*, https://doi.org/10.1007/978-3-031-37985-7_8

know what they are paying attention to. An exchange of glances communicates, I-see-you-seeing-me, and also I-recognize-what-we-are-both-looking-at". This perception of perceiving and experiencing others and sensing that we ourselves are being perceived is termed "co-presence" (Goffman 1963) and has traditionally required physical co-location. However, moving interaction into an online sphere not only risks disrupting eye contact, but it also risks disturbing perceptions of co-presence (Campos-Castillo and Hitlin 2013; Rossner and Tait 2021). Indeed, we suspect that many readers have thought to themselves "it's just not the same" at some point when interacting with others via video link. In this chapter we show how ethnographic studies can be used to understand this perceived difference.

Face-to-face eye contact is important in courtroom settings, for instance, to modify intimacy (Argyle and Cook 1976) or communicate persuasively (Ball 1994). It is also widely believed to be central to assessments of credibility (Neal and Brodsky 2008) despite uncertainty regarding how credibility is actually displayed (Bandes 2014) with direct eye contact assumed to be an indicator of deception, despite findings that dispute this (Sporer and Schwandt 2007). Eye contact can also be used strategically by legal actors in order to convey certain impressions in the courtroom, known as "eye-work" (Flower 2019a). In this chapter we show how ethnography can be used to more fully understand the importance of eye contact and eyework in traditional physical trials and how this translates in remote settings.

Each of the authors of this chapter has studied the courtroom extensively and, despite each coming from different disciplines (architecture for Rowden, sociology for Flower, and feminist legal geography for Klosterkamp), we have all been interested in the role of eye contact in court in various ways. When we began our fieldwork, in 2008 (for Rowden in Australia), 2013 (for Flower in Sweden), and 2015 (for Klosterkamp in Germany), video links were at various stages of establishment as an everyday form of communication in society. As the use of video links in wider society burgeoned, a concomitant presence and development in the courts began to appear too, albeit at varying rates and extents in each of the jurisdictions we studied. The COVID-19 pandemic supercharged this trend as courts—many already battling enormous backlogs—strove to function during lockdowns and social distancing restrictions (Remotecourts.org 2022, Legg and Song 2021). For instance, 12 848 video links were used in Swedish trials in 2011, rising to 181 570 in 2021 at the height of the pandemic (Domstolar 2022), with similar trends in Germany and Australia.

Of the three jurisdictions explored here, Australia's use of video link has the longest history, dating back to the late 1980s. Australia first introduced routine remote participation for child witnesses and defendants, however video links were quickly adopted for a wider range of purposes, not least in highly inaccessible communities (Rowden 2011). It is unsurprising then that during the COVID-19 pandemic all personal court appearances other than continuing jury trials moved online in Australia (Legg and Song 2021). In contrast, video link capabilities, while installed, have been used sparingly over the past 25 years in Germany and Sweden, however increased during the COVID-19 pandemic (Deutschlandfunk 2021; Domstolar 2022). In Germany, video links were first introduced to protect witnesses in criminal procedures who remain the only party permitted to participate remotely with video links mainly restricted to use in civil cases (Sanders 2021). In Sweden, parties, including defence lawyers and prosecutors, may participate via video link if deemed appropriate with regard to safety, costs, and other practicalities. As many courts across the globe have now invested in video link technology and moreover, have strategic plans highlighting digitalization, video links seem likely here to stay.

In this chapter, we first show how ethnography can be used to understand the importance of eye contact in courtrooms with particular focus on impression management. We then develop this to show how video links challenge and disrupt eye contact and risk justicial implications. Finally, we present how autoethnographic experiences can be employed to more fully understand how and why video links can unwittingly create misrepresentations of self. Before we embark on these themes, we present an overview of the extant research on video links in courts.

Courtroom Ethnographies on Video Links

Although video links have gained academic attention, our literature review reveals only a handful of existing ethnographic studies on their use in court proceedings, with even fewer focusing explicitly on eye contact. Instead, the literature is dominated by psychological, criminological, and or legal and socio-legal reviews on remote hearings. For instance, studies have explored whether defendants taking part via video link receiver higher bail or are denied (Eagly 2015; Seidman et al. 2010), whether credibility is impacted by video links (e.g. Landström et al. 2015 find credibility is reduced; Orcutt et al. 2001, and Ellison and Munro 2013 find no difference, Taylor and Joudo 2005 find mixed results), how camera positioning impacts upon our perceptions (Bruan and Taylor 2012), as well as how video links change our perception of emotions (Wiggins 2003). To this, we can add a number of overviews of legal findings which explore the benefits and challenges of video conferencing in a legal setting (e.g., Donoghue 2017, Mulcahy 2008).

Although such studies contribute to a wider understanding of the phenomenon of video links, an ethnographic approach provides something extra. By focusing on social activity in situ (Atkinson 2014) within these legal settings, it enables us, as ethnographers, to explore how legal actors in court interact, engage, and deal with cameras and video links when practising justice. It is the "being thereness" (Borneman and Hammoudi 2009) of ethnography that reveals the symbolic meanings, situatedness, sensorial experience, social identities, and daily routines which are difficult to attain from other methods (Paik & Harris 2015). Moreover, it is the continued, repeated ethnographic presence, revisiting the field over and over, that enables the ethnographer to see the deviations from the mundane thereby revealing the underlying rules of interaction (Goffman 1963).

As noted in the introductory chapter, ethnographic studies of courtroom interactions are not new (e.g., Rock 1993; Roach Anleu & Mack 2017; Tait 2001), nor is an interest in the use of technologies in courts and the resulting tensions (e.g. Carlen 1976). However, such studies tend to focus on nonverbal interactions more broadly, rather than on eye contact (for instance, see Bergman Blix and Wettergren 2018; Flower 2019b; Mack and Anleu Roach 2010). One of the early ethnographic studies which did include a focus on eye contact in interactions in French remote hearings explored the impact of camera placement on sightlines and showed how on-screen impressions are managed, for instance that the counsel's greeting to the court may not be visible on screen due to camera positioning (Licoppe et al. 2013, see also Licoppe and Dumoulin 2010). McKay (2018) similarly explores ruptures in communication in Australian courts stemming from video link usage which restricts the effectiveness of communication and leads to feelings of remoteness and stress. Moving to an English study, the importance of camera positioning to eye level and choice of background is also shown to be important in impression management (Rossner and McCurdy 2020). These later studies were preceded by the *Gateway to Justice Project: Improving video-mediated communications for justice participants* in Australia between 2008 and 2010, which found that video links may alter the nature of proceedings, potentially undermining the "experience and legitimacy of justice" (Rowden 2018: 263; Wallace and Rowden 2018).

Exploring and Understanding the Absence and Presence of Eye Contact using Ethnographic Methods

We now move on to our discussions of how ethnographic means can be used to understand the importance of eye contact in trials.

Using Ethnography to Understand Eyework

Flower conducted ethnographic fieldwork, observing over 50 criminal trials at four district courts in Sweden between 2013 and 2018. She sat near the front of the public gallery, diagonally opposite the defence lawyer and defendant in order to observe their micro-interactions (Goffman 1959). She worked abductively (Atkinson 2014), gathering fieldnotes, conducting interviews with defence lawyers, analysing the material gathered using her chosen theoretical framework returning to the field again and again, continuing this loop in a process of detailing, interpreting, and understanding the interactions taking place. One aspect in particular stuck out as a deviation from—what had become—the expected sequence of interactions and she began to hone her ethnographic gaze on eye contact.

Flower's analysis of her fieldnotes shows that defence lawyers make eye contact when questioning witnesses and plaintiffs and when talking to judges or the prosecutor. Also, when a client is addressed by the judge or questioned by the prosecutor, eye contact with the judge or prosecutor is sought for by the defence lawyer. Eye contact thus appears to be routine. However, during certain phases of questioning their own clients, eye contact initiated by defence lawyers is systematically absent. This can be seen in the following sequence which is an excerpt taken from a theft trial:

> The defence lawyer and defendant both look at the prosecutor when the prosecutor diverts from reading from the presentation of facts. Later, the defence lawyer looks straight at the prosecutor and blinks three times when the prosecutor says that two people matching the accused's description were seen at the crime scene. When the prosecutor states that the defendant was caught with a bag containing the stolen goods the defence lawyer blinks three times then looks down again. After 28 minutes there is still no eye contact between the defence lawyer and his client that I have noticed.
>
> When the defendant is questioned by the prosecutor, he admits that he "did stupid stuff" and looks at his defence lawyer who nods and says "tell them what you did" in a soft but stern voice. His client describes what he did and looks

at him again. The defence lawyer nods again. It's the first time they have had direct eye contact.

The defence lawyer now asks questions to his client but without looking at him, he looks down in front of him, in the report or in the empty space in the middle of the courtroom. He asks three questions about the initial interrogation, all without looking at his client.

Defence lawyer:	"Could it be the case that someone else stole the items?" Here he looks directly at his client and eye contact is made.
Defendant:	"Yes"
Defence lawyer:	"You haven't been with [the other defendant]? Is that correct?" Again, direct eye contact is made and the question is delivered in a slightly sterner voice. (Fieldnotes, February 2018)

In this excerpt, we see an array of eyework strategies—making and avoiding eye contact in order to convey social information to the other interactants in the courtroom. The first we see is a display of surprise at the prosecutor's deviation from the expected order of events (Ekman 2004). This is followed by a related form of eyework—blinking—which reveals another type of surprise, this time when evidence is presented that is damaging to the defence (Flower 2019b). When the defendant is questioned by the prosecutor, we see the first use of direct eye contact between defence lawyer and defendant, aimed at directing the defendant into performing the expected role of feeling and displaying remorse. Next, we see the absence of the expected eye contact, when the defence lawyer is questioning his own client. Instead, we see a gaze into the no-man's land of the centre of the courtroom. However, towards the end of the excerpt, we see once again eye contact between defence lawyer and defendant aimed at managing the client into a performance of innocence, perhaps playing on the (erroneous) assumption that eye avoidance is a signal of deception, hence eye contact indicates truth-telling (Sporer and Schwandt 2007). By making eye contact, the defence lawyer is thus supporting an idealized presentation of his client (Goffman's 1963, "face"). The avoidance of eye contact can therefore be a form of civil inattention—actively and strategically choosing to not see the actions of another part, particularly when they may be cause for embarrassment (Goffman 1963; Goffman 1959)—eye contact can also be used to give and gain support (Flower 2016, 2019a). The attainment and avoidance of eye contact is thus used strategically to convey social information to the courtroom.

In this part, Flower has shown that the intricate yet subtle ways in which eyework is performed are revealed through detailed ethnographic observation, strategies that would have remained hidden without an ethnographic eye.

Ethnography can thus help us to understand the importance of eye contact in courtroom interactions. In the next section, Klosterkamp will show how fieldnotes and sketches help us to understand how this is disrupted when video links are used.

Using Ethnography to Understand the Disruption of Eyework by Video Links

In Germany, video links have—until recently—remained unusual. However, this changed when anti-terrorist trials began to use remote participation for defendants in custody, this format often constituting the only available option for including their oral testimonies. These testimonies are essential in Germany as the legal process is grounded in the "principle of orality" (as in the Swedish system). This means that every piece of evidence to be included in deliberations—from tapped phone calls to eye-witness reports—must be orally presented in the courtroom.

Conducting a courtroom ethnography of anti-terrorist trials between 2015 and 2020, Klosterkamp was able to observe some of these otherwise rare digital settings at the Higher Regional Appeal Courts. In total, Klosterkamp conducted a multi-sited courtroom ethnography of more than 45 trials and the courtrooms' antechambers (including restrooms, waiting rooms, cafeterias, and parking lots) covering over 200 hours of fieldwork (see Chapter 4). The ensuing analysis drew on "embodied protocols", "legal pads", and "grounded datasets" (for more details see Faria et al. 2020: 1099; Klosterkamp 2023). Klosterkamp found that her observations of remote oral testimonies were especially pertinent for her analysis which focused on how the court "knows" and what counts as a "reliable witness" for the prosecution, the defence lawyers, and the judges (Faria et al. 2020: 1107).

Ethnographic fieldwork revealed that participation via video link led to new dynamics being introduced into the courtroom; a space traditionally designed and used for face-to-face interactions (Fig. 8.1; see for Klosterkamp 2021 for more details). Hence as video links remain an exception to the rule, the courtroom dynamics were shaped and rendered by uncertainty and many questions stemming from legal-reasoning regarding how to compensate for what *was missing* or what remained *irreplaceable* due to a lack of co-presence. This is seen in the following extract from Klosterkamp's fieldnotes where the judge is unsure how to examine a witness when the witness' facial expressions are not discernable and eye contact is not possible:

Judge:	Thank you for coming. We know, this is an unpleasant situation for you, since it required a great deal for you, and everyone involved, to get you here. Before we start the oral testimony (...) I would like to introduce you to everyone present.
Judge to technical support [present in the courtroom]:	"Can you please position the camera accordingly?"
Technical support:	"That's not possible. He can only see you or the defendant—the camera angle doesn't allow a pan-over."
Judge:	"Ah, okay. I see. Okay, so please let him see the defendant."
Witness:	"I see a person, but I don't know if it's him. He's too far away."
Judge:	"Can we get him closer?"
Technical support:	"Not much, I'll try" [He tries a few angles, but nothing much has changed]
Judge:	"Okay, let's leave it like it is and position him back to me, please. Thank you".

Technical support follows this instruction.

Judge:	"Can you see me now?"
Witness:	"Yes"
Judge:	"Okay, but I can't see into your face. I can't proceed with my examination like this. I want to see his eyes. Please ask him to look directly at the camera".
Witness:	"I am looking directly into it"
Judge:	"It doesn't look like this—okay, I still can't get used to it. Anyways, we are happy to have you here. Let's get started."

After ending the oral testimony, the judge concludes that it is still hard for him to get an idea of how to evaluate the behaviour of the witness. Although the judge chose the camera positioning, not all aspects could be captured and were perceived as "missing links" at the end of the examination. This meant that the guards or prosecutors who had accompanied the witness during their testimony were often asked by the judge to comment afterwards on the witness' bodily behaviour. (Fieldnotes, April 2019)

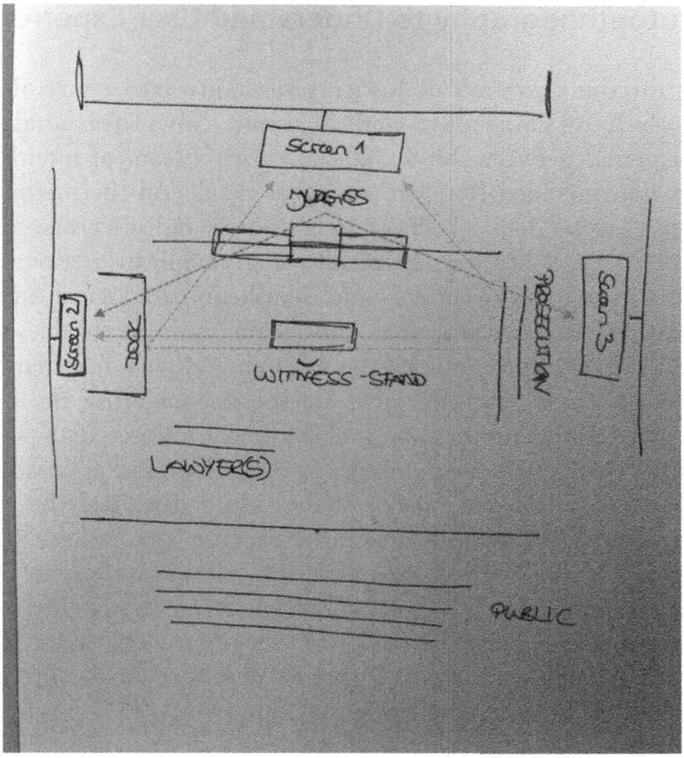

Fig. 8.1 German Courtroom design, seatings, and axes of viewing and co-presence, drafted by Sarah Klosterkamp, based on personal fieldnotes, May 2017

Hence, when direct eye contact is missing, nonverbals are looked to for more information. Eye contact, as well as nonverbal gestures—such as shaking legs or facial expressions—were "hard to grasp" for those involved in these remote settings, especially for the judge and the witness (see Faria et al. 2020: 1107). Furthermore, those physically present in the courtroom, such as the prosecution or expert witnesses, often complained that it was harder to look at all the faces of those taking part (e.g. witnesses, defendants, and the judge) when some participated via video link. This is because, in an ordinary in-person legal setting, the person testifying is seated in the middle of everyone's viewing axes. The technical infrastructure when some participated via video link, as already noted, was not able to offer a similar set-up.

Now Rowden will show how autoethnography contributes to understanding how eyework is disrupted by video links.

Using Autoethnography to Understand User Experiences

Fieldwork for the Gateways to Justice project involved court observations and site visits to 40 courthouses and 20 remote court sites, conducted over a two-year period between 2008 and 2010 with a team of interdisciplinary researchers that included Rowden (for more details on the methodology of the Gateways project data collection on interviews and site visits, see Rowden and Wallace 2018). Wherever possible, Rowden sought to "test out" the court video links herself to better understand the phenomenological experience of communicating via video link in a courtroom setting. Several such "tests" were conducted over the course of the research and were inspired by proponents of autoethnography who advocate for documenting the researcher's own experiences, utilizing them as a valid form of research data (see Méndez 2013). Rather than relying solely on the favoured narrative approach by many autoethnographers, Rowden further analysed and described the encounters through making diagrams and staged photos, later annotating them. While orchestrating these experiences may seem less relevant to current researchers in the field given the ubiquity of video links now in everyday life, at the time it proved enlightening; particularly so given the researcher's then relative unfamiliarity with communicating this way. As described in the literature, this autoethnographic exercise resulted in an "epiphany" (Ellis et al. 2010) for the researcher in comprehending how the design of video linked interactions could distort and construct demeanour and colour participants' opinions of each other over the video link. It is argued that autoethnography enables an embodied insider perspective and hence embodied understanding of video links.

In one particular court in Western Australia, the benefit of this method was revealed. Here Rowden noted during a demonstration of the link she undertook with the help of a court technician:

> While in the remote room I felt as if I was making eye contact with the person speaking from the bar table as they appeared onscreen; when we swapped positions, it appeared to the courtroom that the remote participant was looking away from the speaker at the bar table, and was looking away towards the back of the courtroom. (Rowden 2011: 213)

In discovering this, Rowden staged a photo to capture what was happening (see Fig. 8.2), along with making several sketches of the video link set-up to better understand the camera and screen placement at the remote end (see Fig. 8.3). Through making sketches, she was able to reveal and document that the disjuncture between the remote participant's reality (I-am-looking-at-you-and-paying-attention) and the courtroom's reality (you-are-looking-away-and-not-paying-attention) was mainly because the camera taking the image of the remote person was placed above the screen showing the judge, rather than the screen showing the bar table monitor. Furthermore, it was discovered that the remote witness is captured by a camera placed far above the level of their eyes, so while they are looking straight ahead at the screen in front of them, the camera picks up an image of them having down-cast eyes (see Fig. 8.4). As Rowden concluded the episode:

> Compounding the participant's difficulties in effectively managing the impression they are giving to court, is the possibility of their appearing to the courtroom as if they are disinterested in the proceedings. This is, of course, through no fault of their own, but through a construction of camera angles and screens. (Rowden 2011: 213–214)

This potential for camera and screen placement to detrimentally affect a remote participant's impression management was corroborated when an expert witness interviewee narrated their experience of watching another expert colleague give evidence by video link:

> [O]ne thing I've noticed is (...) you're not necessarily always looking right into the camera. Sometimes you're looking — the camera's right in front of

Fig. 8.2 In this staged photo and subsequent annotations, Rowden attempted to capture the results of the autoethnographic experience: while the person in the remote room believes they are making eye contact with the person at the bar table, to all in the courtroom, however, it appears as if the person in the remote room is disengaged with the proceedings (Images ©EmmaRowden)

Fig. 8.2 (continued)

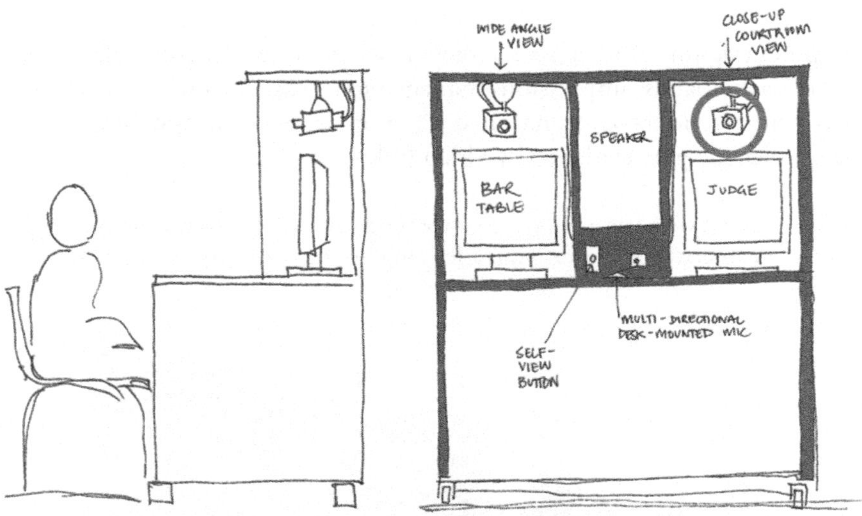

Section of Remote Witness Facility

Elevation View of Remote Witness Technology Cabinet

Fig. 8.3 Sketches showing the remote witness facility in the courthouse. The "Close-Up Courtroom View" camera on the right-hand side, sat above the screen showing the judge, is taking the image of the remote participant that is being displayed in the courtroom (Images ©Emma Rowden)

you, but you're actually looking to the side (…) and it makes the person look very shifty (...) And their eyes are flicking between the two. It's a bad look (…) it just makes, it makes the person look less credible I think than they actually are—and I know the person who is giving evidence on that day (…)

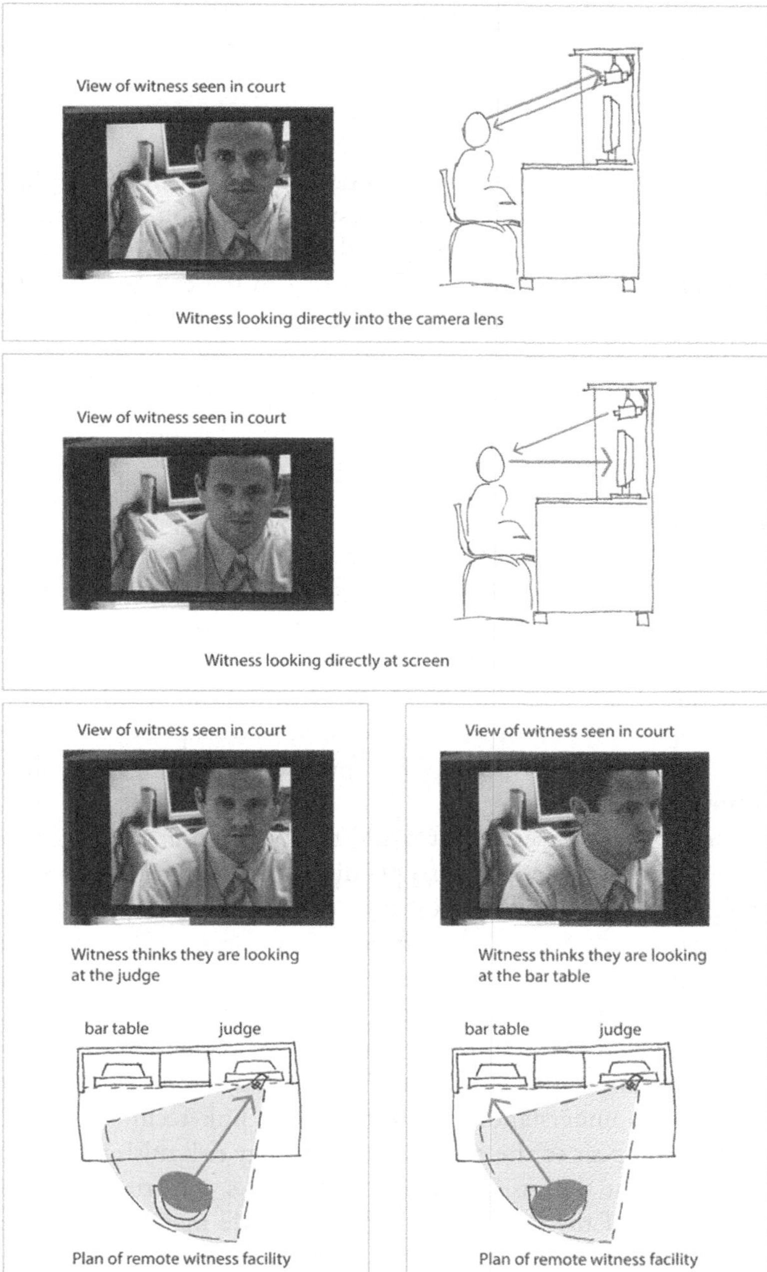

Fig. 8.4 Images and sketches to explain why the remote participant is viewed from the courtroom as looking away from the bar table as their body is turned away from the camera that is relaying their image into the courtroom (Images ©Emma Rowden)

> he's not somebody who I would normally think was shifty or, you know, lacked credibility. But watching him on that video screen doing this [interviewees eyes move from side to side] (...) I just thought "oh, that doesn't come across very well at all".

While the case represents an extreme example, it nonetheless encapsulates the sense that eye contact and, as a result, impression management can be effectively disrupted and misconstrued by some video link set-ups as to render completely different someone's persona to the court. While it might be argued that the above expert witness interview was sufficient to expose this truth of "video links in practice", the autoethnographic approach verified the phenomena, as well as help the researcher unpack and explain *why* this was the case.

Closing Remarks

Video links have progressed towards the everyday and mundane since their inception well over two decades ago. Yet despite their proliferation and despite the technological improvements which continue to improve their quality, the solution to the problem of *what is missing* still evades us. Ethnography can help us to understand how video links disrupt eye contact within courtroom settings in important ways and lead to findings with relevance beyond the courthouse itself.

There are several concerns that come through in our studies. First, the absence of physical co-presence disrupts direct communication between trial participants (such as judges, prosecutors, defence lawyers, plaintiffs, defendants, and witnesses). Second, this absence also disrupts the impression trial participants give to the courtroom with regard to the social image they are attempting to portray, but also and perhaps more worryingly, with regard to how credible they appear. Lastly, the absence and evaluation of other forms of nonverbal feedback in this digitalized interactional process also prevent participants from understanding how the video link technology edits and crafts how they appear to the court and which may risk misinterpretation.

We contend that the insight of how video links construct these impressions and visions of the remote participant is made more redolent through ethnographic approaches. Courtroom ethnography and its related methods thus serve as powerful tools to unpack the tensions, hurdles, and objectives at stake within legal proceedings—something, which might be even more prevalent within upcoming years, as more and more courts aim to keep up with the digitalized infrastructure the global COVID-19 pandemic has brought to them. Nevertheless, despite the wide-reaching juridical inclusion of video links, problems accompanying prevail and warrant further detailed attention. This is distinctly crucial considering that video links have particular ramifications and implications for specific areas of law and may have a specific impact when used in conjunction with certain aspects of trials, for instance, judgements of credibility. Hence, we suggest that pervasiveness of video links demands deeper examination. Furthermore, we suggest that digital eyework is an important area of future research along with a sharper experiential focus on video link participation.

Suggestions and Guidance for Further Readings:

(1) Mulcahy, Linda. 2010. *Legal architecture: Justice, due process and the place of law*. London: Routledge.
(2) Rose, Gillian. 2023. *Visual methodologies: An introduction to the interpretation of visual materials (5th Edition)*. London: SAGE Publications.

References

Atkinson, Paul. 2014. *For ethnography*. London: SAGE Publications Ltd.

Argyle, Mark, and Mark Cook. 1976. *Gaze and mutual gaze*. Cambridge: Cambridge University Press.

Ball, David. 1994. *Theater tips and strategies for jury trials*. Indiana: National Institute for Trial Advocacy.

Bandes, Susan A. 2014. Remorse, demeanor, and the consequences of misinterpretation: The limits of law as a window into the soul. *Journal of Law, Religion and State* 3 (2): 170–99.

Bergman Blix, Stina and Åsa Wettergren. 2018. *Professional emotions in court*. Abingdon: Routledge.

Borneman, John, and Abdellah Hammoudi. 2009. *The fieldwork encounter and the making of truth*. London: University of California Press.

Braun, Sabine, and Judith Taylor. 2012. *Videoconference and remote interpreting in criminal proceedings*. Intersentia.

Campos-Castillo, Celeste, and Steven Hitlin. 2013. Copresence: Revisiting a building block for social interaction theories. *Sociological Theory* 31 (2): 168–192.

Carlen, Pat. 1976. *Magistrates' justice*. London: Martin Robertson & Company Ltd.

Collins, Randall. 2020. Social distancing as a critical test of the micro-sociology of solidarity. *American Journal of Cultural Sociology* 8 (3): 477–497.

Deutschlandfunk. 2021. Digitalisierung der deutschen Justiz. Der langsame Abschied von der Papierakte. Accessed: 8th November 2023. https://www.deutschlandfunk.de/digitalisierung-der-justiz-100.html.

Domstolar, Sveriges. 2022. *Årsredovisning 2021.* Sveriges Domstolar.

Donoghue, Jane. 2017. The rise of digital justice: Courtroom technology, public participation and access to justice. *The Modern Law Review* 80 (6): 995–1025.

Eagly, Ingrid V. 2015. Remote adjudication in immigration. *Northwestern University Law Review* 109: 933–1020.

Ellis, Carolyn, Adams, Tony E., & Bochner, Arthur P. 2010. Autoethnography: An overview. *FQS: Forum Qualitative Sozialforschung/Forum: Qualitative Social Research* 12 (1), Art. 10.

Ellison, Louise, and Vanessa E. Munro. 2013. A 'Special' delivery? Exploring the impact of screens, live-links and video-recorded evidence on Mock Juror deliberation in rape trials. *Social & Legal Studies* 23 (1): 3–29.

Ekman, P. 2004. Emotions revealed: understanding faces and feelings. London: Phoenix.

Faria, Caroline, Sarah Klosterkamp, Rebecca Maria Torres, and Jayme Walenta. 2020. Embodied exhibits: Toward a feminist geographic courtroom ethnography. *Annals of the American Association of Geographers* 110 (4): 1095–1113.

Flower, Lisa. 2016. Doing loyalty: Defense lawyers' subtle dramas in the courtroom. *Journal of Contemporary Ethnography* 47 (2): 226–254.

Flower, Lisa. 2019a. *Interactional justice: The role of emotions in the performance of loyalty*. Abingdon: Routledge.

Flower, Lisa. 2019b. Emotional defence lawyers. *History, Culture, Society* (Special Issue) 3 (2): 282–299.

Goffman, Erving. 1959. *The presentation of self in everyday life*. Harmondsworth: Penguin Books Ltd.

Goffman, Erving. 1963. *Behavior in public places: Notes on the social organization of gatherings*. New York: The Free Press.

Kendon, Adam. 1990. *Conducting interaction: Patterns of behavior in focused encounters*. Cambridge: Cambridge University Press.

Klosterkamp, Sarah. 2021. Geographien des Ein- und Ausschlusses: Strafvollzug und -prozesse im Kontext der Aufarbeitung von Beteiligungshandlungen im syrischen Bürgerkrieg. *Geographica Helvetica* 76: 205–219.

Klosterkamp, Sarah. 2023. Affectual intensities: Toward a politics of listening in court ethnography. *Gender, Place & Culture. A Journal of Feminist Geography,* 30 (11): 1529–1551.

Landström, Sara, Karl Ask, and Charlotte Sommar. 2015. The emotional male victim: Effects of presentation mode on judged credibility. *Scandinavian Journal of Psychology* 56: 99–104.

Legg, Michael, and Anthony Song. 2021. The courts, the remote hearing and the pandemic: from action to reflection. *UNSW Law Journal* 44 (1): 126–166.

Licoppe, Christian, and Laurence Dumoulin. 2010. The 'curious case' of an unspoken opening speech act. A video-ethnography of the use of video communication in courtroom activities. *Research on Language & Social Interaction* 43 (3): 211–231.

Licoppe, Christian, Maud Verdier, and Laurence Dumoulin. 2013. Courtroom interaction as a multimedia event: The work of producing relevant videoconference frames in French pre-trial hearings. *The Electronic Journal of Communication* 23 (1&2): 1–20.

Mack, Kathy, and Sharon Roach Anleu. 2010. Performing impartiality: Judicial demeanor and legitimacy. *Law & Social Inquiry* 35 (1): 137–173.

McKay, Carolyn. 2018. *The pixelated prisoner*. Abingdon: Routledge.

Méndez, Mariza. 2013. Autoethnography as a research method: Advantages, limitations and criticisms. *Colombian Applied Linguistics Journal* 15 (2): 279–287.

Mulcahy, Linda. 2008. The unbearable lightness of being: Shifts towards the virtual trial. *Journal of Law and Society* 35 (4): 464–489.

Neal, Tess M. S., Stanley Brodsky, and L. 2008. Expert witness credibility as a function of eye contact behavior and gender. *Criminal Justice and Behavior* 35 (12): 1515–1526.

Orcutt, Holly K., Gail S. Goodman, Ann E. Tobey, Jennifer M. Batterman-Faunce, and Sherry Thomas. 2001. Detecting deception in children's testimony: Factfinders' abilities to reach the truth in open court and closed-circuit trials. *Law and Human Behavior* 25 (4): 339–372.

Paik, Leslie, and Alexes Harris. 2015. Court ethnographies. In *The routledge handbook of qualitative criminology*, ed. Heith Copes and J. Miller. Abingdon: Routledge.

Remotecourts.org. 2022. Accessed 25th January 2023. https://remotecourts.org

Roach Anleu, S., & Mack, K. (2017). *Performing judicial authority in the lower courts*. London: Palgrave.

Rock, Paul. 1993. *The social world of an English crown court*. Oxford: Oxford University Press.

Rossner, Meredith, and Martha McCurdy. 2020. *Video hearings process evaluation (phase 2)*. London: Ministry of Justice.

Rossner, Meredith, and David Tait. 2021. Presence and participation in a virtual court. *Criminology & Criminal Justice*. 23 (1): 140–157.

Rossner, Meredith, David Tait, and Martha McCurdy. 2021. Justice reimagined: Challenges and opportunities with implementing virtual courts. *Current Issues in Criminal Justice* 33 (1): 94–110.

Rowden, Emma. 2011. *Remote participation and the distributed court: An approach to court architecture in the age of video-mediated communications*. PhD Thesis, University of Melbourne, Melbourne, Australia.

Rowden, Emma. 2018. Distributed courts and legitimacy: What do we lose when we lose the courthouse? *Law, Culture and the Humanities* 14 (2): 263–281.

Rowden, Emma, and Anne Wallace. 2018. Remote Judging: The impact of video links on the image and the role of the judge. *International Journal of Law in Context* 14: 504.

Sanders, Anne. 2021. Video-hearings in Europe before, during and after the COVID-19 pandemic: Lessons for the courts. *International Journal for Court Administration* 12 (2): 1–21.

Seidman Diamond, Sharon, Locke E. Bowman, Manyee Wong, and Matthew W. Patton. 2010. Efficiency and cost: The impact of videoconferenced hearings on bail decisions. *The Journal of Criminal Law and Criminology* 100: 869–902.

Sporer, Siegfried, and Barbara Schwandt. 2007. Moderators of nonverbal Indicators of deception: A meta-analytic synthesis. *Psychology, Public Policy, and Law* 13 (1): 1–34.

Tait, David. 2001. Popular sovereignty and the justice process: Towards a comparative methodology for observing courtroom rituals. *Contemporary Justice Review* 4 (2): 201–218.

Taylor, Natalie, and Jacqueline Joudo. 2005. *The impact of pre-recorded video and closed circuit television testimony by adult sexual assault complainants on jury decision-making*, Research and Public Policy Series No. 68. Online: Australian Institute of Criminology.

Wiggins, Elizabeth C. 2003. What we know and what we need to know about the effects of courtroom technology symposium. *William & Mary Bill of Rights Journal* 12 (3): 731–744.

9

Hate Crime and Reverse Engineering the Law

Kerstin Bree Carlson

Introduction

The June 2020 brutal murder of a black man on the idyllic Danish island of Bornholm dominated the news cycle even outside of Denmark. Beyond the terrible violence in a community with a low crime rate, the facts of the case and Danish authorities' response to it captured global attention. The murder seemed racialized and it was perpetrated by two brothers with professed affinities to white power groups and ideologies. The murder as a hate crime[1] was nonetheless quickly rejected by Danish authorities. Within 48 hours of the discovery of the victim's pulverized body, Danish police and state prosecutors had determined not to investigate whether racial hate was a motivating factor in the crime. The brothers were friends with the victim, and beat him to death during a drinking session. They planned the attack to 'teach the victim a lesson' in response to the victim's alleged sexual relationship with the brothers' mother. For the Danish authorities, the personal relationship between victim

[1] 'Hate' is an aggravating factor in a criminal offence. Hate crimes are recognized in the Danish criminal code § 81, nr. 6. Hate crimes are crimes motivated in whole or in part by prejudice against a social group.

K. B. Carlson (✉)
The American University of Paris, Paris, France
e-mail: carlson@ruc.dk

L. Flower and S. Klosterkamp (eds.), *Courtroom Ethnography*,
https://doi.org/10.1007/978-3-031-37985-7_9

and the perpetrators erased the possibility of 'hate' as a motivating factor. Therefore, even though Danish law recognizes hate crimes, and even though hate crime doctrine does not specify that personal motivation obviates hate, hate as an aggravating factor was not investigated or subsequently charged in the case.

This chapter explores how ethnographic observation of the trial and appeal reveals the applied judicial logic regarding how to assess criminal hate. Importantly, in the Bornholm murder case, court ethnography illuminates an interesting contrast between judicial constructions of intent and motivation. Both are legal fictions, designed to connect facts as committed to laws and the ideologies they represent. Ethnography reveals how the parties (prosecutor, defense, judges) in the Bornholm first-instance and appeals trials engaged in creative, active judicial constructions as regards intent, but narrow, static constructions regarding motivation. This is interesting, since motivation is arguably the more readily demonstrable psychological impetus. Yet in the Bornholm murder case, the parties used 'intent' to investigate and 'motivation' to declare.

The chapter proceeds in two parts. First, it discusses the crime, its context, and the trial. It then examines how trial ethnography, specifically, can help illuminate and understand hidden elements of how and what courts know. In the Bornholm murder case, hate was not investigated and therefore was not officially part of the state's case against the perpetrators. The question of what role racism played was nonetheless raised during both the trial and the appeals procedures by the prosecutor and the court. This contrast—an official denial to legally address race, followed by considerations of race by state parties in court—illustrates the value of courtroom ethnography. In the Bornholm murder case, ethnography provides an otherwise unobservable view into how legal authorities reason.

Categorizing Phillip Johansen's Murder

On 23 June 2020, Phillip Mbuji Johansen, a black Danish man, was beaten to death by two of his friends, brothers Mads and Magnus Møller. Johansen's death shocked the small country of Denmark, population less than 6 million. This is partly because murders are infrequent,[2] partly because it occurred on the otherwise-idyllic island of Bornholm, and partly due to the brutality of the crime.

[2] Typically fewer than 50 murders per year. See https://www.statista.com/statistics/576114/number-of-homicides-in-denmark/.

Since both brothers admitted that they had beaten their victim and left him to die, the facts were not in contention. The only questions the authorities were investigating concerned intent and motivation, which are distinct categories under Danish law and qualify the charges brought by the state. As regards intent, if the brothers meant for Phillip to die, this would make the crime murder, which involves either direct, likely, or dolus eventualis intent to kill. If the death was unintentional, unimagined, or otherwise unexpected, it would be manslaughter.[3] Sentence lengths for the two crimes vary significantly. The prosecution qualified the killing as murder; the brothers qualified it as manslaughter.

Motivation is significant because certain motivation charges, such as 'hate,' can increase sentence lengths. In the Bornholm murder case, the question of whether the crime constituted a 'hate crime' was contested. Several aspects of the defendants' behavior pointed toward race playing a role in the murder, such as one defendant's swastika and 'white power' tattoos, and the other defendant's early admission to police that he pinned the victim to the ground with a knee on his neck, imitating the gesture police used to murder George Floyd in the USA three weeks earlier. Even the brothers' stated rationale for the attack—the non-consensual nature of Phillip's alleged sexual relationship with their mother—could have been impacted by Phillip's race, echoing a well-versed trope of the supposed threat that black men represent for white women (Burton 2012; Hodes 1997).

Yet despite these factors, the Danish authorities refused to investigate or concede any racial motivation for the crime, finding that the crime was 'purely personal.' Under Danish authorities' reading of hate crimes law, the personal relationship between the victim and the defendants extinguished the possibility of legally construing hate as a motivating factor. 'As we see it, it is a completely different motive than skin colour. It is a personal relationship,' the head prosecutor concluded, a few days after the murder (Nørmark 2020). 'Nothing points to racism,' the second in command of the Bornholm police said, the same day (Lund 2020). In August 2020, in a scheduling hearing, the prosecutor held fast to the position she articulated in June, saying 'We still haven't come across any racist motive.' She continued:

> The motive that has emerged today is the only motive we have heard. So we have of course been open to whether there could be other motives. We do it in such a way that in our investigation we look at whether there is anything that could indicate that it is racist, but this is not the case for the time being. (Hagemann-Nielsen and Lou 2020)

[3] In Danish, these categories are 'drab' and 'vold med døden til følge,' respectively.

Thus, although hate crimes are recognized under Danish law, Danish authorities systematically refused to investigate, charge, or test the possibility of judicial recognition that Phillip Johansen's murder represented a hate crime. How should we understand this official, and subsequently judicial, silence? And how do the court and its members interpret the silence?

I attended the two-day first-instance trial conducted in November–December 2020 and the two-day appeals trial conducted in October 2021.[4] Danish court cases are not transcribed and written judgments are not fulsome. Trial ethnography is thus a singular method of following the public face of a trial to see the law in action. It often provides the only window into what motivates the final judgment.

The Trial (30 November–1 December 2020)

Rønne, the largest town and harbor on the island of Bornholm, is host to one courthouse, Bornholm's first-instance court. The stone building, identified by a modest plaque by the door, faces a square in the center of the town. Inside, unadorned white walls and pale wooden floorboards represent a classic Danish style closer to a Lutheran church than a public building. Outside, a few media outlets had set up shop on the square, to cover the trial in real time. This is where the first-instance trial of the Møller brothers took place in late 2020.

The small Bornholm courthouse made concessions for the media presence in the much-discussed case. The audience seats available in the first-floor trial chamber itself were reserved for family and personal acquaintances. The few seats still available and given to the press were reserved for local media. Or at least this is what I gathered from the discontented murmuring of the national media representatives in the overflow room where I sat on the ground floor, just off the entry way. Here a live stream feed from the court room was being broadcast for the approximately 20 seats the room could accommodate. Spectators included a number of national print and audio media representatives, the head of Black Lives Matter ('BLM') Denmark, a freelance journalist working for *The New Yorker*, and myself. Our names and affiliations were placed on chairs in the room, each chair claimed by a specific applicant. Public observation was thus only possible for those who had reserved in advance. I had secured a spot by writing the court and requesting access, explaining that I am a researcher with a Danish university. I was at first denied

[4] Dom 1 december 2020, 1-760/2020 (Retten på Bornholm); Ankedom 28 oktober 2021, S -3463-20 (Østrelandsret).

a place by the court administrator due to lack of space, after which I wrote the head judge personally asking to see if any place could be secured for me, and received an email a few days later granting me a seat. To my knowledge, I was the only researcher to attend either the first-instance or appeals trial, which itself seems interesting, given how publicized the case was, as well as the contentious legal questions it evoked.

The atmosphere in the room was low key and chatty, as many of the journalists knew each other. There were moments of shared collectivity for many of them, including the excited tapping of computer keys when the trial commenced by announcing that the defendants' anonymity had been lifted (several media outlets nonetheless refrained to name the defendants in their live tweets). There was also a collective group groaning and even conspiratorial discussion when a moratorium was placed on live blogging while the two defendants testified (to preserve the integrity of other witness accounts).

The trial took place over two days, presided over by a professional and two lay judges, as well as a jury.[5] Two prosecutors pressed the case against the two defendants, each of whom had his own attorney.

The facts of the case emerged in court. In the early hours of 23 June 2020, brothers Mads and Magnus Møller drove into the woods with their friend Phillip Mbuji Johansen. Philip thought that he and the Møller brothers were going out for an evening drinking in the woods. The evening started this way; the group even left their woodsy spot to go buy more beer and vodka—paid for by Johansen. But the brothers had a plan to 'rough Phillip up a bit' as payback for what they characterized as a sexual assault against their mother. After an hour of drinking and chatting by the fire they had lit, the brothers began their attack. It was a litany of horror that took the prosecutor nearly an hour to describe in court. It was so physically ferocious that the brothers took breaks (two or three, they testified) during the onslaught, to rest and drink more beer. They left Phillip with both his legs broken, his fingers broken, his nose broken, his testicles crushed, and branded with a hot iron on his ears, face, and torso. Their last act was to throw Phillip's cell phone and shoes into the fire.

The brothers testified that when they left him, Philip was breathing; they could see this by the light of the fire, they said. The coroner could not ascertain the exact time of death, but determined that Johansen died by asphyxiating on his own blood sometime between 3 and 6 am.

[5] Danish criminal trials, at both the trial and appeals level, feature both judges and jury, who convoke to produce a verdict. The verdict need not be unanimous, and the number for and against (but not their role), is announced in the final judgment. The negotiations that produce the final vote and verdict are confidential. See Helms (2023) (Danish language ethnography regarding how proof is weighed and guilt adjudicated in Danish courts).

The two men who killed Phillip, Mads and Magnus Møller, were his childhood friends/acquaintances. Mads was Phillip's age and worked with livestock on Bornholm. He described Philip as his 'best friend.' Magnus, Mads' younger brother, also knew Philip. Both Mads and Magnus had troubled school reports and childhoods. The younger brother Magnus had a spotted history of multiple interventions by social workers and violent episodes in school.

Courtroom Testimony

The prosecution called two witnesses: the coroner (who testified about the state of Phillip's body, for more than an hour), and a friend of the defendants (who testified about the question of racism, for less than five minutes). This second witness testified that Mads Møller wasn't racist because she 'never saw him do anything racist' and because he was 'friends with [Johansen] and other non-white people.' Regarding his swastika and white power tattoos, she opined that they were meant 'to provoke.'[6]

Both defendants answered questions from the prosecutor, who asked the Møller brothers directly about racist motivation for Phillip's murder. Mads Møller (Phillip's 'best friend' with the swastika tattoo and 'White Lives Matter' posts on his Facebook page), in response to the question, 'are you racist?' answered 'It would have been strange I was friends with Phillip, if I was a racist.' Regarding Magnus Møller's alleged George Floyd reference with a knee to Phillip's neck, the defendant in court said that he said 'yes' to all questions police asked him, unthinkingly, but that in fact he could not remember if he had his knee on Phillip's neck, or rather breast or shoulder, and that he was not sure when he first heard about George Floyd's murder, whether it was before or after Phillip's murder (Molin and Kulager 2020b).

Prosecutor: "So you didn't know people could die from having a knee to the neck on June 23rd?"
Magnus Møller: "No".

The coroner was not able to definitively state that damage to Phillip's body came from a knee to the neck. The information that Magnus Møller held Phillip down in the same way that George Floyd was murdered came from Magnus Møller himself, in his initial interviews with police. Phillip's murder

[6] Witness for the prosecution, First-Instance Trial November 2020 (author's field notes; testimony can only be accessed through attendance or, in this case, any content available via live blog. Thus quotes are approximate, as best as could be noted during speech).

occurred three weeks after Floyd was killed by Minnesota police, at the height of the BLM global movement.

The prosecution cited three cases to support their interpretation that the facts demonstrated intent to kill (murder); the defense cited more than a dozen cases in support of manslaughter. Ultimately, a unanimous jury found the defendant's guilty of murder and sentenced them to 14 years (two years more than the 12-year minimum for the crime); both defendants appealed on the spot.

The Appeal (October 2021)

For the appeal, the Østrelandsret (one of Denmark's two appeals courts) took itself to Bornholm, so the appeal was heard in the same Bornholm courtroom as the trial. There was far less media attention for the appeal and therefore no live-tweeting of the verbal blow-by-blows. Extra seating with a dedicated live feed was set up in a small room next to the courtroom; seats were not reserved and a small group of fewer than 10 people sat in the room. Relatives of the victim and defendants, supporters from BLM Denmark, and some media outlets found places in the courtroom itself.

In Denmark, appeals processes rehear the facts of the case and employ a jury to sit in and decide with the judges, the same as at first-instance trials. As with first-instance trials, the decision is made by the majority (unanimity is not required). The appeals court reheard only one witness from trial: the coroner. The appeals court also considered the civil question of damages for Phillip's death brought by Phillip's parents (expenses for the burial; loss of enjoyment and companionship with their son). The appeals judgment confirmed the trial court's finding of guilt, by majority increased the sentence from 14 to 15 years, and did not recognize Phillip's parents' claims.

Addressing the Question of Race on Appeal

Race was more directly addressed by parties to the appeals trial than at the first-instance hearing. Unlike before the first-instance court, Phillip's parents addressed the court, requesting damages. Phillip's family's attorney concluded his request for damages to the court with the phrase 'colored lives also have value.'[7]

[7] Author's fieldnotes, 27 October 2021.

The prosecutor began his concluding statement by discussing the racial aspects of the killing, and the way that this racism had been portrayed in international coverage of the murder.

> Why was Phillip Johansen out in this forest? Was it racially motivated? There were discussions, and it was reportedly about racism. This is due to many things: there was the knee on the neck, which drew parallels to what was happening in USA. In the US, there was a murder committed by a policeman, one month before these events, who choked a man by putting a knee on his neck. Can it be a coincidence? These circumstances were widely discussed. *The New York Times* ran a big story on it, 'a racist attack perpetrated by brothers with a racist background.' (Erdbrink 2020)
>
> We don't know what happened in their mind. We can't say what their motive was. But that said, there is nothing that says it was a racist motive. Both the defendants say it's all personal, that it was about their mother, and that Phillip needed to be punished. Both the defendants were friends with Phillip Johansen. So, to come back to the episode in the forest, the defendants both decided Phillip should be punished, and this is the basis for everything that followed.[8]

Here the prosecutor makes the contrast with how law knows regarding intent versus motivation very clear: as regards motivation, the defendants say it was personal, and so: it was.

Likewise, Magnus Møller's attorney addressed the question of race in her closing statement:

> There are no other motives except the mother. There are no racist motives, about treating people of certain colors certain ways. This is about a friend, who has to be now seen in another light. Maybe this is why it took so long [once they reached the drinking spot] to get started, and this is really what happened. This rejection [of his friend], as the first-instance court said, was very violent. It is not an unnatural response, to be physically affected, but this wasn't a good way to handle it.[9]

Finally, on a break during the first day of hearings, I had a short conversation with one of Mads Møller's attorneys, who asked me what my interest in the case was. We had arrived at the Bornholm airport early in the morning together, where I discovered that everyone had prebooked taxis, and there

[8] Prosecutor's closing argument, Appeals Process, 28 October 2021 (author's fieldnotes, quotation approximate, *New York Times* citation provided by author).

[9] Magnus Møller's defense attorney closing argument, 28 October 2021 (author's fieldnotes, quotation approximate).

were no taxis available to take me to town. He allowed me to ride to the courthouse with him. The following is taken from my fieldnotes:

> I told him I was following the case as a legal researcher based on the absence of a hate crime charge. He reacted instantly, aggressively, responding, 'Because there's no hate crime!' He asserted that he had been through all the documents and there was nothing indicating there was a hate crime, because it's not a hate crime, and the prosecutor had made a very thorough investigation, which I of course could not be privy to. After making this pronouncement, he abruptly walked away.[10]

This is an example of the tension and resistance surrounding the racialized elements of Phillip Mbuji Johansen's murder.

Contextualizing (and Racializing) Phillip Johansen's Murder

Outside of official circles, the extenuating circumstances of Phillip's murder suggested a racialized motive to many observers. Phillip, 26 years old at the time of his death, was an engineering student in Copenhagen. He had moved back to Bornholm, the island on which he'd grown up, with the onset of the Covid-19 lockdown. The son of a Danish man and a Tanzanian woman, Philip had extensive networks on the island. Outgoing and affable, Philip was one of the few people of color on the island. His local nickname was '*n-ger-Phillip*' ['n–gger Phillip'].

In the weeks following the murder, civil society groups and progressive politicians publicly and repeatedly criticized the police and prosecutor for leaving investigations of racial animus out of the investigation. For example, member of parliament Rosa Lund (*Enhedslisten*, a left-wing party) tweeted that the police should investigate the murder as a hate crime (Lund 2020). This tweet brought scads of criticism, much of it focusing on Lund's inappropriate meddling in official processes. The conversation about how crimes could be discussed as hate crimes took on its own news cycle. Lund explained to the newspaper *Information*:

> I believe that we have problems with structural racism in Denmark. One way to deal with this is to ensure that the police are better trained to solve hate crimes and have more resources… [W]e have a structural problem, and the

[10] Author's fieldnotes, 27 October 2021.

> debate that has taken place about the murder on Bornholm shows it. I think we talk about these things in a completely different way than we talk about other crimes. We also know that it is difficult to get an internship if you have a foreign surname - and difficult to get a job if you wear a headscarf. It also shows that we have a racism problem in Denmark. (Villesen 2020)

The observation regarding structural racism in Denmark has been raised before and not only by left-leaning Danish politicians. Human rights groups in Denmark have noted that hate crimes are significantly under-prosecuted in Denmark (Danish Institute for Human Rights 2021). In the 2016 Universal Periodic Review of Denmark before the United Nations Human Rights Council, the issue of hate speech and hate crime was referenced no fewer than 27 times in suggestions made to Denmark (Danish Institute for Human Rights 2016). Denmark's treatment of racialized categories constitutes a significant human rights shortfall, as recorded in these reports.

The question of race and racism and how the authorities were or should manage it defined the way the case was covered by media. Following the first-instance trial, independent investigative outlet *Zetland* covered the question of racism before the court in an article named, 'Now we know why Philip had to die. And why racism did not become part of the Bornholm murder case' (Molin and Kulager 2020b). The article discusses the questions related to racism in depth and states at the end that the answer as to why racism was not a part of the court's judgment was because hate was never charged by the prosecutor. BLM Denmark organized protests, calling the murder on Bornholm a 'lynching.' BLM Denmark organized a protest/vigil on Bornholm scheduled to coincide with the trial and verdict. This prompted outrage from some local residents who spoke to news media, who asserted that it was BLM Denmark that transformed the killing, a tragedy, into a racist event. One headline read, for example: 'Friends of those killed on Bornholm: The case is not about racism. Black Lives Matter demonstrated on Tuesday in Rønne after the murder case. Friends had organized a counter-demonstration (Ritzau 2020).' This echoed what locals familiar with the actors had said at the beginning of the case; in the words of one friend of both Philip and Mads Møller, making the case about racism 'would turn [Phillip's] death into a lie (Molin and Kulager 2020a, 2020b).'

Contrasting How the Law Knows: Intent v. Motivation

Law is a discipline that seeks to 'do things with words' (Austin 1962). While it is beyond the constraints of this chapter to examine the specific social and governance rationales behind either criminal law's murder/manslaughter distinction or the recognition of hate as an aggravating criminal law motivation, it is necessary to recall that law constitutes and is constituted by social expectations (Teubner 1993), thus serving both as social reflection and social control. As regards social control, criminal law is specifically purposed with this goal (Garland 2002), which must be communicative (not merely punitive) in liberal societies (Duff 2001). It is here that trial ethnography can help explain the extralegal content of law (Latour 2010).

'Intent' and 'motivation' both constitute legal fictions, because they are constructed via a semiotic imaginary connecting observable/provable facts to unknowable internal processes. The central question this chapter considers is how Danish authorities investigated and argued one (intent) yet stipulated as given by the brothers (motivation) the other. This section considers the specifics that were raised during the Bornholm trials to demonstrate that there is nothing particular to intent or motivation in themselves that explain how the court determined the brothers *intended* to kill Phillip (despite their testimonies to the contrary) versus why the violence they inflected upon Phillip wasn't *motivated* by Phillip's race (because of their testimonies to the contrary). As regards both intent and motivation, facts and actions belie the defendants' direct testimonies, but it is only as regards intent that Danish authorities (police; prosecutor; court) empowered themselves to use these facts. This is particularly significant in the area of hate crimes, which seeks to recognize and redress endemic and often wily social harms. As discussed above, data indicates that in spite of the fact that hate crimes are recognized under Danish criminal law, and notwithstanding evidence that hate crimes constitute a social problem in Denmark, few hate crimes prosecutions take place.

Trial ethnography is useful in considering hate crimes prosecutions—or, as in this case, their absence—because it provides a singular method to investigate intellectual construction regarding social facts and/or government policies and obligations. The terse nature of Danish law judgments does not reveal much of what convinced the judges (or, indeed, who of the court was convinced, since decisions are made by a majority which includes both judges and jurors, a black box that outsiders cannot enter). Therefore courtroom questions, behavior, and content are the slim clues provided to understanding eventual judicial conclusions, and none of these are recorded except by any ethnographers present (cp. Chapter 5, Chapter 12); see also Atkinson (2014).

Intent to Kill

There is no definition of intent in Danish criminal law. Article 19 of the Danish criminal law mentions intent only to clarify that intent is necessary, but does not define it. A 1924 legal resolution had suggested adding an article 20 defining intent. That definition reads: 'Intent is present when the perpetrator, by his action, wants to bring about what is required by law for the crime, or considers its occurrence as a necessary or predominantly probable consequence of the act, or only considers the occurrence of the crime as possible, but would have acted as if he had considered it safe.'[11] This definition, while not present in Danish law, has evolved into the three forms of intent that Danish criminal law recognizes: direct, likely, and dolus eventualis (Rasmussen & Dietz 2019).

The court heard testimony from the defendants regarding how they intended to beat Phillip up 'to teach him a lesson' regarding his alleged relationship with their mother; how they agreed between themselves not to hit him in the head as this can be deadly; how they were so drunk they had to rest while beating him and had trouble remembering the events. Nonetheless, both trial and appeal courts found the defendant's guilty of murder based on facts that spoke more loudly than the defendants' testimonies. For both courts, these facts concerned the extraordinary violence unleashed against Phillip's body (burning, stomping, crushing, and breaking bones), as well as the defendants' final actions when they left Phillip (throwing Phillip's cell phone and shoes into the fire, making it impossible for him to get himself help, had he been able otherwise to do so).

Racist Motivations

Studies of bias reveal that people voice more conservative opinions when holding a cold beverage in their hands, that judges give higher sentences in the period right before lunch because they are hungry, and that threatening someone's self-esteem increases their prejudice toward minorities (Agarwal 2020). In other words, bias studies confirm the existence of vast, harmful, complex prejudices which we do not consciously recognize or control (Agarwal 2020; Kahneman 2013). This type of 'implicit bias' might explain many facets of the case that were left unaddressed. For example, the personal motive named by the prosecutor was Johansen's alleged behavior toward the

[11] Rigsdagstidende 1924-25, tillæg A, sp. 3153-3154 (available here: https://webarkiv.ft.dk/?/samling/19971/udvbilag/00351706.htm).

brothers' mother. Long-established racist tropes regarding the danger that black men pose to white women might help explain how the brothers saw Johansen's alleged behavior as 'assault' and 'rape'—allegations which were widely reported in the Danish press (Nielsen 2020) but remain entirely unsubstantiated—as well as why Danish authorities believed this rationale when offered. Implicit bias also might help explain the brothers' decision to address a conflict with their friend through violence, as well as explain how that violence spiraled so brutally and tragically out of control.

As the prosecutor mentioned many times during the trial, it's not possible to look inside a defendant's head and know what they intended. Courts must assess intent through actions. The Bornholm processes demonstrate how two Danish courts assessed intent through actions, and rejected a similar application of actions to describe motivation. In these two cases we see how intent is a legal category capable of producing investigation, argument, and contradiction, whereas motivation is not.

The Bornholm processes invite us to consider whether Danish legal culture and practice is prepared to use motivation in the same way it does intent, i.e. as an investigatory tool designed to help us see past what the defendant says/thinks he was doing to a truth about facts that the law can recognize as universal. Modern categories of intent and the law's application of them have been practiced for at least 100 years (see footnote 11). The practice itself perhaps allows practitioners to avoid the messy process of looking inside what the purpose of the law's categories is. In terms of motivation and hate crimes, this evolution of legal categories, discourses, and practices haven't yet occurred.

This indicates that recognizing racism is a knowledge problem. How law knows is a question that encompasses what law thinks it can know and what is necessary to construct a proof that meets the standard of inquiry (beyond a reasonable doubt or *conviction intime* in criminal cases, a preponderance of the evidence in civil cases). The question of what the law knows is fraught. It can often reveal deep subjectivities and prejudices, particularly when applied across diverse communities with differing values and practices. We have long recognized the difficulty the law can encounter when my freedom fighter is your terrorist. But culturally bounded ways of knowing have far greater and more pervasive roots in what law assumes and how knowledge is constructed (Levine 2003; Renteln 2005).

The law in action approach (Travers and Manzo 1997) of trial ethnography reveals two significant juridical understandings of hate crimes in Danish court practice that are not affirmatively written into Danish legal doctrine. The first juridical understanding is that hate crimes must involve anonymous, not known, victims. As the *Johansen* case shows, in order for hate to motivate crime in Denmark, it must motivate the crime in its entirety, not merely play a role in the crime. The second, related, juridical understanding is hate's relationship to racism. In this juridical understanding, hate/racism must exist as a singular driving force in order to be judicially recognizable. These juridical understandings are significant because they arguably diverge from the scope and rationale of the recognition of hate as criminal. By making them visible, trial ethnography permits discussion and contestation of law as practiced, pushing for a broader, more cogent application of laws designed to address endemic social violence.

Closing Remarks: The Slow Pace of Law as Social Change Agent

Prosecutors have the discretion to select the claims they believe can be established in court. The brass-tacks approach to constructing a criminal prosecution often appears incomplete or unjust. The 1931 conviction of notoriously violent and murderous American mafia boss Al Capone for the subdued crime of tax evasion is one oft-cited example. Trial ethnography is an essential tool in understanding how court actors understand which claims can be established in court, and why. Trial ethnography in this case contrasts how Danish courts accept the fiction that they can know a defendant's guilty mind by his acts regarding criminal intent how little Danish authorities believe they can interrogate racial animus.

The Bornholm murder case and its rejection of racialized motivation outlines a larger legal and social challenge: how can law make an impact in areas where there is social reluctance or opposition to its dictate? In Denmark, hate crimes are recognized in the criminal code, in keeping with supranational human rights obligations. This legal recognition can only be socially impactful if it is applied in practice, however. The case of Phillip Mbuji Johansen's murder indicates how difficult this social recognition remains, and trial ethnography sheds some light as to why.

Suggestions and Guidance for Further Readings:

(1) Carlson, Kerstin Bree. (2024). Ties that Sever: Losing the Right to Belong in Denmark. In *Law & Critique.*
(2) Carlson, Kerstin Bree. 2023. Punishment, legality, and other challenges of International Criminal Law. In *International Criminal Law Review* 23, 1, pp. 123–144.

References

Agarwal, Pragya. 2020. *Sway: Unravelling unconscious bias*. London; New York: Bloomsbury Sigma.

Atkinson, Paul. 2014. *For ethnography*. London: SAGE Publications Ltd.

Austin, J.L. 1962. *How to do things with words*. Cambridge, Mass: Harvard University Press.

Burton, Nsenga K. 2012. White women and "Blame a Black Man" Syndrome. *The Root*, February 1.

Danish Institute for Human Rights. 2016. *UPR of Denmark 2016: List of selected recommendations*.

Danish Institute for Human Rights. 2021. *Parallel report Denmark—UN Committee on the elimination of racial discrimination (CERD) 2021*. Copenhagen: Danish Institute for Human Rights.

Duff, R. Anthony. 2001. *Punishment, communication and community*. Oxford University Press.

Erdbrink, Thomas. 2020. *A black man was tortured and killed in Denmark. The police insist it wasn't about race*. The New York Times, June 30.

Garland, David. 2002. *The culture of control: Crime and social order in contemporary society*, 1st ed. Chicago: University of Chicago Press.

Hagemann-Nielsen, Frederik, and Jane Lou. 2020. *Anklager i drabssag fra Bornholm: Vi er stadig ikke stødt på racistisk motiv*. DR. Retrieved 30 April 2023 (https://www.dr.dk/nyheder/indland/anklager-i-drabssag-fra-bornholm-vi-er-stadig-ikke-stoedt-paa-racistisk-motiv).

Helms, Lotte. 2023. *Beviskravet i Strafferet*. Karnov Group, Copenhagen.

Hodes, Martha. 1997. *White women, black men*. Yale University Press.

Kahneman, Daniel. 2013. *Thinking, fast and slow*, 1st ed. New York: Farrar, Straus and Giroux.

Latour, Bruno. 2010. *The making of law: An ethnography of the Conseil d'État*. Cambridge: Polity Press.

Levine, Kay L. 2003. Negotiating the boundaries of crime and culture: A sociolegal perspective on cultural defense strategies. *Law & Social Inquiry* 28 (1): 39–86.

Lund, Rosa. 2020. *Tweet*. Retrieved https://twitter.com/RosaLundEl/status/1275902525032542216?ref_src=twsrc%5Etfw%7Ctwcamp%5Etweetembed%7Ctwterm%5E1275902525032542216%7Ctwgr%5E%7Ctwcon%5Es1_&ref_url=https%3A%2F%2Fpolitiken.dk%2Fkultur%2Fmedier%2Fart7846546%2FDet-tragiske-mord-pC3A5-Bornholm-har-gjort-det-tydeligt-at-medierne-ikke-forstC3A5r-deres-lC3A6sere.

Molin, Theis Ehler, and Frederik Kulager. 2020a. *Hvorfor skulle P dø? Vi gravede os ned i historien om drabet på Bornholm og fandt nyt*. Zetland.

Molin, Theis Ehler, and Frederik Kulager. 2020b. *Nu ved vi, hvorfor Phillip skulle dø. Og hvorfor racisme ikke blev en del af sagen om drabet på Bornholm*. Zetland.

Nielsen, Majken Munk. 2020. *Bornholm-drab: Mor beskyldte 28-årig for voldtægt*. Newsbreak.dk, August 19.

Nørmark, Jakob. 2020. *Drabssag: Anklager vil afvæbne racismerygter—motivet er en personlig relation.* https://tidende.dk/bornholm/drabssag-anklager-vil-afvaebne-racismerygter-motivet-er-en-personlig-relation/101278, Last Access November 8th, 2023.

Renteln, Alison Dundes. 2005. *The cultural defense*. Oxford: Oxford University Press.

Ritzau. 2020. *Venner til dræbt på Bornholm: Sagen handler ikke om racisme*. Berlinske, December 1.

Travers, Max, John Manzo, and F. 1997. *Law in action: Ethnomethodological and conversation analytic approaches to law*. Dartmouth: Ashgate.

Teubner, Gunther. 1993. *Law as an autopoietic system.*

Villesen, Kristian. 2020. *Rosa Lund: »Politiet bør efterforske mordet på Bornholm som en hadforbrydelse«*. Information, July 3.

10

Towards Child-Friendly Asylum Justice

Sara Lembrechts

Introduction

When unaccompanied minors or families with minor children obtain a negative decision on their asylum application in Belgium, they can appeal at the Council for Alien Law Litigation (CALL). This leads to an administrative procedure of full judicial review in which asylum judges can either confirm, reform or annul the first instance decision. An appeal at the CALL is first and foremost a written procedure. However, unpublished statistics show that several hundreds of children and young people visit the CALL premises in Brussels yearly for an oral hearing with a judge. Some children merely join their parents without taking up an active role in the procedure, while others are also heard in person. This chapter aims to inspire legal institutions worldwide to install a system of child-friendly justice in appellate asylum cases involving minors. To that end, empirical data from about 350 hours of legal ethnography at the CALL are critically analysed through the lens of children's rights.

Children's rights are the human rights of children and young people. They are fundamental norms aimed at realising social justice and human dignity

S. Lembrechts (✉)
Migration Law Research Group, Ghent University, Ghent, Belgium
e-mail: Sara.Lembrechts@UGent.be

L. Flower and S. Klosterkamp (eds.), *Courtroom Ethnography*,
https://doi.org/10.1007/978-3-031-37985-7_10

for every person between 0 and 18 years of age. Children's rights are codified in national and international instruments such as the United Nations Convention on the Rights of the Child (1989) and the Council of Europe Guidelines on Child-Friendly Justice (2010). This legal framework stipulates that children and young people, including those involved in judicial and administrative procedures of asylum and immigration, are entitled to protection and participation in matters affecting them, as well as to appropriate care and support (CoE Guidelines 2010; UNHCR 2012, 23; Rap 2022). Ethnographic fieldwork at the CALL reveals an increased awareness among judges and CALL staff of the need to accommodate children, young people and families throughout an appellate asylum procedure. Nevertheless, for the procedure to align with children's human rights, additional spatial and communicative adjustments are required.

Following this introduction, a concise overview of the study this chapter is based on is presented. Next, the chapter dives into some of the spatial and communicative dynamics at play before, during and after a hearing of children and young people by an asylum judge in Belgium. The reader is taken on a virtual guided tour of the CALL premises with a focus on the spatial aspects of courtrooms and waiting areas. During the tour, seven young people aged between 11 and 15 years share their experiences of a recent appeal procedure at the CALL. The stories of Rahim, Rafael, Noor, Leila, Amir, Besa and Meryam[1] each reveal different dynamics of what it means for minors to navigate through an asylum procedure at the CALL. In conclusion, the empirical findings are translated into a set of recommendations which could inspire the CALL and asylum tribunals worldwide to become a flagship of child-friendly asylum justice, in line with children's human rights.

Doing Ethnographic Fieldwork at the CALL

The data for this chapter were gathered through a legal ethnography of the CALL. Between August 2021 and May 2023, I spent approximately 350 hours at the heart of the CALL's decision-making practices.[2] In the asylum

[1] These are all pseudonyms. All references to the details of actual cases, dates and individuals involved have been omitted.

[2] I progressed with fieldwork in two phases. Between August 2021 and March 2022, COVID restrictions were in place during hearings and behind the scenes. Initially, these measures restricted my physical presence on the CALL premises and slowed down the development of relationships of trust and cooperation. I was granted access only once a week, not for all public hearings and only when wearing a face mask. In addition, CALL staff, including judges, were encouraged to work from home as much as possible. As the pandemic progressed, restrictions loosened and allowed for more

courtroom, I was able to observe 16 different judges during 45 public hearings involving minors between 0 and (almost) 18 years of age. Twenty-four of these were hearings in which the judge had a conversation with minors from as young as seven years of age.[3] Additionally, from my table in a back office shared by two judges, I could observe judges in their everyday activities at the CALL and conducted a desk study on 30 pending cases involving minors. Furthermore, I had informal and in-depth discussions with 18 asylum judges,[4] four clerks, five attachés and 23 members of the staff. Finally, I conducted in-depth interviews with eight minors (two of them were 9, two were 15 and the others were 11, 13, 14 and 16 years old), three young adults (18, 19 and 24 years old), six (foster) parents and two guardians[5] who had already experienced an appeal procedure before the CALL.[6]

My ethnographic approach has proven to be a unique and helpful pathway to unravel the complexity of the spatial and communicative experiences which shape children's human rights in asylum appeals. Firstly, the empirical data start from the experiences of children and young people. This allows the addition of a children's rights perspective to earlier ethnographic work about appellate asylum procedures (e.g. Gill and Good 2019; see also Chapter 30). Secondly, observations obtained through ethnographic research are complementary to other qualitative, quantitative and doctrinal contributions in the current academic debate on the human rights of children in the context of migration adjudication (e.g. Bhabha 2019; Desmet 2018; Rap 2020, 2022). Thirdly, when recommendations aimed at promoting child-friendly laws, policies and practices in appellate asylum procedures are grounded in ethnographic observations, they are more likely to be attuned to the day-to-day reality at the court. This allows for a nuanced, feasible—but by no means less ambitious—perspective on the challenges, opportunities and good practices at hand.

---

flexibility in collecting relevant data. In the second phase (February–April 2023), all COVID-related restrictions had been waived.

[3] In the other 21 cases, minors were present during the hearing but not heard by the judge. In most cases, these were young children accompanied by their parents.

[4] Two of these took place via Teams and Zoom, all other interactions took place in person.

[5] Data collection through interviews is still ongoing at the time of writing.

[6] The Ethics Commission of the Faculty of Law and Criminology at Ghent University granted ethical clearance for all these activities.

Space, Place and Interaction in the Asylum Courtroom

The Run-Up to a Hearing

> Noor is 13. Together with her parents and her two younger sisters Samira (3) and Amina (1), she was invited to the Council today. It will take at least 20 minutes until the hearing starts, but Noor and her family have already taken their seats in the courtroom. The youngest children are having a great time. They are running around the stage where the judge will soon take his seat. The exuberance of their play, their assorted pink onesies and their shrill laughter provide a stark contrast to the subdued atmosphere in the now increasingly crowded courtroom. (Fieldnote, February 2023)

When applicants such as Noor and her family present themselves at the CALL premises on the day of their hearing, a staff member at the reception desk immediately directs them towards the courtroom in which their case will be heard. The CALL has seven courtrooms for asylum cases, situated on both sides of a long corridor. During the pandemic, half of the courtrooms were used as waiting rooms. Post-COVID, however, these rooms have regained their original function as courtrooms, with sometimes up to five hearings taking place simultaneously. At present, two remaining areas have been designated as waiting spaces for applicants: one open space at the reception (Fig. 10.1a), and one down the corridor in between two courtrooms (Fig. 10.1b).

Applicants can pass their time in relatively comfortable sofa seats or high chairs. At the reception, they can take a free cup of water or purchase a simple coffee. Further down the courtroom corridor, they can buy a soft drink from a vending machine. While no child-friendly adjustments have been made to the spatial environment of the courtrooms, the waiting areas do show positive intentions to accommodate (young) children and families. The use of different sizes in the furniture at the reception implies that children are welcome to take a seat. As is shown in Fig. 10.1b, children can also play with a selection of toys, books and magazines while waiting.

A receptionist explains that this play area was intended to ensure that children would not unnecessarily disturb the course of action in the courtroom. Toys, puzzles and furniture were collected among the staff for children to play with during their parents' hearing (fieldnotes, September 2021). However, observations illustrated by the example of Noor, Samira and Amina show that this corner is rarely used for its intended purpose. Families with young

Fig. 10.1 **a** Reception area (with the courtroom corridor on the left and a corner for children on the right). **b** Waiting area

children are often not informed about their option to use this area. As the corner is not fully visible from the corridor, parents are not aware of the possibility to play with their children while waiting for their turn. Moreover, with receptionists immediately directing applicants towards the actual courtroom, the waiting area at the reception remains underused as well. Instead, young children such as Amina and Samira often end up playing inside the courtroom.

Each courtroom is set up similarly as shown in Fig. 10.2a (COVID) and Fig. 10.2b (post-COVID). There are no spatial differences between hearings involving adults and hearings involving children.

As in most asylum cases, Noor's hearing is chaired by one judge. The judge is seated in front (1 on Fig. 10.2a, b), flanked by the clerk (2). Judges and clerks wear a black gown with a white jabot and have an elevated seat on the podium. When the judge calls their case, all applicants—irrespective of their age (6)—are invited to stand up (COVID) or come forward (post-COVID). They are supported by an interpreter who interprets into a language of their choice, if requested (3). As 1.5m physical distance and wearing a face mask was not feasible in simultaneous translation, COVID-proof courtrooms were

Fig. 10.2 **a** An empty courtroom at the CALL (COVID-proof) (*Note* [1] judge, [2] clerk, [3] interpreter, [4] defendant, i.e. representative from the Commissioner General for Refugees and Stateless Persons (CGRS), [5] applicant's lawyer). **b** An empty courtroom at the CALL (post-COVID) (*Note* [6] applicant [7] applicant's parent, guardian or other supporter, [8] other applicants, lawyers and audience, [9] reception assistant, [10] observer)

fitted with a plexiglass panel between the applicant(s) and the interpreter. Now that COVID restrictions have been waived, plexiglass, facial masks and regular disinfection are no longer required.

> Noor sits quietly on a chair between her parents. As the judge comes in, Noor is invited to come over and sit in the front centre. The interpreter, who swears an oath she does not understand, takes the seat next to her. This is somewhat uncomfortable for Noor: she moves her chair slightly to the side and shrugs her shoulders. Her mother comes to stand behind her. Noor's lawyer and the representative from CGRS also take their place for the hearing. They will get to speak first. This is Noor's first time meeting the lawyer who is pleading her case. Apparently, her own lawyer sent a colleague to plead in her name. (Fieldnote, February 2023)

When COVID measures were in place, the representative of the first instance authority (CGRS) (4) and the applicant's lawyer (5) took a seat (a) in the centre. Post-COVID, their seats were moved to the sidewalls, allowing the applicants (6) to take up a more central space in the courtroom. During the oral hearing, both the lawyers—also wearing a black gown—and the CGRS representatives use a lectern (b). For unaccompanied minors, the guardian, foster parent(s) and/or any other person the child trusts can join them (7). Often lawyers do not plead personally, but send a colleague (*loco*) to represent their client during the hearing, for instance in Noor's case.

> The lawyer's plea reveals to everyone present that Noor has mental development problems. (Fieldnote, February 2023)

Since hearings at the CALL are public, the door to the courtroom is open. Other applicants, lawyers, family members and, theoretically, members of the general public can attend (8). They are either seated or standing in the courtroom (8a), in the corridor (8b) or, in COVID times, in one of the waiting rooms down the corridor. The number of people present at a hearing was limited to the number of available chairs in COVID times. Currently, however, it is not uncommon for hearings to be attended by a mixed audience of up to 40 lawyers, applicants, members of the applicant's family or friends and other outsiders, all of whom can listen in to what is said about Noor's case.[7] In that sense, Besa, 14 years old, has a radically different experience:

> The judge had noticed in Besa's file that she suffers from extreme emotional distress in relation to her asylum procedure. Even though Besa's lawyer does not ask for any additional safeguards for the hearing, the judge decides at his own discretion that it would be more appropriate to hear Besa behind closed doors (*huis clos*). When Besa has taken her seat in front, the judge asks all people present to leave the room. Besa smiles at the judge and is clearly relieved. (Fieldnote, April 2023)[8]

---

[7] As an observer, I could take any free seat in the room (10) or remain standing at the doorway. I was not the only outsider observing hearings: in several cases, newly hired attachés, students or migration professionals were also present. In one hearing, a group of 17 social workers attended to learn about the CALL dynamics (fieldnote April 2023).

[8] The judge explained the purpose of my research and asked the applicant's permission for me to stay as an observer. The applicant, the applicant's mother and the lawyer agreed to my presence. As in all hearings, but especially in this case where my presence was made explicit, it cannot be excluded that my role as an observer might have had an impact on the course of the hearing (fieldnote, April 2023).

The Hearing with the Judge

Unlike Noor, whose case is heard at the start of the session, 13-year-old Amir has to wait his turn for almost three hours:

> With more than 20 cases scheduled, this is an exceptionally busy session. The judge started at 9:00, but it is not until 11:50 that the clerk finally calls Amir's name. Amir shares that the waiting is very boring. He would have preferred an earlier turn so he could go home sooner. Amir is well taken care of while waiting, as he is accompanied by his older brother, his foster parent and his guardian. During his hearing, Amir does not speak much, despite an active encouragement of the judge and his guardian. Amir says he didn't mind, but his guardian hesitates: "I think his battery was just low from all that waiting. He actually did have a lot to say." Amir shares with me that he feels a bit lost: even though so many people told him what to do and what was going to happen, he could not really anticipate the whole situation. (Fieldnote, February 2023)

Hearing children *huis clos* or moving children's cases to the start of the hearing are two examples of the often laudable initiatives some judges take to improve children's experiences. Where *huis clos* is quite a radical measure and only happened once during my observations, hearing children's cases first can be described as a frequent practice. At the same time, when children's cases are heard first, such as in Noor's situation, they may be more exposed to the gaze of others. This exposure was much less tangible in the case of Amir, even though it did not help him much in taking the floor (fieldnote, February 2023). A second disadvantage may be that judges experience more time pressure in the first cases of a session, because "other applicants are also waiting" (fieldnote, November 2021). Moreover, towards the end of the public hearing, the walk-in and walk-out decreases, as does the number of spectators. Irrespective of whether children are speaking or are being spoken about, the atmosphere often becomes more relaxed towards the end (fieldnotes February 2023, March 2023, May 2023).

Some children do not mind speaking in front of a large audience. For others this is more difficult, especially if they cannot anticipate what is expected from them, for example in Leila's case:

> The asylum procedure asks a lot of 11-year-old Leila. Leading up to her first interview at CGRS, she was sick with stress. Today, her open gaze, her hand gestures and her quick steps clearly show that she feels agitated and tense. She knows she will get to speak to the judge soon. Just before the hearing, she discusses with her lawyer how she wants to go about it. Leila looks forward

to telling her story, and would like to try to express herself in French. Leila encourages herself and clenches her fists. Fortunately, she has some time before it is her turn, as her name is only tenth on the hearing sheet.

Then the judge enters. All those present are greeted kindly. Her lawyer reassures Leila and nods encouragingly at her. Leila is confused when the judge calls her name first. The fact that she will be the first to be heard and allowed to take a seat in front of all these people comes as a complete surprise. When Leila's lawyer and the CGRS-representative have spoken, the judge smiles at her: "Leila, do you want to add anything?" The judge notices a slight hesitation from the child. "You may choose, do it at your own pace, take your time." Suddenly, Leila starts to cry. The judge responds very kindly and understandingly, bends towards Leila and says: "You don't have to say anything if you don't want to. Your lawyer has already spoken for you. Maybe it would be better if you take some time for yourself? It is also impressive right, there are so many people present." (Fieldnote, February 2023)

Children and young people can choose to be represented by a lawyer, or to come to the CALL in person. Many of them come in person, both as applicants or as children of applicants seeking international protection. In cases involving larger families, it occurs that there are not enough chairs for parents and children to sit together. My fieldnotes show that when the judge hears their parents, children may remain standing, or sit on their parents' lap, in a buggy next to their parents, or in the back of the courtroom. One mother was heard from her seat in the audience with her sleeping baby in her arms. None of the children I observed were using the play area outside the courtroom during their parents' hearing. One possible explanation is that the toys are mainly designed for very young children, who are not easily left without the supervision of their parents.

Young children below the age of seven were not heard by any of the judges observed. For children of seven years and older, experiences vary greatly. This depends for instance on whether they are accompanied or unaccompanied, on the judge who leads the hearing and on the level of support children experience around them. Despite overall positive intentions to meet children's needs, significant differences in judges' style, attitude, verbal and non-verbal communication with children and young people could be observed. For instance, in the following excerpt taken from my fieldnotes we follow Noor again and compare her experiences to those of Rafael, who is 15:

When Noor has taken her seat in the centre of the room, the judge explains how the hearing will proceed. While doing so, the judge looks Noor and her mother straight in the eye with a friendly, calm and patient expression. Verbally, however, the judge speaks about them in the third person: "First, the lawyer and the defendant will get to speak. Afterwards, the mother, and if she wishes, the eldest child, will also be given the floor." (Fieldnote, February 2023)

Rafael is directly addressed by the judge, who uses his first name and explains what is about to happen: "Rafael, your mum obtained a negative decision. Then you filed your own application. You received a negative decision as well, because reference was made to the same facts your mum cited, which were not considered credible. You have asked that I review the case. We are going to do that today." (Fieldnote, March 2022)

In all observations with unaccompanied minors, judges have systematically offered them the floor to speak. However, accompanied children are usually represented by one or both of their parents. In those cases where they file an autonomous application in their own name, they may be speaking on their own behalf, but only at the judge's discretion. This results in notably different experiences for young people as we see in the following excerpts taken from my fieldnotes concerning Meryam, Besa and Rafael:

Meryam is 14 years old. When she arrives at the Council with her parents, the courtroom is already completely full. The family is asked to wait in the corridor. When the judge enters a couple of minutes later, their case is called first. Without any further explanation, the judge hurries to address the family's lawyer. Before Meryam and her parents can properly walk from the corridor to the lectern, the lawyer has already finished his plea. The judge asks through the interpreter whether "the people want to say something themselves, but without repeating what I already know from the file". Meryam's father, overwhelmed, indicates he does not. Meryam is not asked anything. After the defendant asks the judge to confirm the contested decision, the judge takes the case under review and the next case is already called. The whole procedure has taken less than two minutes. Meryam is left with a questioning look in her eyes. (Fieldnote, March 2023)

Despite her well-documented psychological problems, Besa clearly feels at ease during her hearing *huis clos*:

The judge has a few questions for Besa. She answers in a quiet voice. When the judge uses a term she does not understand, she asks what this word means before she replies. This is one of the rare examples I could observe where a minor applicant actually asked a clarifying question to the judge. (Fieldnotes, April 2023)

Rafael also experiences a positive interaction with the judge:

> Even though the interpreter translates the judge's questions into his mother tongue, Rafael answers them in Dutch. When asked at the end if he has anything to add, Rafael presents a well-prepared and convincing speech about his experience of Belgium and his fear of being forced to return to his country of origin. The judge concludes by praising Rafael for his eloquence, a compliment he answers with a delightful smile. (Fieldnote, March 2023)

After the Hearing

During the pandemic, a reception staff member (9 on Fig. 10.2a) at the doorway supervised the schedule, notified applicants and lawyers in the waiting rooms when it was almost their turn and showed applicants out when their case was closed. However, post-COVID, the role of the receptionist has largely disappeared from the courtroom setting. Applicants—minors and adults alike—are often left wondering at the end of their hearing what is expected from them. When even the lawyer has no time to briefly touch base with them and explain what will happen next, applicants are often left to fend for themselves:

> When the judge has closed her case, Noor and her mother are confused what to do next. They take their seats again with the girls and their father. The interpreter reminds them that their case is over and they may leave the room. Since the lawyer is pleading again in the next case, there is no time for feedback or debriefing. (Fieldnote, February 2023)

Rahim's example shows that this experience differs between children:

> Rahim is 12. Both before and after the hearing, the lawyer takes Rahim and his family outside of the courtroom and sits with them in the sofa seats of the play area. Rahim has the chance to ask his lawyer a few questions. After the hearing, he wants to know how long it will take now to receive a decision. "That usually takes a month or two," the lawyer explains. "Do you think it was good that I came today?" "Yes, definitely. You did a very good job, I'm impressed. And now the judge knows who the decision is about, which is always good." "I have a lot of stress now because I have to wait so long for an answer." "I understand that. Maybe we can go out and get some fresh air?" "I hope I receive a positive decision. It really has to be positive." (Fieldnote, February 2023)

Closing Remarks: Towards Child-Friendly Justice in the Asylum Courtroom

The empirical data presented above highlight the diverse experiences of children and young people with the appellate asylum procedure in Belgium. In order to develop a system of child-friendly asylum justice at the CALL and globally, the observations can be translated in a set of recommendations on how these spatial and communicative experiences can become more aligned with children's human rights. Without aiming to be exhaustive, children and young people should be appropriately informed and given the possibility to be heard if they want to. Spaces and communicative interactions during an appellate asylum procedure should be safe so that children and young people can feel at ease in their confrontation with the judge. Additionally, there should be adequate care and support for the particular needs they have in relation to their young age, their evolving capacities and their status as applicants or children of applicants seeking international protection (CoE Guidelines 2010). These measures could help overcome key challenges for children and young people seeking international protection, irrespective of the substantive outcome of their asylum appeal.

The diverse examples presented throughout the chapter show first of all that not all minors have access to trustworthy information concerning the procedure. Moreover, even if they do, such as in Amir's case, they may feel it does not adequately describe the actual experience of the courtroom. It would have been helpful for Noor's family if a reception assistant would have guided them towards the play area for children. For Leila, who did feel well-prepared to speak to the judge, a degree of predictability and clear expectations about the conduct of the hearing could have alleviated painful surprises on the spot. In turn, Noor had no idea what she was supposed to do when her hearing was finished and her lawyer was not available for debriefing. Arguably, a certain level of stress and anxiety may be unavoidable during an appellate asylum procedure. However, when children are well informed, they may experience a degree of ownership and predictability on what is going to happen. This allows them to feel relatively at ease and, like Rafael, take pride in their presence.

It is therefore important for asylum institutions and governments to invest in reliable information for all asylum-seeking children—online, on paper, and in personal interaction. Ideally, this information includes visuals and is tailored to the needs and understanding of minors involved. A virtual guided tour, a short clip with testimonies of other children, a leaflet and/or a child-centred page on the court's website may bring the procedure to life for children. Whereas judges can only play a limited role in informing children about the actual hearing, key figures such as guardians, lawyers, social workers and reception staff are crucial in ensuring that this information reaches children *before* they enter the courtroom.

Inside the courtroom, a case involving children and young people requires judges (and, for instance, reception staff and interpreters) to adapt their language and style to a child's level of understanding. Learning how to put children at ease and how to ask them careful questions without re-traumatising them is a priority for several CALL judges. Unlike their colleagues in family law or juvenile justice, asylum judges are not trained and supported in hearing minors (fieldnotes, September 2021). Nevertheless, they have mastered and applied small communicative adjustments—albeit with great variations between individual judges, as the examples in this chapter show.

Verbally, an asylum judge can address the child on a first-name basis and in the informal you-form.[9] The judge can also explain why the child is there, who the different actors in the courtroom are and how the hearing will proceed. They can check whether the child has understood everything, and ask the open question whether the child has anything to add to what has been said by others. Additionally, Rafael's story demonstrates that judges' non-verbal communication showing a genuine interest through their tone of voice and posture can make a notable difference in children's experience.

In line with children's human rights, judges should consider making an invitation for the child to speak become a standard element in every hearing involving children. Even if children could refuse to speak without any consequences, this would ensure accompanied children and young people like Meryam are not left out. Leila's story is illustrative for the many judges at the CALL who are aware of this and have included sensitive formulations in their invitation to the child to speak (fieldnotes September 2021, February 2022, February 2023, March 2023, April 2023).

The observations also show that at the CALL, children, young people and families are part of the regular court role, appearing before the same judges and in the same courtrooms as adults. To support judges and other stakeholders in their awareness of the need for spatial and communicative adaptations, and to maintain this focus throughout an entire hearing, appellate asylum hearings could be organised thematically. A thematic hearing consists solely of cases involving children and young people, either as applicants or as children of applicants seeking international protection. Thematic

[9] The difference in English may be futile, but in the procedural languages at the CALL—French (*tu/vous*) and Dutch (*jij/u*)—this is a meaningful nuance.

hearings could be conducted by judges who are specifically trained in hearing children and could take place in a separate, child-friendly courtroom where children can feel safe and at ease.

Furthermore, observations highlight the lack of privacy as a recurrent challenge for asylum-seeking children and their families. Hearing children *huis clos*, as was the case with Besa, reduces their stress levels and shows that the judge cares about their wellbeing. Understandably, judges have raised the concern that systematically hearing all children behind closed doors could fit uneasily with the principle of transparency in asylum justice (fieldnotes, May 2023). However, adaptations enhancing children's safety and privacy could start smaller, for instance with the introduction of a child-friendly waiting room and by keeping the number of people present in the courtroom to a minimum.

Other possible measures that could not be observed until today but that could transform the asylum appeal to a more child-friendly procedure include the choice of the judge and lawyer not to wear a gown, to have all actors sit at equal height with the minor and to use neutral, pleasant colours and comfortable furniture in the courtroom. These types of adjustments could lower the threshold for children and young people to engage with the judge and augment the experience of procedural justice.

To conclude, the recommendations that derive from my observations came about within the reference framework of children's rights and are therefore specifically aimed at the situation of minors in an asylum procedure before the CALL in Belgium. However, the proposals to enhance children's experience of asylum justice may be equally relevant for asylum-seeking minors in other parts of the world. Furthermore, they may also benefit adult applicants, particularly those who are in a situation of increased vulnerability, such as persons with disabilities, the elderly, pregnant women, persons who have been tortured or raped or who have suffered other serious forms of psychological, physical or sexual violence throughout their migration trajectories.

Suggestions and Guidance for Further Readings

1. Where academic publications on children and their rights in migration have increased, few scholarly articles specifically deal with children's rights in *appellate* asylum proceedings (with the exception of Arnold [2018] on Ireland and Josefsson [2017] on Sweden).
2. Similarly, literature on child-friendly justice is abundant, but few academics have focused on adaptations in the justice system for children in migration (with the exception of Rap [2020, 2022] on the first instance procedures in The Netherlands).

3. Two exploratory studies on children's rights in the asylum case law of the CALL, published in Dutch, were based on desk research and case law analysis (Desmet 2018; Vernimmen and Reyntjes 2019).
4. No ethnographic research specifically on the rights of children in appellate asylum proceedings seems to have been published elsewhere.

Acknowledgments This chapter is based on findings collected during my ongoing doctoral research project (2020–2025), funded by the FWO, project file number G015520N.

References

Arnold, Samantha. 2018. Child refugee and subsidiary protection appeals in Ireland. *Child and Family Law Quarterly* 30 (4): 350–371.

Bhabha, Jacqueline. 2019. Governing adolescent mobility: The elusive role of children's rights principles in contemporary migration practice. *Childhood* 26 (3): 369–385.

Council of Europe. 2010. Guidelines on child friendly justice. https://rm.coe.int/16804b2cf3. Last Access: November 8th, 2023.

Desmet, Ellen. 2018. Minderjarigen in de volle rechtsmachtprocedure van de Raad voor Vreemdelingenbetwistingen. *Tijdschrift voor Vreemdelingenrecht* (3): 198–214.

Gill, Nick, and Anthony Good. 2019. *Asylum determination in Europe. Ethnographic perspectives.* Cham: Palgrave Macmillan.

Josefsson, Jonathan. 2017. Children's rights to asylum in the Swedish Migration Court of Appeal. *The International Journal of Children's Rights* 25 (1): 85–113.

Lundy, Laura, Aisling Parkes, and John Tobin. 2019. Article 12: The right to respect for the views of the child. In *The United Nations Convention on the Rights of the Child: A commentary*, ed. John Tobin. Oxford: Oxford University Press.

Rap, Stephanie. 2020. Access to justice and child-friendly justice for refugee and migrant children: International and European legal perspectives. *Europe of Rights & Liberties* 2020 (2): 277–292.

Rap, Stephanie. 2022. 'A test that is about your life': The involvement of refugee children in asylum application proceedings in The Netherlands. *Refugee Survey Quarterly* 41 (2): 298–319.

United Nations High Commissioner for Refugees. 2012. A framework for the protection of children. https://www.unhcr.org/media/31720. Last Access: November 8th, 2023.

Vandenhole, Wouter, Gamze Erdem Türkelli, and Sara Lembrechts. 2019. *Children's rights—A commentary on the United Nations Convention on the Rights of the Child and its protocols*. Northampton: Edward Elgar.

Vernimmen, Jonas, and Louise Reyntjes. 2019. De erkenning en toetsing van kindspecifieke vervolgingsgronden in de asielprocedure van NBMV. In *Rechten van niet-begeleide minderjarige vreemdelingen in België*, ed. Ellen Desmet, Jinske Verhellen, and Steven Bouckaert. Brugge: Die Keure.

11

Moral Communication in Court

Louise Victoria Johansen and Julie Laursen

Introduction

This chapter compares moral communication in low penalty-range common assault cases with serious cases where the prosecution has called for a harsh indeterminate sentence in Denmark. Indeterminate sentences of imprisonment are rare in Denmark, but possible if the crime caused serious harm to others and if a fixed term sentence is insufficient to protect the life, health or freedom of other people; whereas cases of common assault constitute one of the most frequent types of offence in the Danish criminal system. Our research is based on several long-term fieldwork studies conducted in criminal courts in Denmark and institutions affiliated to them (such as the Department of Corrections, the Prosecutor's office and prisons). When comparing our field notes from these studies, we were struck by how different the written and oral communication about defendants, and between defendants and the judges seemed in the two kinds of cases. We use this observation to engage in a systematic analysis of differences and similarities in order to address critical aspects of courtroom communication. Our ethnographic

L. V. Johansen (✉) · J. Laursen
Faculty of Law, University of Copenhagen, Copenhagen, Denmark
e-mail: louise.victoria.johansen@jur.ku.dk

J. Laursen
e-mail: julie.laursen@jur.ku.dk

L. Flower and S. Klosterkamp (eds.), *Courtroom Ethnography*,
https://doi.org/10.1007/978-3-031-37985-7_11

approaches and thorough organised comparison between our fieldnotes and interviews allowed for a nuanced understanding of important communicative differences. In both studies, we followed a significant number of cases from their initial phases in other institutional settings, such as the Department of Corrections or remand prison, and thus before they were presented in the courtroom, through to the execution of the sentence. We interviewed convicted persons and/or the legal actors both before and after the trial. We thus view the criminal court cases from a processual perspective, and one of our conclusions is that in order to understand moral communication in the courtroom, it is necessary to take an ethnographic approach to its study which situates it as being interconnected with other institutions surrounding the court.

According to penal philosopher Anthony Duff (2001), trials, convictions and punishment are communicative processes. They are also a locus for the expression and interpretation of emotions (Bergman Blix and Wettergren 2018; Flower 2019). Bandes (1999) explores the role of emotions and morality within criminal justice systems, arguing that although morality plays a crucial role for judicial decision-making, legal professionals often regard morals as being incompatible with objective justice. This resonates with our own findings in the Danish judicial context where legal actors such as judges, prosecutors and defence lawyers hesitantly and ambiguously embrace the idea of sentencing having moral aspects.

In this chapter, we narrow these moral, communicative and emotional aspects of judicial decision-making down to only include moral communication *about* the defendant's criminal actions, abilities and behaviours as expressed through expert documents, such as the pre-sentence reports and psychiatric evaluations that feed into the sentencing process, and in judges' communication of the final verdict *to* the defendant. Morality may be expressed through the evaluation of defendants' remorse for deeds committed, in explanations of how the crime could occur, and in the judges' communication of the intention of punishment (Hawker-Dawson 2021; Scheffer 2010; van Oorschot et al. 2017). We analyse moral communication as both oral and written communication, with a view to emphasising that it is not possible to strictly delineate between speech and text communication. In court cases, various documents are read aloud in the courtroom, i.e. the text is 'spoken' and sometimes commented upon during the trial by either the prosecution or the defence: conversely, much of what is expressed orally during the trial itself is documented in writing (cf. Scheffer 2010). The texts may also be 'performed', in the sense that defence lawyers or prosecutors may engage more or less enthusiastically with the documents that communicate the defendant's moral abilities (Johansen 2015).

The court's verdict also conveys assessments about the defendant's moral status in relation to punishment. In Denmark, this written verdict consists of a very brief statement seemingly devoid of emotion (Wandall 2008), but we argue that the prosecution and appellate courts are able to 'decode' this legalistic information. Judges' communication is thus partly directed outwards and upwards at audiences, institutions and actors other than the court (such as the public), or to a court of higher instance, or even the prison that eventually gives host to the sentenced person (Gubrium and Holstein 2009; Hawker-Dawson 2021; Innes 2014). Finally, we argue that moral communication in the courtroom is dependent on the *type* of criminal case in question. Literature on communication in criminal trials has tended to emphasise different communication styles according to jurisdictions and legal traditions (e.g. Field 2006; Field and Nelken 2010; Scheffer et al. 2010); we add to this research by highlighting internal variations within the same jurisdiction depending on the *kinds* of criminal cases, legal documents and professional actors involved.

Methodology

We draw on two separate long-running ethnographic fieldwork studies. Ethnographic methodologies are particularly well-suited for studying morality in the court (and beyond) because ethnographic fieldwork enables long-term and 'deep' involvement in a particular field (Hastrup 2004). Long-term observations and conversations with central actors in the courts were particularly important for the purposes of these studies because asking direct questions about morality and sentencing is often difficult and yields 'thin' answers (Ievins 2023). Ethnographic studies in court thus allows the researcher to observe 'morality in action' (Hawker-Dawson unpublished Ph.D. thesis) and facilitate conversations about subtle, convoluted and difficult topics such as morality, personhood and dangerousness. The first research project was conducted from 2009 to 2011, as a multi-sited study in three different institutional settings within the Danish criminal justice system: the Prosecutor's Office, the Probation Service and the District Courts (see Johansen 2018). The study focused on violent crimes in the form of common and aggravated assaults. Johansen studied the practices surrounding presentence reports with a focus on the editing process as well as interactions among investigators, defendants and judges. 32 cases of common assault were followed from the Prosecutor's office through to the probation service where 32 conversations between defendants and probation officers were observed. The cases were then observed in court, and additional participation during judges' deliberations was granted in order to assess the significance of particular pieces of information in the reports for the judges' understanding of the case and the defendant (see Chapter 3; this chapter). Interviews were conducted with 12 judges, 12 prosecutors, 11 defence attorneys and 19 probation officers immediately after they had interacted with the case and defendant in question.

The second research project analyses the connections between the wider aims and functions of the penal state and the everyday practices, experiences and interactions in prison. It consists of an ongoing examination of the experience of being indeterminately sentenced by a court and of serving an indeterminate sentence in prison. Indeterminate sentences of imprisonment are only given in cases where the crime caused serious harm to others, if the defendant's characteristics make him dangerous and if a fixed term sentence is insufficient to protect the life, health or freedom of other people. The latter categories are difficult for the courts to determine, so the judges lean on forensic expertise in determining the personality traits and dangerousness of a defendant. We draw on fieldnotes, informal conversations with legal actors in courts, written trial transcripts and rulings as well as observational and conversational data from 10 cases brought forward between 2021 and 2022. The written transcripts and rulings across these diverse sites are usually devoid of emotive language. Thus, the judges' feelings or moral sentiments are never included in sentencing remarks, such as they may be in the court systems of, for example, England and Wales (see Hawker-Dawson 2021). Rather than relying solely on direct remarks in the preventive detention cases, we have paid particular attention to the mental health reports made by psychiatric experts and to language deployed by the prosecution when they (try to) justify preventive detention.

The analysis in this chapter stems from a systematic comparison of our fieldnotes and interview excerpts as well as lengthy conversations about our key ideas and themes. We also observed a few preventive detention cases together in court, which stimulated fruitful dialogues on similarities and differences in our data material. The names of persons and places in our empirical examples have been anonymised.

Moral Communication

Hawker-Dawson (2021, 14) argues that communication in sentencing is important both for "our understanding of the nature of punishment and because it may impact the extent to which punishment is perceived to be legitimate and morally justifiable". He develops a fourfold typology of communication: the first is *communicative aridity*, which demonstrated little attempt to engage with defendants—including on the moral level—and wherein judges used technical language, obscured by professional codes. The second typology, *counselling communication*, entailed some verbal censure and offers of respectful and supportive advice, albeit in a way which may involve warning or challenging a defendant. The third typology, *specific deterrence*, involved censuring defendants verbally in a fierce tone intended to shock and ultimately deter. Finally, *ritual denunciation* was emphatic, condemnatory verbal censure which resembled intense morality lessons. We draw primarily on the *counselling* and *deterrence* typologies found in common assault cases and the *communicative aridity* of judges in indeterminate sentence cases since Danish judges seldom make use of strong *denunciatory* communication.

Talking openly about any moral dimensions of crime and punishment during a trial was not prevalent among the judges we observed in the Danish courtroom context, although prosecutors and defence lawyers sometimes engaged more actively in this kind of communication. Research from other countries and jurisdictions tell different stories about judges' explicitness in their communication about a given defendant's moral status. Field (2006), for instance, compared communication about the defendant's character in French courtrooms to their English and Welsh counterparts. He found that judges in France put effort into relating a particular crime to the life of the defendant as an ordinary French citizen, whereas courts in England and Wales put less emphasis on personal 'character'. While German courts (similarly to Danish courts) allow the defendant to have the 'last word' before closing arguments, English Crown Courts do not grant the defendant this opportunity of 'self-moralising' by accounting for their deed in court (Scheffer 2010). Scheffer et al. (2010) identified differences between German, English and American communicative styles in the courtroom, attributing these differences to procedure and cultural expectations. Judges' roles may be influenced by these different legal cultural contexts, but our own studies show that important variations even exist within our own national jurisdictions depending on different types of cases and sentencing options that judges are considering.

Both direct, indirect and 'self' moralising may take place in the courtroom (cf. Luckmann 2002; Scheffer 2010). Through direct moralising, judges and other legal actors may ask defendants to explain why they acted as they did at the time the crime was committed thereby probing into their moral reactions. Defendants are encouraged to 'self-moralise' via these questions. Indirect moralising, on the other hand, is often offered by the 'expert' documents that feed into courtroom knowledge, which include pre-sentence reports and psychiatric reports that also convey information about the defendant's (in)appropriate emotional and moral reactions. In what Scheffer (2010) calls 'indirect moralising' or 'moralising outsourced', other professions and institutional bodies thus convey knowledge to the court, which can be used to assess the defendant's moral character.

Institutional Translations of Knowledge

Knowledge about a case as conveyed through either speech or texts often passes through several institutional settings, such as the prison and probation service, the Board of Forensic Medicine, or even from the court of first instance to appellate court. The legitimacy of this knowledge is dependent on the level of trust that these institutions and their actors have in each other. Documents are not only read based on the facts they communicate, but also based on the knowledge and trust that consumers of these documents may have about their origin (Gubrium and Holstein 2009; Cicourel 1976). In his study of the French 'Conseil d'État', Latour (2010) analyses the 'career' of cases by following them through different phases of the legal process. He shows how documents are issued with the purpose of being used in other legal settings than the courtroom, and the institutional interests in the documented information may thus be translated according to these interests. Translation contains both spatial and professional dimensions because knowledge is translated between institutions as well as localities and professions (Latour 1999). While judges may be interested in certain aspects of the defendant's case, subsequent institutions such as the prison and probation service will need other kinds of information conveyed via the document. Documents should be seen as having been issued in order to enable these different institutional needs.

A similar point can be made regarding judges' verdicts that convey information and justification to both the defendant, the victim, the wider audience and possible appellate courts. In this sense, the court also tries to legitimise its decision 'upwards' and 'outwards' (Hawker-Dawson 2021).

Between Speech and Text: Performance and Silence

Documents concerning the defendant's actions and their social, personal and psychological situation are pivotal in modern jurisprudence. Aided by these documents, judges are able to reach decisions by, among other things, referring to this written information. Scheffer (2010, xxxiii) characterises documents that are used during trials as being hybrid forms of "written speech and spoken texts". Texts are not just read aloud; they are often *activated* when legal actors draw the court's attention to specific, important parts of information in the document. Documents thus shape courtroom interaction and communication (Latour 2010; Prior 2003). The defence attorney may hone in on a pre-sentence report or a medical report, while the same documents may go uncommented upon in other cases. To judges, this shifting engagement may indicate some important characteristics of the defendant and whether they are 'worthy' of an extra engagement or not, just as it points to the dynamics of courtroom communication in relation to speech and text: it is not just about *what* is being read aloud, but *how* it is done. Flower (2019), for instance, notes that documents may be used as 'props' for impression and emotion management in the courtroom.

Research on communication in courts has predominantly focused on the way in which language shapes meaning and constructs information (e.g. Atkinson and Drew 1979; Conley and O'Barr 2005; Garfinkel 1967), while much less attention has been given to the absence of information and its impact (Johansen 2018). Foucault (1978) highlights silence as 'an element that functions alongside the things said' (1978, 27). Foucault urges us to look at what is *not* being said and the ways in which it connects with power relations in authorised discourse. This points to the fact that certain aspects of defendants' persons and personalities may be cut out and silenced even before documents reach the court. On a slightly different note, research on emotions in Swedish courtrooms has shown how professional emotions and performances function as silenced backgrounds in the daily work of courts (Bergman Blix and Wettergren 2018; Flower 2019). In the following analysis, we focus on both the textual and performative aspects of silence in moral communication in court.

Modes of Moral Communication in Courts

Our analysis falls into three different categories, reflecting different modes of communication in the court cases we observed. Firstly, we discuss moral communication stemming from other professionals and institutions, such as pre-sentence reporters and psychiatrists, which feeds into the courts. The second analytical category describes the performance as well as silencing of moral information *about* the defendant, while the last category focuses on sentencing communication directed to and taking place with the defendant, and communication upwards—to the court of appeals—and outwards to a wider audience, including victims and the media.

Moral Communication Outsourced

It is difficult and uncomfortable to sentence someone to imprisonment in general (Tombs and Jagger 2006). Foucault's (1991) genealogy of the fusion of the court and the psy-sciences shows how the issue of imposing a penalty became increasingly 'embarrassing' for the judiciary during the nineteenth century, which compelled them to lean on 'new' disciplines such as psychiatry to aid them in their decision-making. By extension and in order to explain how Danish judges draw on other sources of expertise when they sentence a person, we utilise Scheffer's (2010) concept of 'moralising outsourced', describing how psychologists, psychiatrists and other experts feed courts with additional information about defendants.

In order to advocate for an indeterminate sentence, the prosecution has to request a psychiatric assessment of the defendant, which includes the Board of Forensic Medicine's recommendation to the court regarding whether an indeterminate sentence is required. In cases of common assault, on the other hand, the prosecution or subsequently the defence will only request pre-sentence reports from the Probation Service if they estimate that judges might instead consider a suspended sentence with possible treatment conditions or community service. Another important difference that surfaced through our ethnographic observations of different criminal cases was the fact that these documents contained quite diverse moral meanings and content. Legal professionals regard pre-sentence reports as an asset to the defendant, aimed at giving context to the crime in question by constructing the defendant as a *person* rather than an abstraction of traits (cf. Tata 2019). The defendant's childhood and parental situation, school trajectory, etc., were described in detail even for defendants of mature age, and their life story was framed within a wider social context. The pre-sentence reports that were read aloud in the cases we observed conveyed normative ideas about childhoods and homes through sentences such as "a mother who was normally at home", or "an ordered economy", just as reports may mention if defendants come from "a broken home".

Mental health assessments in indeterminate sentence cases, on the other hand, seemed to focus purely on problematic and anti-social aspects of the defendant, framed in a medical-technical language devoid of personal tone (Board of Forensic Medicine Annual Reports 2005–2008, 2009, 2013). We noted psychiatric and psychological specialist terms such as defendants' lack of "regret, shame and empathy", emphasis on their "grandiose self-image" and their "difficulties in understanding other peoples' emotions", mentions of "deviant personality", 'aggressive and sadistic personality traits', 'anti-social narcissistic traits', 'rigidness', 'immaturity', 'self-centeredness', 'lack of empathy', 'affective instability', 'superficiality', 'lack of the ability to establish and maintain social relationships' and traits such as 'tendencies to blame his surroundings for his problems' (Fieldnote, September 2021). We found it surprising that little mention was made of defendants' childhood situation and wider social context. While pre-sentence reports tried to portray the defendant as a social person, the mental health assessments almost seemed to break the person down into purely psychological dispositions.

In line with the different values attached to these documents, the defence tended to read aloud and comment on pre-sentence reports, while the prosecution presented the mental health assessments and elaborated them during their closing remarks. This also means that moral communication was not only outsourced in the sense that documents were issued through other institutions and professionals—even within the courtroom itself, the presentation and performance of these documents was outsourced to legal professionals other than the judge. Since judges were merely presented with this extralegal knowledge by other legal actors, they were able to uphold a notion of judicial impartiality and objectivity. The result of this outsourcing of moral communication also meant that it was not always clear where punishment came from; in other words, communication about punishment came from many different directions and not just the judge representing the State.

Performing and Silencing Morality

Our different courtroom ethnographies showed variations in the ways in which the defence and prosecution communicated documentary 'evidence' of the defendant's moral abilities (see Chapter 9).

In common assault cases, the defence would often just read the *abstract* of the pre-sentence report aloud without further comments. We observed that this was the case when defendants had had difficult upbringings or a life riddled with criminality and social deprivation. These defendants' life stories often remained 'written' texts because they were only read aloud relatively neutrally and not activated in any other way in the courtroom. On the other hand, defence lawyers would make an 'extra' effort if they sensed that the defendant might be close to receiving a suspended sentence because of their personal circumstances and appropriate emotional and moral reactions:

> The lawyer starts reading excerpts from the *extended* part of the report, which is quite unusual. Every time he cites from it, he mentions the page number, and both the judge and the prosecutor start leafing through their copies of the report in order to read along with the defense. In this way, the lawyer prompts the other legal actors to engage in this story of a person who despite difficult social odds had succeeded in living an otherwise irreproachable life. (Fieldnote, May 2009)

Another, related way of handling these reports concerned the ways in which the defence would capitalise on any sign of possible remorse in the reports:

> Erhan is charged for threatening a public servant. The report states that he tried to apologize to the victim several times. In the courtroom, his defence lawyer reads this aloud and then asks Erhan if he feels sorry? Erhan says, 'of course I do'. The defence looks at him and then at the judge while Erhan says this. In her sentencing remarks, the judge explains her mild, suspended sentence with the fact that Erhan apologized repeatedly. (Fieldnote, May 2009)

If the report did not mention some kind of repentance, on the other hand, the defence would seldom ask the defendant to elaborate their feelings about the case in the courtroom.

As aforementioned, mental health reports were devoid of any signs of possible mitigation, relying instead on a range of psychological parameters to explain the supposed dangerousness of the defendant. The prosecution read these assessments aloud in court and re-narrated them during their closing remarks in which they often gave speeches filled with highly emotive remarks, as this excerpt from our fieldnotes demonstrates:

> The prosecutor is about to present her final submissions and tells the ethnographer that she will be more *emotional* than usual. She seems quite nervous. During her final remarks she uses bombastic pronouncements, and changes her

tone of voice so that it is light and childish when she enacts the abused child's perspective, and dark and severe when she cites the defendant. She raises her voice when she tells about the severe child abuse and how she has "never seen such a definitive statement from the Board of Forensic Medicine". (Fieldnote, May 2021)

In another case of indeterminate sentence, the defence left the mental health report uncontested and instead proceeded to ask the defendant, who was charged with a brutal murder, some quite trivial questions about his present mood in prison, which he answered by saying that he felt good and slept well. Considering the severity of the case, this dialogue was somewhat bizarre and hinted at the defence lawyer's total resignation and even silencing of the defendant's possible remorse about the deed.

Summing up, the performative aspect of moral communication was most prevalent in indeterminate sentence cases. Prosecutors tended to perform in a way that highlighted the defendant's immorality and dangerousness. The performative aspect seemed much more downplayed in cases of common assault and became most evident in the gap between what details were highlighted and which were left uncommented upon. The ethnographic examples show different aspects of silencing in the sense that silence can take the shape of a performative or textual absence and can also be expressed in the total absence of mitigating aspects of defendants' persons in cases of indeterminate sentence that serve to shut down any redeeming aspects of morality or humanity. These silences and absences can only be grasped ethnographically since they will not surface in any court transcripts and also require in-depth knowledge of what usually occurs in the courtroom.

Communicating the Sentence

In common assault cases, judges utilised a fusion of what Hawker-Dawson (2021) coins as *counselling style* with a sharp form of communication aimed at deterring defendants from future crime. In this context, counselling should be understood in the sense of "giving advice respectfully and supportively, albeit in a way which may involve warning and challenging someone" (ibid., 98). Counselling entailed some verbal censure and the most concerted attempt to engage with defendants. Judges attempted to communicate to offenders that their actions were wrong, perhaps especially so when a harsh penalty was *not* imposed, but were also oriented towards the future good of the defendant. The judge in the following example explicitly referred to the pre-sentence report, which acted as a mitigating factor in Brian's case:

> Judge (raising his voice and looking directly at Brian): This is the last chance [...] Brian; you need to learn to control your temper. Your pre-sentence report shows that deep down; you're a really nice boy. You ought to be more like him. This is such a shame!
>
> Brian: Yes.
>
> Judge: Try to stay away from situations where you know you'll struggle controlling yourself. (Fieldnote, August 2009)

The judge leveraged the pre-sentence report to remind Brian of his inner-self ("a really nice boy") and spoke directly to Brian's sense of morality. The judge's evaluation of the shamefulness of the action framed the whole interaction in a slightly paternalistic, albeit benevolent, manner. Judges often addressed defendants directly without much space for the latter's own self-reflection; this reflection is not the point of the judge's sentencing remarks which are more a monologue than a dialogue. While we found that the judges condemned the assault as both a moral and legal wrong, they often spent an equal amount of time discussing the defendants' future, as they sought to elicit change. The judges sentencing remarks would vary in their strictness, but did not generally degrade or exclude defendants from the moral community. For instance, in the following excerpt, a 16-year-old boy was charged with common assault against a fellow passenger on a train. The judge emphasised that the defendant would have received a much tougher sentence had he been an adult:

> If you were an adult, you would have received 60 days or 3 months in prison just like that! Now you've been given 60 days whereof most is conditional. You'll go to prison for 14 days – you exhibited a crude behaviour. The lady [who was assaulted] might have said something to you – but it is still not right to put your shoes on the train seat – even though the lady was impolite, you have no right to behave like that. (Fieldnote, June 2009)

The judge in this particular example actually chose explicit, condemning moral language by addressing the "crude behaviour" of the defendant and framing the incident as a matter of rights and decency. She used a combination of denunciatory and specific deterrence communicative styles, but ultimately handed the defendant down a mild sentence due to his young age. In another case, Lars, a 35-year-old man, was sentenced to a 3-month conditional sentence including 80 hours of community service and treatment for alcohol dependency. The judge looked directly at Lars and explained that he gave him a relatively mild sentence, because he did not have any prior convictions and had suffered a difficult period with a bereavement and alcohol abuse. This was said in a relatively soft tone of voice. The judge then raised his voice and went on to say more sharply that, 'I would advise you to refrain from - in any way - repeating what you have done, because then you will go straight to [prison]'. Judges seemed to communicate through both language and intonation, speaking either softly or in accessible terms when 'counselling' the defendant, and shifting to a louder, sharper tone of voice when using the specific deterrence approach and emphasising the defendant's proximity to custody (cf. Hawker-Dawson 2021).

In cases receiving indeterminate punishment, the judges' communication remained technical and devoid of emotion with an overall neutral tone of voice. They often gave their sentencing remarks very quickly without additional explanation and hurriedly withdrew from court thereafter. All that remained was silence, which, according to a judge we interviewed, in this context means that all moral judgement takes place "implicitly", hence unspoken in an indeterminate sentence. The judge goes on to say that his role in these cases was "not rehabilitative", but to implicitly communicate "how seriously you [the defendant] misbehaved" purely through the sentence itself. Similarly, in the same case, the prosecutor we interviewed said that judges' communication was clearer when "defendants get a chance and can be lifted upwards" which is not the case in indeterminate sentencing.

In Denmark, the written verdict constitutes a very brief statement devoid of emotion, but we argue that the prosecution and appellate courts are able to 'decode' this information. Other professionals understand certain expressions and technical language, which is incomprehensible to outsiders.

This upwards communication is characterised by highly 'legalistic' sections intended primarily for barristers and the Court of Appeal rather than defendants (cf. Hawker-Dawson 2021). In this communicative framework, there is little attempt to morally engage with defendants or other lay attendees in the court. Judges' communication is thus—at least partly—aimed at institutions and actors beyond the specific courtroom (Gubrium and Holstein 2009). In some cases of common assault, and in nearly all cases with an indeterminate sentence, the Court of Appeal became "the unseen audience in sentencing hearings" (Hawker-Dawson 2021, 101).

In cases with an indeterminate sentence, judges' sentencing remarks were often shaped by communicative aridity (Hawker-Dawson 2021; Walgrave 2003), which means they used highly technical judicial communication, especially when communicating upwards and outwards to audiences beyond the courtroom such as the wider public (including victims), the press and the Court of Appeal, especially in cases with broad media interest. Judges' concern with the very real possibility of appeal in preventive detention cases culminated in the use of technical language obscured by professional codes:

> Judge: "We have taken the Board of Forensic Medicine's assessment into consideration who described Peter's personality as anti-social, and found him to be dangerous to his surroundings. Beyond that, we have taken Peter's previous sentences into consideration where he displayed what the law calls quick recidivism".
>
> In this particular case, no one explained what an indeterminate sentence is and what it entails and no one looked directly at the defendant or spoke to him while the ruling was read aloud. (Fieldnote, May 2021)

Both the written verdict and the judges' oral remarks thus serve multiple purposes, in line with Latour's (2010) point concerning the presentation of knowledge in court as a translation of different institutional interests. Furthermore, we argue that judges' omission of moral explanations directed towards the defendant constitutes 'silent' communication about the deed *and* defendant as being beyond repentance, reform and reconciliation.

Closing Remarks

If we wish to understand communication in courts, we need to expand our analytical framework *beyond* the court's parameters. Danish judges generally take on a reserved role during trial, and they depend on a range of other professionals to make their judgement. They 'morally outsource' their judgement to other experts such as psychiatrists, psychologists and probationers. Communication in the court cases we observed is thus shaped by affiliated professional actors as much as it is by what goes on inside court. These findings have implications for researchers embarking on fieldwork in courts in the sense that the richest data on moral communication might be found among what is written and said—and not least, *how* things are said. The tacit knowledge of the professionals in a court setting is intertwined with other experts' knowledge and can thus not be understood in a vacuum.

Our comparative approach allowed us to highlight key differences in the ways in which written documents such as pre-sentence reports and the Board of Forensic Medicine's assessments are utilised in very divergent ways. The reports have different purposes and cannot be compared directly with one another, but their influence on the court's understanding of the defendant's moral abilities is equally profound.

Communication in courts is important because it represents the ways in which the "state legitimates and justifies its power to punish" (Daly and Bouhours 2008, 502). In line with recent scholarship on the objective and subjective meanings of punishment and on sentencing as moral communication, we argue that it is important to pay attention to how communication in court targets different audiences, what judges' aims are, whether the parties engage in a moral dialogue and how defendants absorb the messages. We add layers of complexity by taking other institutions and actors into account and argue that future research needs to develop this line of inquiry.

Suggestions and Guidance for Further Readings

1. Latour, Bruno. 2010. *The making of law. An ethnography of the Conseil d'Etat*. Cambridge: Polity.

   Latour's ethnographic study of the French administrative Supreme Court analyses judges' exchanges when preparing and deciding cases. Latour argues that law is created and shaped by the tension between legal reasoning, expert knowledge and common sense.
2. Scheffer, Thomas. 2010. *Adversarial case-making. An ethnography of the English Crown Court*. Amsterdam: Brill.

   Scheffer develops a transsequential approach to the preparation and decision of cases at the English Crown Court from the perspective of law firms, barristers' chambers as well as the courtroom itself, particularly showing the interrelated role of talk and text in these legal processes.

References

Atkinson, J. Maxwell, and Paul Drew. 1979. *Order in court: The organization of verbal interaction in judicial settings*. Atlantic Highlands, NJ: Humanities Press.

Bandes, Susan. 1999. *The passions of law*. New York: New York University Press.

Bergman Blix, Stina, and Åsa Wettergren. 2018. *Professional emotions in court: A sociological perspective*. London and New York: Routledge.

Cicourel, Aaron Victor. 1976 [1968]. *The social organization of juvenile justice*. London: Heinemann Educational Books.

Civilstyrelsen. (2005–2008, 2009, 2013). Board of Forensic Medicine Annual Reports.

Conley, John M., and William O'Barr. 2005. *Just words: Law, language and power*. Chicago, IL: University of Chicago Press.

Daly, Kathleen, and Brigitte Bouhours. 2008. Judicial censure and moral communication to youth sex offenders. *Justice Quarterly* 25 (3): 496–522.

Duff, Anthony. 2001. *Punishment, communication, and community*. Oxford: Oxford University Press.

Field, Stewart. 2006. State, citizen, and character in French criminal process. *Journal of Law and Society* 33 (4): 522–546.

Field, Stewart, and David Nelken. 2010. Reading and writing youth justice in Italy and (England and) Wales. *Punishment & Society* 12 (3): 287–308.

Flower, Lisa. 2019. *Interactional justice: The role of emotions in the performance of loyalty*. New York: Routledge.

Foucault, Michel. 1978. *The history of sexuality: An introduction*, vol. 1. New York: Pantheon.

Foucault, Michel. 1991. *Discipline and punish: The birth of the prison*. London: Penguin.

Garfinkel, Harold. 1967. *Studies in ethnomethodology*. Englewood Cliffs, NJ: Prentice Hall.

Gubrium, Jaber, and James Holstein. 2009. *Analyzing narrative reality*. London: Sage.

Hastrup, Kirsten. 2004. Getting it right: Knowledge and evidence in anthropology. *Anthropological Theory* 4 (4): 455–472.

Hawker-Dawson, Thomas Charles. 2021. Penal communication in Crown Court sentencing. Unpublished PhD thesis, University of Cambridge.

Ievins, Alice. 2023. *The stains of imprisonment: Moral communication and men convicted of sex offenses*. Oakland, CA: University of California University Press.

Innes, Martin. 2014. *Signal crimes: Social reactions to crime, disorder and control*. Oxford: Oxford University Press.

Johansen, Louise Victoria. 2015. *Personen bag straffen. Forhandlingen af viden om sigtede*. Copenhagen: Jurist – og Økonomforbundets Forlag.

Johansen, Louise Victoria. 2018. Between standard, silence and exception: How texts construct defendants as persons in Danish pre-sentence reports. *Discourse & Society* 29 (2): 123–141.

Latour, Bruno. 1999. *Pandora's hope, essays on the reality of science studies*. Cambridge: Harvard University Press.

Latour, Bruno. 2010. *The making of law. An ethnography of the Conseil d'Etat* Cambridge: Polity.

Luckmann, Thomas. 2002. Moral communication in modern societies. *Human Studies* 25: 19–32.

Prior, Lindsay. 2003. *Using documents in social research*. New Delhi: Sage.

Scheffer, Thomas. 2010. *Adversarial case-making. An ethnography of the English Crown Court*. Amsterdam: Brill.

Scheffer, Thomas, Kati Hannken-Illjes, and Alexander Kozin. 2010. *Criminal defence and procedure: Comparative ethnographies in the United Kingdom, Germany, and the United States*. Basingstoke: Palgrave Macmillan.

Tata, Cyrus. 2019. 'Ritual individualization': Creative genius at sentencing, mitigation, and conviction. *Journal of Law and Society* 46 (1): 112–140.

Tombs, Jacqueline, and Elizabeth Jagger. 2006. Denying responsibility: Sentencers' accounts of their decisions to imprison. *British Journal of Criminology* 46 (5): 803–821.

van Oorschot, Irene, Peter Mascini, and Don Weenink. 2017. Remorse in context(s): A qualitative exploration of the negotiation of remorse and its consequences. *Social and Legal Studies* 26 (3): 359–377.

Walgrave, Lode. 2003. Imposing restoration instead of inflicting pain: Reflections on the judicial reaction to crime. In *Restorative justice and criminal justice: Competing or reconcilable paradigms?*, ed. Andrew von Hirsch, Julian Roberts, Anthony E. Bottoms, Kent Roach, and Mara Schiff, 61–78. Oxford: Hart.

Wandall, Rasmus H. 2008. *Decisions to imprison: Court decision-making inside and outside the law*. Aldershot: Ashgate.

12

The Court as a Site of Rediscrimination

Samantha Morgan-Williams and Fiona Donson

Introduction

This chapter provides an ethnographic analysis on the adverse experiences of Travellers who have taken equality cases to the District Court (the Court), Ireland's lowest court level. In doing so, we recognise the inability of existing desk-based research to capture emotional and memorial elements of adversarial court appearances for Irish Travellers. Given the importance of centring Traveller experiences of discrimination and marginalisation, we use ethnographic research and interviews with those who had taken cases to the Court. This chapter speaks to existing literature promoting the importance of understanding how justice is experienced through court observation and lived experience (Pacheco-Vega and Parizeau 2018; Hawilo et al. 2022; Klosterkamp 2023; Roach Anleu et al. 2016). This allows us to be more sensitive to the experience of Travellers, with follow-up interviews providing further insight into individual experiences which would not be accessible via ethnographic observation.

S. Morgan-Williams (✉) · F. Donson
School of Law, University College Cork, Cork, Ireland
e-mail: samantha.williams@ucc.ie

F. Donson
e-mail: f.donson@ucc.ie

L. Flower and S. Klosterkamp (eds.), *Courtroom Ethnography*,
https://doi.org/10.1007/978-3-031-37985-7_12

In this research we adopt an ethnographic approach to understand Traveller experiences before the Courts. Using both fieldwork and formal interviews to create a rich ethnographic understanding of how Travellers experience and perceive the District Court. In adopting this approach we first address the context of Traveller experiences of discrimination, exploring their history of marginalisation before turning to our ethnographic approach and findings. In exploring the experiences of those surveyed, we draw on formal ethnographic interviews to show how Travellers, as a socially excluded and marginalised group, perceive the highly adversarial nature of the Court. These interviews focused on Traveller perceptions of case outcomes and ability to secure 'justice'. Quotes have been anonymised with pseudonyms used throughout. We then draw on ethnographic field notes completed over a six-month period (June 2022–December 2022) wherein we completed visits to the Court to observe hearings and the Court's environment. The ethnographic data presented shows how these harms and experiences which arose from the interviews, feeds into a culturally sensitive understanding of the issues facing Traveller litigants.

Ultimately, this ethnographic lens highlights the adversarial nature of the Court, as one which alienates and 'others' minorities such as Travellers, 'rediscriminating' instead of vindicating them as victims of discrimination. The research and its ethnographic findings therefore feed into the need for a broader recognition and understanding of vulnerable court-users' experiences to adequately inform reform of equality adjudication bodies, enhance judicial training, and enable actions ensuring access to justice for the most vulnerable.

Context

Irish Travellers (Travellers) are an indigenous minority group, also known as *Minceír* or *Minceírí* (pl) (Binchy 1994). Traditionally nomadic (Helleiner 2003), like many other minority groups (Sinti, Roma, and Romani Gypsies) Travellers have been subject to a history of persecution and attempted enforced assimilation (Haynes et al. 2021) facing proliferating levels of exclusion from the most basic of services (Fanning 2012). While the community is small, less than one per cent of the population, Travellers experience significant levels of discrimination, disadvantage, and marginalisation (McGinnity et al. 2017). Discrimination is described by the community as being a normal part of the Traveller life (The Traveller Movement 2017) with little effective remedy within the equality system (Morgan-Williams and Donson 2022).

At the same time, Travellers have a long history of being over-policed and overrepresented in the criminal justice system (Joyce et al. 2022).

Court-based research on Traveller and other minorities (including Roma, Sinti) largely focuses on criminal justice experiences. Joyce et al. (2022) undertook participatory research finding trust in the criminal system to be "low" with Travellers describing their attitude to courts as "fearful". Similarly in England and Wales, Seemungal (2005) reported perceptions of unfairness in treatment by court. Ethnographic research by Albrecht (1997) in Germany highlighted that discriminatory treatment did occur in the criminal justice system even if it could not clearly be established that it affected outcomes of trials. While Song-Richardson (2017) detailed the way in which race-neutral due process protections could be adapted by criminal justice personnel to racialise the justice process. Over-policing of Travellers as suspects and under policing as victims (Joyce et al. 2022), results in trust in the justice system being deeply damaged.

The research in this chapter focuses on the civil law equality process. Little research has been carried out to date in this area, with this being the first ethnographic study in Ireland to examine equality litigation in the District Court. A rare example in the Irish context by Judge Caroline Leonard (2001) takes a judicial focus in reflecting on racism in Ireland and Sweden but provides little concrete findings other than noting a lack of data and acknowledgement that "Travellers are generally fearful of the legal process" (Leonard 2001, 115).

Method

The authors surveyed Travellers and lawyers based within Munster, Ireland, with experience in the District Court. Five focus groups with 48 Travellers took place, to gain an understanding of minority-group experience of the court as a site for equality adjudication. The data presented here sought to investigate Traveller's experience of litigation, interrogating why the Court is unsuitable for equality cases. Individual follow-up interviews, self-selecting in nature, were then completed with 25 Travellers. Women made up the majority of interviewees as in practice Traveller women play key leadership roles within community organisations in this region of Ireland, are more likely to instigate equality complaints, and are often more accessible as research participants. To compliment the qualitative interviews, ethnographic work was undertaken during 13 District Court sittings in Munster, Ireland across a six-month period (June 2022–December 2022).

Ethnography through formal interviews and fieldwork was used to develop a situational understanding of atmosphere, experience, and the general nature of proceedings and is an excellent method for understanding 'Observation is a well-established method for studying courtroom behaviour' (Roach Anleu et al. 2016, 1).

Our findings are presented through core harms identified both during ethnographic research and interviews, including atmosphere, procedural barriers, and the impact of intergenerational trauma and societal exclusion of minorities such as Travellers. These core harms shape how Travellers (and other minorities) engage with the District Court indicating that it is perceived as a site of 'rediscrimination'.

The District Court, Inequality Cases and Barriers to Justice

Building on our existing research considering how the District Court is unsuitable as an equality adjudication body (Morgan-Williams and Donson 2022) our analysis shows that Irish courts, regardless of their level within the system, are understood by the interviewees in this study as operating as largely inaccessible and alien venues for applicants. Basic information as to *how* court hearings work and *what* applicants should expect to happen once in the system is often limited particularly in relation to what might be considered 'less serious' cases at the court of first instance (Leonard 2001). In practice, applicants need legal representation to parse procedural matters including costs, instigation of claims, and to act before judge. Even for us, as legal academics, supporting individuals in accessing court supports and legal information can become an impossible task shrouded in opaque bureaucracy.

Yet for excluded groups such as Travellers initially seeking legal representation to help navigate the system can be daunting (Morgan-Williams and Donson 2022). The very nature of the legal process, whether before a court or an equality tribunal, was found by the interviewees, to be a significant barrier to litigation. Even before a case starts, legal processes can feel overwhelming and exclusionary as Lisa told us, perceptions of the 'elite' and the othered litigants shaping access to the Court process:

> The system is still belonging to the government, and they are still going to protect the people with their businesses. I know they have it out in print why there was this court and we won this, and you can do that and the other thing. But I do believe anyone is powerful enough and rich enough to own pubs and things, they are always linked to these people that's making the power, you

> know. That's why the judges and solicitors and everything like that, you still don't win.

Outside of the main areas of day-to-day litigation—criminal, family, personal injury—there are few lawyers who are willing and/or able to represent applicants (Donson and Morgan-Williams 2023). Traveller interviewees highlighted that even getting to speak to a lawyer does not guarantee legal agency (Brinks 2019). For instance, Sarah told us:

> We got onto a solicitor and the solicitor told us, yeah, we can take the case but if you lose the case you are going to be liable for the whole cost of the court and it wouldn't be worth your while doing it. Never done anything about it. So, they are frightening us, they are putting the fear in us straightaway without giving information on the legal system and what you could do and steps you could take.

The lack of clear information about the law and applicants' legal options in taking cases reinforces the status of Travellers as marginalised (Morgan-Williams and Donson 2022). While this is a broader issue for any potential victim of discrimination, the overwhelming nature of Traveller's day-to-day discriminatory experiences means that it impacts them particularly sharply. It also highlights how equality cases, at least when brought before the District Court, can be regarded as costly, niche, and problematic litigation (IHREC 2022).

This issue was laid bare during our ethnographic work in June 2022–December 2022, where on every visit we found ourselves unable to locate basic information such as court schedules, listings, and basic support with lodgement of claims (all services which should be readily accessible under the Courts accessibility and customer service charter). The difficulties in finding this basic information for us as lawyers, crystalised the issues for our Traveller interviewees.

Procedural Barriers

During interviews many were clearly concerned about procedural matters before the District Court, including the accessibility of information and forms. However a core issue identified by all was the cost of litigation in the absence of civil legal aid. While this is an issue for many potential and actual litigants, Travellers are particularly fearful of this, given high levels of unemployment, homelessness, and deprivation. There is more at stake for the Traveller Community—a highly socially excluded group (88.6% unemployment), but who also experience 38 times more discrimination than white settled Irish (IHREC 2022). The majority of our interviewees were reliant on social welfare and had limited means. The possibility of costs being awarded against them was therefore a significant deterrent to many of those who spoke to us such as Katie:

> You don't know how much it's going to be; you don't know if you are going to be able to pay it or not. It could be out of your range as well, could be ridiculous kind of money. And how are you going to pay for that kind of money anyway. And you might have to go to prison if you don't pay the fine or whatever it might be, if you don't pay that money what's going to happen. Are they going to send the [bailiffs] around to take what you have, while you don't have much anyway. But you have to go to prison to clear the debt or whatever. So, you are the one punishing yourself.

This was also recognised by the lawyers who highlight the unsuitability of the court for first-instance discrimination claims, particularly when compared to more accessible adjudication bodies within the State where no costs arise. Such adversarial court procedures result in a need for legal representation, which in turn increases costs and risks for potential litigants (Russell et al. 2008; Morgan-Williams and Donson 2022).

Joan, a lawyer, noted that bringing these equality cases before the District Court included a "significant risk for clients in terms of costs orders being made against them, together with court fees for filing pleadings." She noted this was particularly dissuasive for Traveller litigants, stressing that "this financial impediment doesn't exist in [other equality bodies]." She also highlighted the "lack of meaningful support for clients with additional needs" going to the Court.

In our own legal work, running the Traveller Equality & Justice Project Clinic, we have seen first-hand the deterrent effect of possible costs being awarded again to those who lose their discrimination cases before the Court. When informed of the possible costs burden (max €15,000), many of our service-users have simply chosen to abandon their cases, rather than face untenable legal cost awards. This is a worrying trend, resulting in a significant impact on equality case progression for minority victims of discrimination.

Atmosphere

Like many courts of first instance, the District Court is often a mixture of chaos and highly bureaucratic formality. For those who do proceed to hearing, notwithstanding the potential costs burden, the intimidating architecture, the atmosphere, and highly adversarial and formal environment, coupled with a high police presence, lends itself to an intimidating and exclusionary space. This further alienates vulnerable litigants, including Travellers. As Gill and colleagues (2021, 63) note "layout, corridors, waiting areas, lines of sight, forms of address and body language all contribute to creating legal atmospheres characterised by formalism and gravity" which can be highly intimidating for litigants (see also Bezdek 1991; Carlen 1976). This manifests as an overtly formal and almost unwelcoming environment within which interviewees spoke often of the sense of the building and "coldness". The idea of being an outsider with the building acting as a physical and emotional barrier to justice is very much part of this, building from unfamiliarity with the formality of the legal atmosphere (Rowden 2018; Rock 1993). This was recognised by Sophie who says:

> It's the stillness and the coldness… you know you are going in there and you are going to be judged because of who you are, and you don't know… are they going to see you as a person. It can be [a] very daunting place.

This was also noted within our ethnographic research (June 2022–December 2022), wherein we felt on edge, alien, and excluded from the lawyers, judges, and court staff going through the motions, while we and the other observers and litigants were mainly sat at their mercy, helpless until given direction (stand, sit, exit, be quiet). This othering is recognised by Klosterkamp (2023) and speaks to the structural violence and normative order of the courtroom and how its expansions limit and restrict not only bodily movements but also the display of emotions, prioritising justice for ideal victims. Victims are expected not to be loud or overly emotional. While observers are often told to be silent or admonished for speaking amongst themselves by judges and clerks. This lends itself to the creation of a feeling of being "on edge" within the space, for fear of falling foul of the process. Yet members of minority groups such as Travellers may not understand or be versed in the archaic deference required in a strict court setting (Flower 2021; Faria et al. 2020). One of the few academic descriptions of the District Court in fact makes specific reference to Travellers adding to the chaos and noise of the court (O'Nolan 2013). The sense of the courthouse then for Traveller litigants is that they are at an immediate disadvantage: "you're already being judged on who you are." This in turn leads to Travellers feeling as though they need to suppress their identity if they want to get through the process, Rosemarie recognised this:

> [Y]ou're thinking, am I respectable enough, do I look OK? What is she going to say, what is he going to say, what's the solicitor thinking?' Those not 'in the loop', the 'Courtroom outsiders,' struggle to understand the highly adversarial and often unwritten rules of the Court often seamlessly navigated by the 'insiders'. (Hawilo et al. 2022)

The interviewees consistently spoke to this perceived alienation and described the idea of court as "frightening" and "daunting." The ebbs and flows of court activity, familiar to lawyers, court officials, and judges, are a mystery to the unfamiliar litigant such as Sharon who says, "I know I was never in a courtroom in my life, I walked in, I did feel intimidated. I felt that I was overpowered by all these people." This unfamiliarity is compounded by what appears to the outsider as the unstructured nature of the proceedings which can result in long waits, sitting in uncomfortable and public spaces as Annemarie tells us: "I think a lot of anxiety had built up over the four hours (waiting), I suppose panic started to set in: the what's if and what not. But when we got in, it still felt very challenging being in the building itself." Court proceedings can therefore be a strange, slow process for the uninitiated; applicants wait in an uninformed confusion worried about missing their case, or some other vital moment (Hawilo et al. 2022).

Gill and colleagues' (2021) research within the asylum appeals process highlights the disorientation that is felt by vulnerable groups as they interact with legal institutions. This is compounded by the lack of autonomy in many experiences, particularly where lawyers act as gatekeepers within the process. Legal representation is largely regarded as a key access to justice component. While interviewees, such as Michelle, highlighted that "there's no one for me, nobody for me only the solicitor walking alongside me," it was also common for litigants to have had no real explanation of the process or what to expect in court (Flower 2019). Vulnerable applicants are therefore heavily reliant upon the guiding hand of the lawyer.

However, even in situations where from the lawyers' perspective a case is settled, the exclusion of clients from discussions can leave them feeling disappointed and powerless. It can also reinforce a feeling that the court system is not for them; a lack of justice even in the face of what the solicitor would regard as a success. As noted by Clara:

> [Y]ou are not getting into the court, you are just in a small room and they are just coming up and telling you, you are not hearing what the judge is saying inside, you are not hearing what people … saying. You are only hearing what the solicitor is saying and they are just coming out and telling you what they are hearing inside.

Mary highlighted that while they won financial compensation, they were unhappy because they did not understand the process and did not feel as though their lawyer had treated them with respect: "I felt devalued as a person dealing with that solicitor [lawyer]."

The interviewees also spoke to issues of privacy and the need to create intrapersonal engagement from judges to facilitate discussion of painful events as victims of discrimination. However, speaking after a positive court experience, Rosemarie noted that the court room had been "scary, it was like [you] felt like you were just like back in school but with more authority in control of you. So, the judge on the day was absolutely beautiful, made us feel so comfortable." Describing the judge as "open and sympathetic towards a discrimination case" interviewees were very aware that many within the system, lawyers and judges, do not appreciate the pain and humiliation that (day-to-day) discrimination inflicts (Hawilo et al. 2022).

Indeed, the public nature of court proceedings means that "where personal information of unknown and disconnected others is disclosed to a broader public audience that centres individual participation in violent events and victimhood, imbued with institutional logic of seeking justice" (Klosterkamp 2023, 1529). This was recognised in our ethnographic research, as we experienced the sense of loss of control as we waited for long periods at the mercy of unintelligible court processes. As legal academics, supposedly more familiar with the court as an institution, we too felt alien and lost within the highly adversarial and oftentimes, school-like, District Court environment during fieldwork (June 2022–December 2022).

Waiting for a hearing to take place, often for hours, results in Travellers sitting in public spaces. This can lead to feelings of being judged by others in the same space. Traveller women are often highly visible owing to their self-described "distinct Traveller-look", leading to feelings of heightened visibility, and fear of being judged as the "typical criminal Traveller up to no good." As Anne-Marie tells us:

> [F]or four hours sitting on a wall waiting outside [the court] because we didn't know when we were going to be called, we had these assumptions that people passing by were saying 'oh look they must be up [for] something'. Not that we were ever there as victims.

Interviewees were highly attuned to their visibility within the court space. Expressing concern that others would doubt their victimhood, making assumptions about their reasons for being at the Court.

Impact of Intergenerational Trauma

Court proceedings have a particular impact upon many marginalised and vulnerable groups, particularly where their experience of authority and law is one of oppression and fear. This is very much the case for Travellers who have historically been over-policed resulting in excessive criminal justice engagement within the community (Joyce et al. 2022).

Interviewees recognised the impact of this intergenerational trauma reporting feeling alienated, as though they were on trial, their victimhood being erased by highly adversarial nature of the proceedings as Anne-Marie says "I felt completely in trial that day. I felt I was going in for a punishment even though what happened on the night wasn't punishment enough."

Many interviewees echoed this, highlighting how the adversarial approach (not often required in other equality settings) can heighten the combative and adverse experience of the hearing process:

> Going in there I didn't feel like a victim, I felt like the person being accused. So that's you see I felt going in there that everyone was against me in there, that it was actually I was on trial, you know instead of being an actual victim, that's how it felt. Because we had never been in there before, that's just my experience.

This has shaped the community's perceptions and experiences of all legal institutions with all courts, whether civil or criminal, being regarded with fear and mistrust as born out in the interview material (see paragraph below—Sophie). This is further reinforced by statistics in relation to the number of Travellers as justice involved persons. The Traveller Justice Initiative highlights that "[a]lthough only accounting for 0.7% of population in the Republic of Ireland, Travellers account for an estimated 10% of the entire prison population and 15% of the female prison population" (TJI 2020). As one interviewee noted: "you only have to go down to any court in this city or in any part of this country. And you would walk in there and you will see a good few Travellers in there up for minor offences". This over-representation is typical of the treatment of Indigenous and minority ethnic groups in other countries (Costello 2021).

Unsurprisingly, then, Traveller interviewees in the research were very cognisant of this and the fear that being in court would reflect an outward perception of their presence as being related to criminality. The result is a stripping of victim status and a rediscrimination, even a reinforcement of Traveller identity as being perceived as linked to criminal identity, Sophie noted:

> [S]tanding outside waiting … as everyone passing thought we were criminals, that were discriminated all over again, because standing waiting outside a court room even though we were the victim, people passing assumed oh what are they up for now? What are they after doing?

This traumatising effect is reinforced by the impenetrable nature of the proceedings highlighted above. The strangeness of the process is both foreboding and alienating. The strength required by members of the community to bring a case is significant and it is characterised by those doing so as part of breaking the intergeneration cycle of trauma and harm. Rosemarie summed this up for us:

> It's intimidating for the community. We've came from a background of people who weren't educated and you're going into a room with highly educated people, and you're coming from a long line of parents and grandparents, and great grandparents that had a different way of life. Textbook learning and education wasn't the way that our culture, it's not the way we lived our lives in the past. So, it's frightening to be facing educated people….

This alienation further reinforcing the sense of 'not belonging' and exclusion that pervades life for Irish Travellers.

Many interviewees, recognising the lasting impact of intergenerational harms inflicted on Travellers through over-policing and criminalisation, highlighted that traditional court systems are not just daunting, but stand as a symbol of injustice for their community. Interviewees highlighted that a less adversarial, tribunal model (which had previously operated) would be more accessible. In the following excerpt Jane talks about this:

> As a Traveller woman I think it should be back (to a more accessible tribunal system), because going to the courts…? Forget about it! no not going up to the courts no, no, people aren't going to go through the hassle of putting in a case. So, the way I describe it is, it was good (…) because you are not half as nervous. Like I said the last case that I took on, I spoke for basically nearly everybody that was in that room. And there was fire in me, and I didn't care. But would I have done that if I was in front of a judge in a court room? I don't think so.

An adjudication system that sits outside of the courts and is focused on an inquisitorial approach, rather than adversarial one, is more likely to provide accessibility, not just for the Traveller interviewees we spoke to, but for all marginalised groups who may experience discrimination.

Closing Remarks

The data presented in this chapter lays bare the harms and intergenerational trauma which Travellers face when taking a case to the District Court. In particular, this ethnographic fieldwork and interviews explores how Travellers, as a highly socially excluded minority group, both access and experience the Court. Our own reflections on the alienating nature of low-level courts despite our privileged status as legal academics, and their resultant inappropriateness as sites of equality adjudication, was reinforced by interview data from Traveller litigants. Applicants from all communities are likely to experience the same challenges, but as Travellers are the most discriminated against group in Irish society the damaging nature of this legal venue is starkly clear. The failure to provide suitable avenues for redress to enable Travellers to challenge discrimination is ultimately an essential part of responding to both historical and contemporary pervasive racist treatment.

As Russell et al. note, general courts, dealing with a myriad of issues from criminal matters to debt, are inappropriate for equality adjudication (Russell et al. 2008). Specialist tribunals are essential to ensuring effective access to justice. The District Court's highly adversarial and opaque procedures, has been shown to effectively 'rediscriminate' victims, enforcing its unsuitability as an equality adjudication body, further entrenching harms, rather than providing recourse.

In speaking to the myriad issues facing Travellers before the District Court, this ethnographic research considers that these include procedural, structural, and environmental barriers perpetrated within the court are compounded by intergenerational trauma, adverse prior experience with legal institutions, and systemic over policing. Findings revealed a rich narrative of mistrust, fear, shame, and helplessness, created by the perceived inability of the Court to achieve a 'just outcome.'

Finally, we note that while more research is needed to explore the District Court and minority experiences, this research must be appropriate and responsive to the needs and challenges of such communities. Marginalised communities are often over researched in a manner that does not respond to their needs, removing agency over research outcomes and usage. There is a significant danger of being regarded as *using* such groups rather than working collaboratively and in partnership. Appropriate research motivations and design should ensure that both the researcher and community benefit from the data results. The ethnographic work we undertake provides a foundation for understanding how the District Court operates for Traveller litigants. In turn, our research *must* be informed by their community experience and user voice. Adopting a complimentary ethnographic approach facilitates deeper understanding, wherein our own observations and emotions of courts allows us to engage in open conversations with the Travellers as researcher partners. Exploring key challenges, adopting a fully participatory approach, centring a 'nothing about us without us' ethos that centres the voices of Travellers.

More broadly, this ethnographic data highlights the need for further research which assesses culturally appropriate redress options in recognition of the mistrust and barriers to justice which Travellers face in challenging discriminatory treatment within the Irish equality system. The combination of ethnographic research alongside empirical data gathering through interviews, provided a nuanced insight for us to the harms and barriers which Travellers face as equality litigants before the highly adversarial court. The research presented identifies clearly that the District Court acts as, at best, a barrier to seeking justice for discrimination, and at worst is a wholly avoidable site of rediscrimination.

Suggestions and Guidance for Further Readings

1. Brinks, Daniel M. 2018. Access to what? Legal agency and access to justice for Indigenous peoples in Latin America. *Journal of Development Studies* 55 (3): 348–365.
2. Gill, Nick, Jennifer Allsopp, Andrew Burridge, Daniel Fisher, Melanie Griffiths, Natalia Paszkiewicz, and Rebecca Rotter. 2021. The tribunal atmosphere: On qualitative barriers to access to justice. *Geoforum* 119: 61–71.

References

Albrecht, Hans-Jörg. 1997. Ethnic minorities, crime, and criminal justice in Germany. *Crime and Justice* 21: 31–99.

Bezdek, Barbara. 1991. Silence in the court: Participation and subordination of poor tenants' voices in legal process. *Hofstra L. Rev., 20*, 533.

Brinks, Daniel M. 2019. Access to what? Legal agency and access to justice for Indigenous peoples in Latin America. *Journal of Development Studies* 55 (3): 348–365.

Binchy, Alice. 1994. Travellers' language: A sociolinguistic perspective. In *Irish travellers: Culture and ethnicity*, 134–154. Belfast: Institute of Irish Studies, Queen's University of Belfast.

Carlen, Pat. 1976. *Magistrates' Justice*. London: M. Robertson.

Costello, Anne. 2021. Travellers in prison presentation to the Joint Committee on Key issues Affecting the Travellers Community, 20 May. https://data.oireachtas.ie/ie/oireachtas/committee/dail/33/joint_committee_on_key_issues_affecting_the_traveller_community/submissions/2021/2021-05-20_opening-statement-and-submission-anne-costello-et-al-programme-coordinator-travellers-in-prison-initiative_en.pdf (last accessed 27 April 2023).

Donson, Fiona and Samantha Morgan-Williams. 2023. Barriers to access to justice for members of the traveller community: Rediscrimination within the equality system. In *Access to justice in rural communities: Global perspectives*, eds. Newman, Daniel and Faith Gordan. Oxford: Hart Publishing.

Fanning, Brian. 2012. *Racism and social change in the Republic of Ireland*. Manchester: Manchester University Press.

Faria, Caroline, Sarah Klosterkamp, Rebecca Torres, and Jayne Walenta. 2020. Embodied exhibits: Toward a feminist geographic courtroom ethnography. *Annals of the American Association of Geographers* 110 (4): 1095–1113.

Flower, Lisa. 2019. *Interactional justice: The role of emotions in the performance of loyalty*. Abingdon: Routledge

Flower, Lisa. 2021. Rumbling stomachs and silent crying: Mapping and reflecting emotion in the sensory landscape of the courthouse. In *Sensory penalities: Exploring the senses in spaces of punishment and social control*, ed. Kate Herrity, Bethany E. Schmidt, and Jason Warr. Bingley: Emerald Publishing.

Gill, Nick, Jennifer Allsopp, Andrew Burridge, Daniel Fisher, Melanie Griffiths, Natalia Paszkiewicz, and Rebecca Rotter. 2021. The tribunal atmosphere: On qualitative barriers to access to justice. *Geoforum* 119: 61–71.

Hawilo, Maria, Kat Albrecht, Meredith Martin Rountree, and Thomas Geraghty. 2022. How culture impacts courtrooms: An empirical study of alienation and detachment in the Cook County court system. *Journal of Criminal Law and Criminology* 112 (171).

Haynes, Amanda, Sindy Joyce, and Jennifer Schweppe. 2021. The significance of the declaration of ethnic minority status for Irish travellers. *Nationalities Papers* 49 (2): 270–288.

Helleiner, Jane. 2003. *Racism and the politics of culture: Irish travellers*. Toronto: University of Toronto Press.

Irish Human Rights and Equality Commission. 2022. Report of a review of section 19 of the Intoxicating Liquor Act 2003 carried out in pursuant to section 30 of the Irish Human Rights and Equality Commission Act 2014. https://www.ihrec.ie/app/uploads/2022/02/Review-of-the-Intoxicating-Liquor-Act-pursuant-to-section-30-of-the-IHREC-Act-Final.docx (last accessed 27 April 2023).

Joyce, Sindy, Olive O'Reilly, and Marianne Joyce. 2022. Irish travellers' access to justice. Report, European Centre for the Study of Hate. Online accessible: https://www.drugsandalcohol.ie/36509/1/ITAJ_Final.pdf. Last accessed: November 8th, 2023.

Klosterkamp, Sarah. 2023. Affectual intensities: Toward a politics of listening in court ethnography. *Gender, Place & Culture. A Journal of Feminist Geography*, 30 (11): 1529–1551.

Leonard, Claire. 2001. Racism and xenophobia: Difficulties facing the court in Ireland and Sweden in dealing with ethnic minorities. *Irish Judicial Studies Journal* 2 (1): 110–123.

McGinnity, Frances, Raffaele Grotti, Oona Kenny, and Helen Russell. 2017. Who experiences discrimination in Ireland? Evidence from the QNHS Equality Modules. Research Series, Economic and Social Research Institute (ESRI). Online accessible: https://www.esri.ie/publications/who-experiences-discrimination-in-ireland-evidence-from-the-qnhs-equality-modules (Last Access: November 8th, 2023).

Morgan-Williams, Samantha, and Fiona Donson. 2022. Barriers to justice for Irish travellers seeking to challenge discrimination. https://www.ucc.ie/en/media/projectsandcentres/tejp/IRCNFReportFinal2022(1).pdf (last accessed 27 April 2023).

O'Nolan, Caroline. 2013. *The Irish District Court: A social portrait*. Cork: Cork University Press.

Pacheco-Vega, Raul, and Kate Parizeau. 2018. Doubly engaged ethnography: Opportunities and challenges when working with vulnerable communities. *International Journal of Qualitative Methods* 17 (1), 1–13.

Roach Anleu, Sharyn, Stina Bergman Blix, Kathleen Mack, and Asa Wettergren. 2016. Observing judicial work and emotions: Using two researchers. *Qualitative Research* 16 (4): 375–391.

Rock, P. 1993. *The social world of an English Crown Court: Witnesses and professionals in the Crown Court Centre at Wood Green.* Oxford: Clarendon Press.

Rowden, Emma. 2018. Distributed courts and legitimacy: What do we lose when we lose the courthouse? *Law, Culture and the Humanities* 14 (2): 263–281.

Russell, Helen, Edel Quinn, and Frances McGinnity. 2008. The experience of discrimination in Ireland: Analysis of the QNHS equality module. The Equality Authority. https://www.esri.ie/publications/the-experience-of-discrimination-in-ireland-analysis-of-the-qnhs-equality-module. Last accessed: November 8th, 2023.

Seemungal, Florence. 2005. Perceptions of fairness: A quantitative assessment. In *Ethnic minorities in the criminal courts: Perceptions of fairness and equality of treatment*, Roger Hood, Stephen Shute, and Florence Seemungaal. Project Report. Lord Chancellor's Department.

Song-Richardson, Leah. 2017. Systemic triage: Implicit racial bias in the criminal courtroom. *Yale Law Journal* 126 (3): 862–893.

Travellers in Prison Initiative (forerunner to TJI) Indigenous and Minority Ethnic Groups in Prison Briefing paper 1. https://www.ssgt.ie/wp-content/uploads/2019/12/TPI-Briefing-Paper-Nov-2019.pdf (last accessed 27 April 2023).

The Traveller Movement. 2017. The last acceptable form of racism? The pervasive discrimination and prejudice experienced by Gypsy, Roma and Traveller communities, (2017) at https://travellermovement.org.uk/policy-and-publications/the-last-acceptable-form-ofracism (last accessed 1 August 2023).

13

Observing Courtrooms in Contexts of Exceptionality

Jeanne Hersant and Fabiola Miranda-Pérez

Introduction

Chile has gone through two consecutive periods of exceptionality between late 2019 and mid-2021. By exceptionality, we refer to the suspension of fundamental rights such as freedom of movement, access to education and justice. The protests known as the "Chilean October" of 2019, characterised by many human rights violations performed by police forces during more than two months,[1] preceded the Covid-19 pandemic, which led to highly restrictive measures in Chile. To be more specific, on October 18, 2019, a constitutional state of emergency (*estado de excepción constitucional de emergencia*) was declared for a fortnight, a mechanism that has never been used in the country in democratic times and which involves a curfew and control of

[1] 8,827 victims were registered with the National Prosecutor's Office, mainly for acts constituting crimes of torture, unlawful coercion and abuse against individuals (Torres 2020: 22-23).

J. Hersant (✉)
School of Social Work, Pontificia Universidad Católica de Chile, Santiago, Chile
e-mail: jeanne.hersant@uc.cl

F. Miranda-Pérez
Faculty of Health and Social Scienes, Universidad de las Americas en Chile, Santiago, Chile
e-mail: fabiola.mirandaperez@etu-iepg.fr

L. Flower and S. Klosterkamp (eds.), *Courtroom Ethnography*,
https://doi.org/10.1007/978-3-031-37985-7_13

civil security by the military. In March 2020 was decreed a constitutional state of disaster (*estado de excepción constitucional de catástrofe*) that lasted 18 months, included a curfew and led to the massive closure of public institutions, including schools and courts of justice, which began operating solely remotely. Both periods of exceptionality had a direct impact on our ethnographic work given they affected the conditions of observation of justice in the making in courts, as well as the possibility to interact closely with our interviewees outside the courtrooms. In this chapter we show how exceptionality disrupted our data collection, and how we negotiated exceptionality by adapting our data collection strategies.

This chapter originates from a collaboration in the framework of a collective ethnography focused on access to justice, and a subsequent dialogue that took place between the authors as we conducted separate fieldwork remotely, during and after the pandemic exceptionality. The research presented in this chapter has in common the observation of incipient judicial and para-judicial work in the Chilean social sciences, in a relatively new judicial scenario and therefore quite unknown even from the socio-legal research point of view. Between 2000 and 2008, huge procedure reforms were implemented to modernise justice. The reform introduced new courts first in criminal justice, with the adversarial system following an oral procedure taking place in public hearings, unlike the former system based on a written mostly secret procedure (Hersant 2017). Subsequent procedural reforms in family and labour law, in 2005 and 2008 respectively, also included the principle of publicity as a key pillar. These three experiences of procedural reforms—criminal, civil and family.

> sought to fulfil through the publicity of hearings various purposes, including bringing justice closer to citizens, favouring a better understanding of how the system worked, reducing suspicions regarding the lack of impartiality, [...] and complying with democratic standards. (Fuentes 2022, 1)

However, in practice, publicity of hearings has been far from a settled practice (Fuentes 2022), even before periods of exceptionality.

In this chapter, we seek to emphasise the way the "plasticity" of the ethnographic approach allows us to adapt to adverse situations and how we have reassessed ethnographic work: on the one hand, by acknowledging our ethnography's political value in times of democratic exceptionality and, on the other hand, by adapting autoethnography—usually focused on the investigator his or herself—to the relationship with our respondents. Our experience draws on previous experiences both of collective research (Collectif Onze 2016) and methodological designs such as autoethnography (Teo 2022; Dyer et al. 2022) and photovoice (Sutton-Brown 2014). We believe that the tools and reflections developed here could inform future ethnographic practices, considering judicial politics is always a contested field and that exceptionality—such as defined above—has become quite common place in many democratic countries' ruling, especially—but not exclusively—in the context of the pandemic. To this respect, it should be noted that since October 12th, 2021, there has been a state of emergency in effect in four provinces in southern Chile, marked by violent protests related to the territorial demands of Mapuche communities and organisations (CEPAL 2012, Pairican 2013). As a matter of fact, "the state of emergency saturate[s] our political, social and democratic life" (Hennette Vauchez 2022, 9) and, in our view, is bound to affect social research. That is why we hope our reflections can nurture future practices and epistemological positions in the field of judicial ethnography, in blurry contexts between "exceptional" and "normal".

Doing Courtroom Ethnography in Times of Exceptionality: Chilean Context and the Virtues of ethnography's Plasticity

In 2018, we began a collective ethnography as part of a research project on access to justice where we consider the subjective experience of users within the judicial institution as part of access to justice. The central research question we addressed was: how open and public is justice to the audience? Here, "the audience" corresponds to accompanying people and relatives of prosecuted or detained individuals, common citizens or researchers. Certainly, the publicity of legal proceedings is a recent innovation in the Chilean judicial system, implemented in the last 20 years, replacing one of the most inquisitorial penal systems in the world (Hersant 2017). During that fieldwork, massive protests broke out in October 2019, which lasted until December 2019. These mobilisations were met with significant violence and human rights violations performed by law enforcement and state security personnel and resulted in more than 20,000 arrests.[2] The criminal courts of first instance suddenly became the focus of public attention because of their control over the legality of police arrests (Morales et al. 2022). In this chapter's first part, we aim to show the way this context impacted us as ethnographers regarding our access to the field. Apart from the increased difficulties

[2] During the first month of protests, there was a 10% increase in the number of defendants who went through detention control hearings compared to the same period the previous year.

in gaining access to the courtrooms, this experience of exceptionality sharpened the research team's need to draw on writing strategies that acknowledge the public incidence of ethnography (Fassin 2013).

Just when we thought we were getting back to normal in regard to conducting observations of courtroom hearings, along came the Covid-19 pandemic. The constitutional state of emergency decreed in Chile between October 19th and October 28th, 2019, was followed by an extended one, starting on March 18th, 2020, and finishing on September 30th, 2021. All court hearings were then replaced by remote hearings via the Zoom platform or simply postponed (Law 21.226, April 2nd, 2020), causing a significant backlog.[3] This led to an almost total closure of the judicial scenario to the public for obtaining access to virtual hearings requires a previous authorisation from and coordination with the *Poder Judicial*. Ethnography allows a great flexibility in approaches and data collection, its scientific reliability depending on how ethnographers deal with what we call its "plasticity": "ethnography is necessarily a singular enterprise mediated by the person of the ethnographer" (Avanza 2016, 996) where research strategies may be adapted to new events and are commonly compared to "craft" or "bricolage" (Hammersley 2004, Dequirez et al. 2013, Au 2022). In this respect, research questions and tools can be reassessed and adapted after initial field phases. In order to deal with this new scenario, Miranda-Pérez introduced an adaptation of autoethnography in her study of psychosocial professionals involved in criminal and family court proceedings. Here, contrary to the idea that interviewees' collaboration makes them feel more valued, she realised that ethnography through self-report and the usage of Information and Communications Technology (ICT) could lead to exhaustion in her interviewees and even strain her relationship with them. They were indeed unintentionally asked to use the same tools as their employer did, which risked to convert self-report, in their perceptions, into one more work accountability requirement (Harrel et al. 2022, 61).

Exceptionality's First Moment: Detention Control Hearings During the "Chilean October"

The following reflections' first part is based on a collective ethnography carried out between 2018 and 2020 in lower criminal courts of different sizes (regional capitals and semi-rural communes) in four regions of the

[3] At the beginning of 2023, in-person hearings were reintroduced but most of the hearings continue to be conducted remotely or in a hybrid way.

country including the capital region. Unlike conventional ethnography, the collective practice of ethnography implicates the simultaneous participation of more than one ethnographer in the field. Accounts of collective ethnography experiences are quite fresh in scientific literature (Tuula et al. 2006; Clerke and Hopwood 2014; Collectif Onze 2016), and mostly come from Latin America (Ospina Martínez 2018; Herrera Bautista et al. 2021, among others). New accounts also appeared in the wake of the generalisation of remote interactions in the context of the 2020 pandemic (Martínez et al. 2021).

What is Courtroom Collective Ethnography About?

Our hearing observation protocol was inspired by the only experience of collective ethnography carried out in the judicial field we are aware of, by Collectif Onze (2016) in France, in family justice. This collective fieldwork was conducted in pairs, rarely even in trios, where each person was assigned a role based on a pre-established guideline. One member of the pair focuses on aspects of verbal interaction and the other on bodily expressions and non-verbal interactions. From there, pair's members gathered their fieldnotes in a single document and shared it with the whole team, so that everyone could review and use it. Having a large team and working with shared fieldnotes allows for greater feedback on the fieldwork conducted from within the team. In addition to promoting collaborative work, detailed shared fieldnotes allow the context and conditions of the hearings to be taken into account for analysis' purposes. Last, collective ethnography allows the recollection and process of a larger amount of information than individual ethnography (see Chapter 7).

Unlike the work of Collectif Onze (2016) and other studies of judicial ethnography that assume sustained interactions with agents and/or the materiality of the field (Latour 2002; Barrera 2012), we focused on observing interactions in the courtroom during public hearings, without seeking to engage in those interactions. We aimed to highlight the experience of people with no knowledge regarding the law and strange to the judicial context, as well as the treatment they receive in court. Collective ethnography is invaluable for observing court hearings where interactions take place in technical language, at a sustained pace, making them difficult to record fully. It also allows us to mitigate the emotional costs of prolonged involvement in the settings studied (Clerke & Hopwood 2014; Yeghicheyan & Jaspart, 2018) or, precisely, in contexts of exceptionality with strong police repression such as those we have experienced in Chile since 2019.

Access to Courtrooms in Times of Exceptionality and Dilemma About Writing and Public Interpellation

Before the beginning of the "Chilean October", the difficulties of access to the field were manifested through diffuse and random practices of control of our entry to the court, both by the guards and the administrative staff who sometimes considered it disrespectful to the judge not to ask for prior authorisation to enter a courtroom as members of the public. These practices, contrary to the principle of publicity and outside the law, were confirmed to us a posteriori, one day when we went to observe detention control hearings[4] in Santiago, during the revolts. On that day, there were officials from the Chilean Gendarmerie at the entrance to the Justice Centre, asking for identification information from people who wanted to enter:

> We introduced ourselves as an investigation team and when we asked, one of them kindly commented: "We have been taking this measure for a long time, but it is not coming from above, it is something that we coordinate among ourselves to maintain order and security, even though we know that it is illegal". He adds that in the context of protests "The Supreme [Court] ruled the other time accepting the measure". (Fieldnotes, December 2019)

With the beginning of the 2019 riots and the state of emergency, even the doors of the courtrooms began to close, filtering the public that could enter and limiting the capacity of the courtrooms. Even so, we managed to enter detention control hearings almost every time we asked and attended 72 of them between October and December 2019, in 9 courts in Santiago and Araucanía (Hersant et al. 2020, Le Bonniec et al. 2021). During this period, practices that are outside the criminal procedure code, such as group detention control hearings, which already existed in the capital and in some courts in the country, became widespread (Segovia, Henríquez and Osorio 2022). We were also able to observe, on several occasions, that the conditions of detention were neglected, preventing the investigation of possible irregularities and police mistreatment of detainees. These difficulties to access public spaces as well as the violations of rights that we witnessed during those weeks were intermingled with the emotions generated by the very tense atmosphere in the courtrooms and the fear and sadness that enveloped us inside and

[4] The purpose of the detention control hearing is to monitor the conditions of detention to ensure that police officers acted in accordance with the law. The same hearing can then proceed to the description of the crime and the formalisation of the investigation, which is the moment when the Prosecutor's Office files charges, and the person is informed of the crime they are charged with (Hersant et al. 2020).

outside the courtroom as we witnessed the brutality of the repression. This led us to reflect on the public role of our research and to question much of what we had assumed so far, specifically regarding the contrast between the times of scientific research and journalistic times, as well as axiological neutrality. Overcoming our concern of an "epistemologic blur between a rigorous approach and a normative drift" (Fassin 2013, 625), we defined a strategy of "popularization" (Fassin 2013, 625) and made our observations public in an opinion column where we took a stance in relation to what was happening in the detention hearings (Hersant et al. 2020). Doing so, we hoped that, in a certain way, the publicity of hearings would be restored and that due processes and the safeguarding of people's rights would be under public scrutiny.

Exceptionality's Second Moment: The Pandemic and the Shift to Virtual Autoethnography

The Covid-19 pandemic brought with it another form of exceptionality as "a point of change, or a series of events, that disrupt the social world, introducing a period of uncertainty" (Koppe 2022, 30), in which all face-to-face social encounters were suspended and even incriminated, without any possibility of physical displacement.

Autoethnography usually focuses on the researcher's own feelings, history and experience (Teo 2022; Dyer et al. 2022), whereas photovoice methodology allows groups—usually marginalised urban groups (Sutton-Brown 2014)—to explore their physical and social environment through their own lens (see Chapter 4). The latter indeed draws on ethnographic techniques that combine photographs taken by the respondents, critical dialogue and experiential knowledge (Sutton-Brown 2014). Miranda-Pérez decided to switch her strategy of data collection and combined autoethnography with photovoice, following Ashley Rubin's liberating motto: there is no "one right way" to do qualitative social research (Rubin 2021, 1). All authors use autobiographical accounts, some also use art (Dyer et al. 2022) or poetry, visual and performance (Landu 2014). For us, auto ethnography has indeed proved to be "a way of examining how the private troubles of individuals are connected to broader public issues" (Denzin 2014, vii).

Adapting Autoethnography to Focus on Respondents

In this section we aim to describe the way Miranda-Pérez adapted autoethnography, to approach her interviewees—psychosocial workers in family and criminal courts—in a context where face-to-face interactions—the most common way of doing qualitative research in the field—were no longer feasible. With the lockdown and the need to "create" a totally virtual ethnographic study, Miranda-Pérez was forced to consider other ways of conducting ethnography that would entail collaboration and co-production with the people under study (Koppe 2022). She also decided to pay attention to her respondents' emotions and perceptions drawing on critical social work theory to "visualize oppression and inequality that relates to the social worker herself, her professional role and her private life, and not just to the client's vulnerability and exclusion" (Mattson 2014, 9). It is well-known that social workers operate with high level of stress in the workplace and that "serving as a social worker during the pandemic proved to include additional mental, physical and emotional challenges that added to the taxing nature of the position" (Cooke, Hastings 2023, 3). In these conditions where justice operators move from physical institutions to their homes, virtual ethnography presents itself as a possible way of accessing spaces of sociability and to explore how professional practice is reinvented.

The widespread use of the Zoom platform in the judiciary and in the justice institutions we investigated allowed, on the one hand, to bring together citizens who, generally, were unable to attend hearings due to work-related reasons. On the other hand, it revealed the very strong digital divide in Chile, exposing the strong socio-economic and territorial inequalities that characterise the country. Thus, work diaries show what professionals must do in order to allow their clients to access justice. Their commitment to the users, and often their frustration towards the institution of the judiciary, led them on some occasions to go beyond their assigned tasks to ensure the appearance of persons at the hearings, as shown by the following extract of a self-report sent through WhatsApp audio:

> About the trial we had talked about! (laughs) [...] [T]hat the victim was going to testify through Zoom, but then he changed his mind... Well, at first, he didn't want to testify, but later we were able to convince him to testify through Zoom, but he ran out of internet data, so I had to arrange for him to be picked up, but by the time I got a taxi, he had already paid his internet bill. In fact, I have the impression that the prosecutor paid his bill, but I'm not sure (laughs in between) ... I had to monitor [the whole situation], whether the taxi arrived to pick him up for the hearing [...]. I also had to make sure that someone

> could meet him [at court]. But well, in the end it wasn't necessary, he did the hearing online. (Self-report, December 2021)

These inconsistencies reflect problems of communication between the judicial institution and the citizenry, which had already been observed in the research on access to justice. Respondents also report a noticeable addition to their workload due to hyper-connectivity, as a result of remote work and adjustments such as those described in the self-report above, although many of our respondents perceived this as an improvement of the efficiency of the justice system (see Chapter 8). This considerably increased their work hours, as the number of cases they were assigned increased—especially in the family justice system.

Work Diaries

Life diaries are a rich source of contextualised information, which allows for inquiry into practices, events and interactions of subjects in a natural way (Alaszewski 2006). In the present case, Miranda-Pérez asked her respondents to write a work diary, handled as a self-reporting instrument, which they could complete with the assistance of the research team. She conducted an in-depth interview with 36 psychosocial workers and invited them to keep in touch with her thanks to the writing of a work diary. Respondents were asked to record a week's work, which in practice took one month. Miranda-Pérez also asked them to take some pictures of their workspace at home. She finally got 11 diaries from 8 women and 3 men. Work diaries became a consensual record of their daily lives at their own pace. It sought to capture their working environments and the progress of their working days, as well as emotions, feelings, problems, needs and successes that arose from their working context (Henríquez et al. 2021). This way, Miranda-Pérez gradually succeeded in capturing the meanings attributed by her respondents to their work, how they experienced their new routines and working practices, in a context where a large part of their work was mediated by confinement and remoteness.

Although work diaries were a tool that sought to adapt to exceptionality, Miranda-Pérez quickly realised that she had to make adjustments once its application began. Throughout conversations with her respondents regarding work overload, she indeed became aware of the fact that diaries were seen as an extension of her respondents' workload. For example, she initially considered filling out work diaries using the Google docs platform, but as she implemented it, respondents commented that this method meant working an additional time and that it was difficult for them to maintain the routine asked. Miranda-Pérez then gave them the possibility of making voice recordings through the WhatsApp application, which allowed her to have both synchronous and asynchronous contact, and this was good valued by her interlocutors. Using WhatsApp generated a relationship of trust, and provided rich audio records with different voice tones (tiredness, joy, enthusiasm, frustration, etc.) and environmental sounds. Consequently, little by little, as a result of the dialogue that arose in the construction of the work diary, and through the interaction with her, other multifaceted resources such as photographs, audios, instant communication media were added spontaneously to the communication with Miranda-Pérez, allowing her not only to read their account, but also to get closer to participants' feelings. Her aptitude to show flexibility and empathy proved to be essential to mediate respondents' initial situation of discomfort (Miranda-Pérez et al. 2022). This led her to acknowledge the importance of establishing limits and caring the formulation of questions (Henríquez et al. 2021).

As the virtual relationship became more fluid and closer, the respondents shared more resources. This was essential to deepen and detail questions and spontaneous reflections that arose through the filling in of the diary (Henríquez et al. 2021; Ahlin and Li 2019). Particularly the visuals, when we received photographs, allowed us to enter their every day in a temporary immersion, to be able to see and know how practices, behaviours and customs are conceived, as a way of understanding how the personal becomes the social, in this case, work (Pink 2007; Banks 2010). In some cases, there were comments on the photographs sent, others simply sent photos of their environment to excuse themselves for not being able to respond to the instrument, either because of excessive workload or because they were with their families.

In any case, all of the above opened up the possibility to access respondents' surrounding atmospheres (Ingold 2016), namely the physical and emotional space in which they moved and lived during the lockdown. It also opened the way for spontaneous, self-reflective accounts, as if it were a conversation with oneself. In addition, sensations of the research team that accompanied the elaboration of diaries were recorded too. We are far from ensuring this experience replaces "being there", which has been so highly valued in anthropological work, however, it leads to delving into the practices of professionals from their own reflexivity. In this sense, this self-reporting exercise of writing life diaries, where respondents' own subjectivities are incorporated and evidenced, challenges the common position of the ethnographer in the field as a mediator between fieldwork and interpretation.

In the light of controversies such as the well-known case of Alice Goffman's "On the run" (2014) ethnographic study, where her reflexivity as an ethnographer was questioned (Avanza 2016), one may argue that including participants' own subjectivity act as a methodological guardrail.

Closing Remarks

Research requires a constant exercise of self-reflection of our work, where we must adapt to the reality of our informants depending on the specific context we find ourselves in, we must consider the possible ways from where and how to learn about reality (Maxwell 2005). Courtroom ethnography is also an institutional ethnography (as opposed to the observation of informal groups), which refers to the manifesto of the feminist sociologist Dorothy Smith (2005), who perceived the importance of institutions in the perpetuation (or transformation) of gendered social relations.

Suggestions and Guidance for Further Readings:

1) On criminal courtroom ethnography, a classical journalistic report:

Bogira, Steve. 2005. Courtroom 302. A year behind the scenes in an American criminal courthouse. New York: Vintage Books.

2) On comparison and family courtroom ethnography:

Biland, Émilie, Steinmetz, Hélène. 2017. Are judges street-level bureaucrats? Evidence from French and Canadian family courts. *Law & Social Inquiry* 42 (2): 298–324.

3) On diary methods:

Hyers, Lauri. 2018. *Diary methods.* United Kingdom: Oxford University Press.

Acknowledgements We would like to thank Fabien Le Bonniec, Pablo Segovia, Felipe Aguila, Eduardo Contreras, Valentina Henríquez, Montserrat Larrondo, Fernanda Osorio, Juan José Martínez, Wladimir Martínez, Claudia Poblete, Diego Poblete, Jocelyn Prat and Millaray Vicuña who participated in different stages of the collective ethnography described in this chapter. Fabiola Miranda-Pérez also thanks her research assistants Natalia Cabrera and Maite Henríquez. We are particularly grateful to Fabien Le Bonniec for his comments on a former draft of this chapter, and to the Chilean Agencia Nacional de Investigación y Desarrollo (ANID) who funded our respective research by allocating the grants Fondecyt Regular n°1180038 and Fondecyt Iniciación n°11190123.

References

Ahlin, Tanja., and Li, Fangfang. 2019. From field sites to field events: Creating the field with information and communication technologies (ICTs). *Medicine Anthropology Theory* 6.

Alaszewski, Andy. 2006. *Using diaries for social research.* California: Sage Publications.

Araujo, Kathya, ed. 2020. *Hilos tensados.* Santiago: Ediciones Universidad de Santiago de Chile.

Avanza, Martina. 2016. Le 'cas Alice Goffman' et les risques d'un backlash méthodologique. *Revue Française De Science Politique* 66 (6): 995–1001.

Au, Anson. 2022. A black feminist approach to antiracist qualitative research methods: commemorating the legacy of bell hooks. *Current Sociology* 0(0): 1–19 (online first, https://doi.org/10.1177/00113921221146583)

Banks, Marcus. 2010. *Los datos visuales en investigación cualitativa.* Madrid: Morata.

Barrera, Leticia. 2012. *La Corte Suprema en escena. Una etnografía del mundo judicial.* Buenos Aires: Siglo Veintiuno.

Bautista, Herrera, Moszowski Van Arturo, Aäron Loon, Acevedo Martínez, Moreno Víctor, Yeyectzin del Angel, López Rodríguez, and Karen and Pérez Merlos, Diana. 2021. De la etnografía colectiva y sus vicisitudes: Un balance crítico. *Diario De Campo* 8–9: 170–188.

CEPAL. 2012. *Desigualdades territoriales y exclusion social del pueblo mapuche en Chile.* Santiago de Chile: Naciones Unidas.

Clerke, Teena., and Hopwood, Nick. 2014. *Doing ethnography in teams. A case study of asymmetries in collaborative research.* London/New York: Springer.

Collectif Onze (Le). 2016. Enquêter, écrire et publier en collectif. ethnographiques.org, No 32. Online available: https://www.ethnographiques.org/2016/Onze. (Last access November 8th, 2023).

Cooke, Collina D, Hastings, Julia F. 2023. Black women social workers: Workplace stress experiences. *Qualitative Social Work* 0 (0): 1–16 (online first https://doi.org/10.1177/14733250231151954)

Denzin, Norman, ed. 2014. *Interpretive autoethnography.* New York: Sage.

Dequirez, Gaëlle., and Jeanne Hersant. 2013. The virtues of improvisation. Ethnography without an ethics protocol. *Current Sociology* 61 (5–6): 646–660.

Dyer, Jennifer, Sarah Pickett, Jennifer Davis, Kathleen Hackett, Cindy Holmes, Julie James, Daze Jefferies, Kimberley Manning, Pullen Sansfaçon, Annie and Temple Newhook, Julie. 2022. Collaborative autoethnography for feminist research. In

Rethinking feminist theories for social work practice, ed. Christine Cocker and Trish Hafford-Letchfield, 97–116. London: Palgrave Macmillan.

Fassin, Didier. 2013. Why ethnography matters. On anthropology and its publics. *Cultural Anthropology* 28 (4): 621–646.

Fuentes, Claudio. 2022. ¿A quién le importa el principio de la publicidad en la justicia reformada? *El Mercurio Legal*, May 4, 2022. Online avaibable: https://www.elmercurio.com/Legal/Noticias/Opinion/2022/05/04/principio-publicidad-justicia-reformada.aspx (Last access November 8th, 2023).

Goffman, Alice. 2014. *On the run. Fugitive life in an American city*. Chicago: Chicago University Press.

Hammersley, Martyn. 2004. Teaching qualitative methodology: Craft, profession or bricolage. In *Qualitative Research Practice*, ed. Clive Seale, Giampietro Gobo, Javier F. Gubrium, and David Silverman, 549–560. Thousand Oaks, CA: Sage.

Harrell, Sam, Ben Anderson-Nathe, Stéphanie. Wahab, and Christine Gringeri. 2022. Feminist research and practice; reorienting a politic for social work. In *Rethinking feminist theories for social work practice*, ed. Christine Cocker and Trish Hafford-Letchfield, 59–76. London: Palgrave Macmillan.

Hennette Vauchez, Stéphanie. 2022. *La démocratie en état d'urgence. Quand l'exception devient permanente*. Paris: Éditions du Seuil.

Henríquez Olivares, Maite, Delgadillo Campos, Javiera, Cabrera Morales, Natalia. 2021. El diario de vida como material etnográfico: estrategias de diseño e implementación. *Revista Intervención* 11 (2): 163-188.

Hersant, Jeanne, Le Bonniec Fabien, Águila, Felipe, Martínez, Wladimir, Prat, Jocelyn. 2020. La zona gris de las audiencias de control de detención en el context del estallido social. CIPER Académico, 12 February: https://www.ciperchile.cl/2020/02/12/la-zona-gris-de-las-audiencias-de-control-de-detencion-en-el-contexto-del-estallido-social/ (Last access November 8th, 2023).

Hersant, Jeanne. 2017. Patronage and rationalization. Reform to criminal procedure in Chile. *Law & Social Inquiry* 42 (2): 423–449.

Ingold, Tim. 2016. *Lines. A brief History*. London, New York: Routledge.

Koppe, Zania. 2022. Ethnography in crisis: Methodology in the cracks. In *Qualitative and digital research in times of crisis: Methods, reflexivity and ethics*, ed. Helen Kara, Su., and -ming Khoo, 30–42. Bristol: University Press.

Landu, Victoria. 2014. Conecting the dots. A review of Norman K. Denzin's Interpretive autoethnography. *The Qualitative Report* 19 (50): 1–4.

Latour, Bruno. 2002. *La fabrique du droit: Une ethnographie du Conseil d'Etat*. Paris: La Découverte.

Le Bonniec, Fabien, Martínez Cañoles, Wladimir., and Vicuña Salas, Millaray. 2021. Detención, formalización y judicialización de la protesta social en el sur de Chile: el continuum de la violencia estatal durante el estallido social de Octubre 2019. *Izquierdas* 50. Online available: http://www.izquierdas.cl/images/pdf/2021/n50/art30.pdf (Last access November 8th, 2023).

Martínez, Francisco, Eeva Berglund, Rachel Harkness, David Jeevendrampillai., and Marjorie Murray. 2021. Far away, so close: A collective ethnography around remoteness. *Entanglements* 4 (1): 246–283.

Mattsson, Tina. 2014. Intersectionality as a useful tool: Anti oppressive social work and critical reflection. *Affilia: Journal of Women and Social Work* 29 (1): 8–17.

Maxwell, Joseph. 2005. *Qualitative research design: An interactive approach*. California: Sage Publications.

Miranda-Pérez, Fabiola, Andrade Guzmán, Carlos. 2022. Psychosocial professionals in Chilean justice institutions. Reflections based on the experiences and practice of psychologists and social workers. *British Journal of Social Work* 0 (0): 1–16 (published online first).

Morales, Ana María, Ulda Figueroa., and Catalina Bustamante. 2022. El sistema de justicia penal durante el estallido social chileno. Legalidad y trato justo en el control judicial de las detenciones realizadas durante los disturbios de 2019. *Política Criminal* 17 (34): 432–473.

Martínes, Ospina, and María Angélica. 2018. Flirteando con el mal. Los avatares de la etnografía colectiva en una atmósfera ritual. *Revista Corpo-Grafías: Estudios Críticos De y Desde Los Cuerpos* 5 (5): 192–208.

Pairicán, Fernando. 2013. Lumaco: La cristalización del movimiento autodeterminista Mapuche. *Revista De Historia Social y De Las Mentalidades* 17 (1): 35–57.

Pink, Sarah. 2007. *Doing visual ethnography: Images, media, and representation in research*. California: Sage Publications.

Rubin, Ashley T. 2021. *Rocking qualitative social sciences. An irreverent guide to rigorous research*. Stanford: Stanford University Press.

Segovia, Pablo, Valentina Henríquez., and Fernanda Osorio. 2022. Análisis de audiencias de control de detención colectivas en un Juzgado de Garantía de Concepción: Un acercamiento desde el Análisis del Discurso. *Boletin De Filología* 57 (2): 399–431.

Smith, Dorothy. 2005. *Institutional ethnography. A sociology for people*. London: Rowman & Littlefield.

Sutton-Brown, Camille. 2014. Photovoice: A methodological guide. *Photography & Culture* 7 (2): 169–186.

Teo, Aaron. 2022. A timed crisis: Australian education, migrant Asian teachers, and critical autoethnography. In *Qualitative and digital research in times of crisis: Methods, reflexivity and ethics*, ed. Helen Kara, Su., and -ming Khoo, 191–203. Bristol: University Press.

Torres, O. 2020. *El Estallido de las Violaciones a los Derechos Humanos. Informe sobre los Derechos Humanos 18 de octubre 2019—12 de marzo 2020*. Chile: Heinrich Böll Stiftung Cono Sur.

Tuula, Gordon, Pirkko Hynninen, Elina Lahelma, Tuija Metso, Tarja Palmu., and Tarja Tolonen. 2006. Collective ethnography, joint experiences and individual pathways. *Nordisk Pedagogik* 26: 3–15.

Yeghicheyan, Jennifer., and Alice Jaspart. 2018. La recherche collective, rempart contre "l'inconfort ethnographique"? Le cas d'un terrain partagé en prison. *Ethnologie Française* 48 (3): 539–552.

14

Courtroom Performances of Masculinities and Victimhood

Tea Fredriksson and Anita Heber

Introduction

The courtroom has been described as a theatre (Carlen 1976; Christie 1986; Goffman 1959; Mattsson 2014; Modéer and Sunnqvist 2012), where scripts structure how "the parties act out a human drama" (Levenson 2007, 3). In this chapter, we explore how different masculinities and victimhoods are performed on the courtroom stage, and how these performances are intertwined within the courtroom's "sensory landscape" (Flower 2021).

Scripted performances let audiences observe actors' behaviours and emotional displays at length—like in court (Goffman, 1986). Studies show that courtroom scripts govern both behaviour and emotions (Bergman Blix and Wettergren 2018; Törnqvist 2017). Within the courtroom's "emotional regime" (Flower 2018, 246), moreover, not all emotions are acceptable. While the courtroom is "an emotional place" (Flower 2018, 227), its script demands that emotions are expressed delicately. The roles of plaintiff and defendant thus follow specific scripts that adhere to, and underpin, courtrooms' "specific

T. Fredriksson (✉) · A. Heber
Department of Criminology, Stockholm University, Stockholm, Sweden
e-mail: tea.fredriksson@criminology.su.se

A. Heber
e-mail: anita.heber@criminology.su.se

L. Flower and S. Klosterkamp (eds.), *Courtroom Ethnography*,
https://doi.org/10.1007/978-3-031-37985-7_14

affective quality" (Bens 2018, 349). These roles, and the emotions associated with them, are defined in relation to each other (Mattsson, 2014). Opposition is key—"sad", "scared" plaintiffs contrast "regretful" or "angry" defendants, while the prosecution contrasts the defence (Törnqvist 2017). Studies have shown that for plaintiffs, following these scripts is crucial for enacting victimhood successfully (Ask and Landström 2010; Christie 1986; Stevenson 2000).

Performing Masculinities

Courtroom performances are deeply affected by gender norms. Masculinities, like any gender, are shaped by power relations intersected by structures of class, ethnicity, and sexuality (Hearn et al. 2012; Messerschmidt 2000). Across these intersections, one defining aspect of masculinities is their relationship with (physical) violence, which has been described as a resource for (re)producing masculinities (Messserchmidt 2004; Lander et al. 2014). Exposure to physical violence has been labelled as a masculinity challenge, since violence, and an (in)ability to handle violence, can be seen as questioning masculinity performances (Messerschmidt 2000, 13). This masculinity challenge also includes a protector norm, where men are expected to shield women from other men's violence (Hollander 2001; Heber 2017). This reinforces images of men as heroes, and women as victims (Uhnoo 2011).

Men may deal with violence differently depending on social contexts and types of violence, meaning that whether violence is considered acceptable depends on several contexts (see Chapter 9). In conventional society, violence is hardly tolerated (Karlsson and Pettersson 2003; Jon 2014). Thus, violence-avoidance is part of conventional masculinities. In the courtroom, the emotional script demands subdued emotions (Flower 2021), thus further suppressing aggression and violence, impacting what masculinity performances are available or acceptable. In short, masculinities can be (re)produced through different ways of enacting, avoiding, or opposing violence (Hollander 2001; Lander et al. 2014). In the courtroom contexts observed in this study, masculinity enactments are related to men's official roles as plaintiffs or defendants in assault cases. Studies show that victimized men have difficulties performing masculinities and victimhood at the same time—especially when men are victims of violent crimes (Åkerström 2007; Burcar 2014; Heber 2017). Violent victimization remains a social stigma for men, since traditional masculinities preclude vulnerability or weakness (Connell 2005; Åkerström 2007; Pettersson 2021). Relatedly, the victim label is predominantly associated with women, children, or the elderly. Thus, it can be difficult for men to express consequences of victimization in the courtroom, even though they are more likely victims than women—not least of violent crimes (Heber 2017).

Studying Courtroom Masculinities

This chapter draws on fieldnotes from twelve court cases of varying length from two different Swedish district courts; each court session lasted between approximately one hour to four hours. The common denominators were that (1) the plaintiffs were men, and that (2) the cases involved (threats of) physical violence. To study how combinations of masculinities and victimhood are performed in court, we noted things like interactions, movement, clothing, and speech. Furthermore, we noted what was being said, especially when it came to descriptions of violence. We also paid attention to how the space set the scene through seating, awkward silences, delays, (un)spoken rules, and the use of technology. This all contributed to how the space and its actors created certain gendered performances. We attended all of the court cases together to be able to write down as much as possible, since recording devices are not allowed in Swedish courtrooms. During the observations and the subsequent analysis, we noted how masculinities and victimhood were interlaced. Reading, discussing, and re-reading the fieldnotes resulted in three overarching themes that sprung from both the empirical data and the study's theoretical framework. These are: heroic rescuers; capable victims; and fearful men.

Heroic Rescuers

A recurring way of conveying masculinity within the plaintiff role was through tales about acts of heroism. Since men are traditionally viewed as able to handle violence, they are also expected to protect women from violence (Jon 2014; Uhnoo 2011; Pettersson 2021). In one courtroom observation, a victimized security guard and his testifying colleague described their encounter with a violent man. They were alerted because this man harassed a woman on a train. However, the woman was long gone by the time the altercation between the guards and the defendant, who was absent from the trial, took place. The woman was not heard during the trial, however, the security guards mentioned her repeatedly, painting themselves as her knights in shining armour. Both the violence they suffered and the violence they enacted became part of this tale of heroic rescue. Relatedly, another plaintiff performing heroism relating to violence against a woman (by her partner), was an intervening neighbour. The call he placed to the police was played in court:

> The call is about twenty minutes long. We hear how the neighbour tries to calm the defendant down. The defendant threatens to beat him up. The neighbour does not seem to take this seriously, instead his responses sound like something a frustrated parent trying to calm down a small child would say—asking him to please go get dressed, and to "please don't use bad words" right now because the call is being recorded. While the call is being played, the neighbour sits completely still, his expression unchanging, while the defendant becomes increasingly red in the face and eventually bursts into loud sobs. (Fieldnote, September 2020)

The neighbour maintained a neutral expression throughout the trial, and sat motionless while the other plaintiff, the battered woman, often cried and turned to her legal representation for comfort and support. Such emotional neutrality is expected of him, both as a man (Heber 2017), and as a performer within the emotional regime of the courtroom (Flower 2018). There was little doubt that the neighbour had been subjected to the threats in question, but he did not enact the victimhood traditionally associated with being a plaintiff. He even left the courtroom twice to top up his parking meter—a move that signalled his reluctance to spend more time or money than absolutely necessary in the victim-role the courtroom gave him.

Another example of heroism was found in a man who was kidnapped and extorted. This plaintiff's story was full of strategic decisions, which gave his ways of navigating the courtroom a strategic air as well. Initially, he participated from a video room with his legal aide. As such, our first impression of him was that he wanted to avoid confronting his assailants. We watched him on screen, as he fidgeted in his seat, hung his head, and looked uncomfortable. The camera was placed above him, making him look small as he looked down, fiddling with a paper coffee cup.

When it is time for him to speak, his legal aid asks if he can join the courtroom. The judge says that this is fine, but that "it would be in the presence of the accused", which the plaintiff is explicitly unbothered by. The accused are three men, who are spread out in the courtroom:

> The plaintiff describes how the defendants "stormed into" his apartment, let in by a woman who was already there. Apparently, this woman owed money she could not pay, so he was supposed to pay in her place. He had only met her a few times, so this seemed odd to us. However, the defendants came in with

> a knife and threatened both the man and his son, so he agreed to pay. The son was not there at the time, and the plaintiff repeatedly expressed doubts that these men even knew his son's name or where to find him. At the same time, he repeated that he felt he had to pay to keep his son safe, and that the woman he barely knew "would be dead on the floor" if he refused. While he was "scared for maybe five minutes", the "situation calmed down" pretty quickly—when he agreed to give the men money. He says that they haggled a bit and "agreed on a price", presenting himself as capable and rational even when threatened. The uncomfortable look he had on camera has disappeared; he seems rather confident now. (Fieldnotes, September 2020)

Throughout, he spoke slowly, with plenty of seemingly annoyed sighs and hesitations. He explained that the money involved (over 90,000 Euro) was "not a big deal" to him, and gave an overall impression of not wanting to waste his energy on this trial. While he verbalized his reluctance to participate, he also navigated his plaintiff status strategically by enacting it in ways that played into both his status as a victim—participating via video, and as a hero—facing his assailants. He performed heroism in several ways: protecting his son, clearing a threatened woman's debt, and walking into court to face his assailants in spite of their threats to himself and his family. Alternating between victim-masculinity and heroic masculinity, however, made his choice to sit in a separate room at the start of the trial seem more like wanting to *look the part* of a victim than wanting to avoid his assailants; especially since he seemed amused when he was later asked to identify them, chuckling while they waved and laughed in response.

Across our observations, men invoked heroism as a way to confront violence in a self-sacrificing, law-abiding way, defending themselves and others. This offset their victimhood: while plaintiffs might have suffered, they did so as traditionally masculine men in powerful positions, protecting women and children from other, wrongfully violent men (cf. Uhnoo 2011; Åkerström et al. 2011). Here, power (physical, social, or financial) becomes a resource for enacting heroic masculinity (Hollander 2001; Jon 2014).

Capable Victims

When men successfully balanced victimhood and masculinities (cf. Åkerström et al. 2011), they performed a sort of capable victimhood: they were injured enough to evoke the court's sympathy, but never enough to lessen their masculinity. We found several attempts at this balance. This finding elaborates on previous research, describing how male crime victims resist traditional victimhood, performing as particularly masculine victims instead

(Burcar 2014; Heber 2017; Åkerström et al. 2011). Unlike such victims, the capable victims observed here were able to strike a mutually beneficial balance between victimhood and masculinity.

These performances were especially prevalent among, but not exclusive to, police officers and security guards, whose professions align with the traditional masculinity challenge—they are expected to meet violence with stronger violence. Such masculinities and professions are also expected to avoid expressions of fear or weakness (Connell 2005; Messerschmidt 2000). Physical violence is considered pervasive in men's lives (Hollander 2001)—especially in professions that expect them to both encounter and enact it. The professionals we observed rarely showed emotions, performing as both capable men and capable professionals. When these balanced performances were successful, professionals managed to perform as capable victims despite having used violence themselves, and without losing their claim to the masculine as well as institutional powers that allow them to use it:

> We are all waiting for the policeman, whom a middle-aged, drunk woman is supposed to have attacked and tried to bite. Apparently, the policeman has forgotten all about the trial, and no one has seen or heard from him. Later, when he is located, he says he will be there in fifteen minutes, which turns out to be forty. Everyone has to wait for him in the hallway. When he comes, he saunters in, in full uniform, his back straight. He is a tall, white, muscular man in his thirties. He does not even glance at the accused woman, who looks frail and nervous. When the court is back in session, the policeman does not excuse himself, nor is he reprimanded by the judge. Instead, the policeman sits down, leans back, and calls his colleague on the phone, even though phones are strictly forbidden in the court room. Later, when he talks about the incident, he reassures us: "I was not afraid, I did not fear for my life, it was not a situation I could not handle, but [the attack] goes beyond what I feel is acceptable". He admits that he has used mild violence to keep the woman from biting him, and he has pressed her head firmly into the police car window. According to the woman however, the policeman was aggressive and unnecessarily violent. The prosecutor asks the policeman to clarify some things about his injuries, to which he responds that he does not really remember, but: "if I have written that in the memo, it is correct". (Fieldnote, September 2020)

The courtroom is restricted when it comes to emotional expressions (Flower 2018), and the policeman acts in line with this. Moreover, his rule-bending actions (e.g. lateness and phone calls) are accommodated (see Chapter 6). Reacting to challenges with ease—whether in the form of violence or courtrooms—is in line with both traditional masculinities and with what society might expect from an officer of the law (Connell 2005). In the courtroom, the policeman performs as a confident, powerful, and violent plaintiff—all of which is accommodated in light of his police-role.

Victimized security guards expressed a similar absence of fear or sadness in relation to their victimhood. Such emotional expressions did not seem acceptable to them (see Flower 2018). Instead, they attempted asserting power by performing dominant masculinities befitting their professional guard-status (Messerschmidt 2000). They would underline physical injuries, describing them as either surprising (if they were severe) or unimportant (if they were not). However, security guard plaintiffs were not accommodated by the court like policemen were—both their professionalism and victimhood were thoroughly questioned by attorneys. While guards often mirrored police in their performance as confident and powerful professionals, their familiarity with "calling the shots" in their profession did not translate to the courtroom.

Oftentimes, when the plaintiff was police or security, the defendants suffered from alcohol-related issues and were themselves (more) injured during the altercations in question. While these people were not in positions of social power, they evoked stronger victimhood in the courtroom—becoming capable *as victims*, despite their defendant status. This was exemplified by a man accused of violently resisting two security guards who wrestled him to the ground:

> A thin, pale man with dark, curly hair sits accused of having assaulted two security guards at a techno party. On the opposite side of the large room, two security guards sit together, one man and one woman. They are both in their fifties, at least ten years older than the accused. The defendant looks to be half the size of the male security guard, who has a big white beard and tattooed arms. The plaintiffs both point this out in their stories, how surprising it was that "someone who is not enormously big" would take "such force" to subdue. Neither security guard has documented their injuries or shown them to anyone—however, the defendant has several photos of injuries taken by both himself and hospital staff.
>
> The photos the defendant took of himself are posed and flattering, while still highlighting cuts and bruises. His expression is almost defiant. Meanwhile, the next set of photos we see are taken at the hospital. These are yellowish, the light gives them blurry qualities, and they were taken without caring if the subject looks good in them. These photos are only a day apart, but the man's physique looks much less toned here. The defendant sighs and shifts around in his seat when the nurse's pictures are shown, looking down, suddenly seeming embarrassed. (Fieldnote, October 2022)

Through his own, carefully posed photos, the defendant shows how violence has become inscribed on a chiselled, resisting, face and body.

However, when the unflattering pictures are shown, the story shifts—he becomes weak and powerless. The defendant uses his photos to construct a strong masculinity, which has endured violence and is in control of how that violence is portrayed to others. This exemplifies possibilities of the gendered body in constructing oneself as a competent, capable man (Messerschmidt 1999; 2000; Connell 2005; Jon 2014). We can also view these pictures as reflections of metrosexual masculinities, allowing men to highlight their appearance (Coad 2008). Contrariwise, the nurse's photos convey a victimized body in all its vulnerability, assailed by multiple attackers. They show the limitations of the defendant's bruised body, as though he did not "handle" violence capably (Messerschmidt 2000, 13). These pictures thus nuance how the defendant's masculinity is constructed. When the pictures on the screen shift in tone, so does the defendant's apparent mood—both his body and his ego seeming bruised when he loses control of his performance. However, his victimhood is strengthened by this, making him a capable victim. As he occupied the victim-role, it became much harder for the plaintiff to claim it.

The security guard justified not treating his own injuries by highlighting that he would not "seek medical help unless… I mean I've called in sick twice in twelve years". Nor would he take photos of himself to document them. Here, he resists performing a masculinity that incorporates either weakness or vanity (Coad 2008; Connell 2005). Instead, he presents himself as a strong, capable man both personally and professionally. He mentions other guards calling the "attack" he underwent "really brutal". To include others' reactions is a common way for men to underline violence while remaining capable and strong in victim-roles (Burcar 2014; Åkerström et al. 2011). However, in this case it does not seem to work, since the violence clearly inscribed on the defendant's body effectively places blame on the security guards.

Unlike the policeman, the guard emphasizes the violence suffered. However, he also resists showing weaknesses associated with victimhood. The guard thus struggles to combine victimhood and masculinity. The defence subsequently questions his legitimacy as a victim—and as a guard. At this, the guard raises his voice, shifts in his seat, clenches his fists, and becomes visibly frustrated by his "brand" of masculinity being in question rather than in control. He responds to the defence's challenge to his masculinity (Messerschmidt 2000), but not in line with the subdued actions and emotions the court script demands of him (Flower 2018). Consequently, both his victimhood and his professional capabilities are questioned—his behaviour and emotional outbursts are not accommodated as parts of his role as either plaintiff or professional. Powerful, aggressive masculinity, where violence is valuable (Hollander 2001; Lander et al. 2014), might strengthen his status outside the courtroom, but weakens his status within it. Contrariwise, the policeman was not questioned as either plaintiff or professional, and was able to successfully translate his performance into a courtroom-appropriate role. Capable victims, in short, balance their victimhood and their masculinity by enacting *just enough* of each—the amounts depending on contexts like violence-types, professionalism, and their role as plaintiff or defendant.

Fearful Men

This section deals with how emotions, predominantly fear, are invoked as ways of performing victimhood. While traditional victimhood emphasizing fear and sadness were rare in our study, they did still occur among both male plaintiffs and defendants. These men expressed a variety of emotional responses such as fear, distress, and sadness, aligning with the traditional expectations placed on victims:

> A bus driver has been attacked, the defendant has taken a stranglehold on him. The driver is a middle-aged black man with short, greying hair and a trimmed beard. During the trial, he sits upright in his chair with his hands clasped as in supplication, except when he describes the assault. Then, he uses them moderately for emphasis. The defendant, a Balkan man in his 20's, is clearly uncomfortable, partially because an entire high-school class is observing.
>
> The prosecutor plays surveillance footage from the bus, showing the attack on big screens. Then, it is time for the plaintiff to tell his story. He narrates slowly, needing a lot of probing from the prosecutor. The driver says that he has met the defendant several times before the attack: "I am always afraid of him". On the day of the attack, the defendant carried a bag, which the plaintiff suggests could contain a gun or a knife, and the driver tried to forbid him from entering the bus. He describes how the defendant became "very aggressive, he hit me several times, he is young, maybe I'm stronger but I didn't want to fight". "I am not someone who fights" the driver adds, his hands raised, folded as in prayer. His story is confirmed by the surveillance, where he seems to be backing down, protecting himself from the attack.
>
> "How have you felt after this incident?", the prosecutor asks. "I have not been well [...] I was on sick-leave for a whole year after...I have seen psychiatry. Until today, I have not been well, but I hope to feel better after this trial". (Fieldnote, September 2022)

The driver openly expresses both fear of the defendant and the psychological tolls the assault has taken on him. His hands clasped in supplication implores the courtroom to believe him and bring relief from his ongoing suffering. His performance in court, and in the surveillance footage, is that of a fearful and vulnerable man who backs away when challenged to fight (cf. Messerschmidt 2000). The plaintiff responds in line with conventional expectations of non-violence (Jon 2014)—however, while not fighting, the driver also maintains that he *would* be strong enough to overpower his attacker, thus claiming a non-violent, yet violence-capable masculinity (Connell 2005; Messerschmidt 2000). In this way, he saves face by avoiding multiple stigmas associated with both fighting and non-fighting enactments of masculinity and victimhood.

While the driver may be our clearest example of a man who claimed ownership of his feelings as a fearful victim, our study also provided other, similar observations. One man received threatening pornographic text messages from a woman, and blushed while saying it made him feel *uncomfortable*. When the prosecutor asks if he was *afraid*, he answered: "yes, both for myself and my family". Like the heroic rescuers, he wanted to protect his family. However, unlike them, he also allowed himself to express fear. We witnessed other such emotional expressions from plaintiffs, regarding their fear of perpetrators. However, these men often needed encouragement, prompting, or direct questions from the prosecutor to be able to express these feelings. Another plaintiff, who was attacked in the city centre's bus terminal, voiced his feelings after similar prompting: "It was really shocking. Nothing called for that barbaric behaviour". Meanwhile, the defendant described similar feelings: "I got very afraid of him because he…he could hurt me". The courtroom thus displays an emotional tug-of-war, as both parties vie for the right to be righteously upset.

The blurring of "victim" and "offender" roles within the more rigid roles of plaintiff and defendant was visible in several court cases. In the following case, the defence opened by noting that a counter-suit had been made—immediately destabilizing the positions of victim and offender. Later, it was time for the defendant to describe events:

> He is visibly uncomfortable, blushing. He alternates between shielding his head in his hands and fidgeting with a ball of paper. Throughout the trial, he looks away from the audience (there is a high-school class also here, and his defence points out that they make him uncomfortable).
>
> His hands are shaking when he describes what happened. He starts slowly, outlining psychological problems and suicidal thoughts that were especially difficult on the night of the event (after a fight with his girlfriend). This led him to several pubs. When he wanted to go home he was denied entry to the underground station by a security guard due to drunkenness. The defendant tried to hit the security guard with a plastic bag, and is wrestled down by the guard and his colleague. Then, the defendant was frisked by the security guard,

> who is the plaintiff in this trial. "It felt like sexual abuse", the defendant says, describing how the guard searched his pant pockets. He proceeds to explain how the guard cuffed him too tightly, and took him to "the torture chamber", where he was beaten. This is a room in the underground station, which guards call "the safety room". (Fieldnote, October 2022)

In this trial, the defendant performs fearful victimhood: vulnerable, sexually assaulted, tightly cuffed, and beaten in a "torture chamber". This image does not align with the defendant-role and its associated aggression, nor with strong, capable masculinity norms (Connell 2005). He denies his capacity for violence, claiming to have waived the plastic bag at the frightening, charging security guards to keep them away. However, he does perform an entitled kind of masculinity in court, interrupting proceedings and speaking out of turn. While he embodies non-violence with his hunched over, fidgeting posture, he still challenges the court's proceedings and portrayal of him. As such, his performance can be viewed in line with masculinity challenges (Messerschmidt 2000). Like the clashing definitions of the space as a *torture chamber* and a *safety room*, there are clashing definitions of what happened—and of who is "really" a victim. The defendant does not accept his assigned role, instead adopting all the attributes, expressions, and experiences of a victim. Here, rather than avoided, the victim-role is actively sought. Meanwhile, the plaintiff neither voiced nor embodied any emotional distress—he seemed unsure of why he was there, only responding briefly to the prosecutors prompts. The plaintiff's victimhood was thus weakened both by his own performance as well as by the defendant's, since they were opposites in the "wrong way" compared to the courtroom's script (Bens 2018; Mattsson 2014).

In the aforementioned neighbour's case, who intervened during domestic violence, we similarly observed how the defendant expressed emotional distress. While the defendant admitted to hitting his girlfriend, his emotional repertoire was in line with the victim-role, as he cried during much of the four-hour trial and made mention of a counter-suit against the girlfriend for having assaulted him, too. As such, while we did observe fearful victim-masculinities among plaintiffs, we also saw defendants adopting these emotional scripts—expressing fear, discomfort, and sadness tied to having *been wronged*, rather than having *done wrong*.

Closing Remarks

This chapter has explored how masculinities and victimhood can be performed and intertwined in the courtroom. One way of doing masculinity as a plaintiff was by constructing oneself as a *heroic rescuer* who protects women and children from violence. This goes in line with traditional masculinity performances. A second way was that of the *capable victim*. These plaintiffs often held professional positions of power, such as police officers and security guards, which they tried to leverage in the courtroom to balance victimhood and masculinity—with varying success. Capable victims were successfully presented (by themselves and others) as *both* men and victims; this category was also observable among defendants. Similarly, we observed *fearful men* among both plaintiffs and defendants, who performed victimhood in line with the traditional expectations of victimhood usually associated with female victims, through emotions such as fear, distress, and weakness.

While the themes explored here were expressed in different ways, they are not mutually exclusive. Rather, they all elucidate interlocking aspects of how courtrooms restrict some gendered and emotional performances, and enable others (Mattsson 2014; Stevensson 2000; Flower 2018). Moreover, they all actualize different strategies for navigating court proceedings—some more deliberate than others. While some victim performances can seem deliberately strategic, the courtroom script demands that plaintiffs and defendants alike adhere to the script, which in and of itself requires more or less strategic performances. In line with previous studies (Burcar 2014; Åkerström 2007), some men opposed their victimhood in order to maintain a traditional, strong masculine status while acknowledging their plaintiff status. For example, by wearing a police uniform, or leaving to fill a parking meter, men approached their assigned role as "plaintiff" while opposing the associated role of "victim". Moreover, as has been established in masculinities studies (Connell 2005; Hollander 2001; Lander et al. 2014; Messerschmidt 2000), violence and vulnerability formed a central tension within which victimhood and masculinities had to be navigated. For instance, by simultaneously emphasizing their unwillingness *and* their ability to fight, men could position themselves within this tension without compromising their ability to come across as either victims or violence-capable.

Through the themes analysed here, we see how the script associated with the victim-role becomes fluid; it is sought after, avoided, or opposed as part of different masculinity performances. While the courtroom positions people firmly as either defendants or plaintiffs, these roles are not always accepted by those who are ascribed these roles. Instead, men might reformulate or challenge them. Such challenges show how the victim-script is not exclusive to plaintiffs. Instead, it is every bit as fluid as the masculinities performed in the courtroom.

While we found commonalities with other studies on masculinities and victimhood, the courtroom setting also added new insights that nuance established claims. In the courtroom, masculinities and victimhood are beholden to specific, scripted rules which often contradict one another—while also being fluid in ways that transcended them. While masculinities often require the capacity for violence to be considered legitimate, victimhood is equally dependent on vulnerability (Burca 2014; Christie 1986). However, this chapter shows how courtroom masculinities can allow men to incorporate vulnerability without losing face. This chapter has also highlighted how the courtroom victim-role can incorporate some capacity for violence without diminishing the role's inherent vulnerability. In summary, this chapter exemplifies how courtroom ethnographies can unveil how victimhoods and masculinities can be performed in ways that compliment, contrast, and coextend with one another.

Suggestions and Guidance for Further Readings:

(1) Bergman Blix, S., and Wettergren, Å. (2018). Professional emotions in court: A sociological perspective. Taylor and Francis.
(2) Herrity, K., Schmidt, B. E., and Warr, J. (Eds.). (2021). Sensory penalities: Exploring the senses in spaces of punishment and social control. Emerald Group Publishing.
(3) Modéer, K. Å., and Sunnqvist, M. (Eds.). (2012). Legal stagings: The visualization, medialization and ritualization of law in language, literature, media, art and architecture. Museum Tusculanum Press.

Acknowledgements This research was funded by the Swedish Crime Victim Authority (*Brottsoffermyndigheten*)

References

Åkerström, Malin. 2007. Coola offer—Unga mäns balansering av brottsofferidentiteten. In: *Brott i Välfärden. Festskrift till Henrik Tham*, ed. Hanns von Hofer, and A. Nilsson, 427–459. Stockholm University.

Åkerström, Malin, Veronika Burcar., and David Wästerfors. 2011. Balancing contradictory identities—Performing masculinity in victim narratives. *Sociological Perspectives* 54 (1): 103–124.

Ask, Karl., and Sara Landström. 2010. Why emotions matter: Expectancy violation and affective response mediate the emotional victim effect. *Law and Human Behavior* 34 (5): 392.

Bens, Jonas. 2018. The courtroom as an affective arrangement: Analysing atmospheres in courtroom ethnography. *The Journal of Legal Pluralism and Unofficial Law* 50 (3): 336–355.

Bergman Blix, Stina., and Wettergren, Åsa. 2018. *Professional emotions in court: A sociological perspective*. Routledge, London

Burcar, Veronika. 2014. Masculinity and victimization: Young men's talk about being victims of violent crime. In *Masculinities in the criminological field*, (pp. 113–130). Routledge.

Carlen, Pat. 1976. THE STAGING OF MAGISTRATES'JUSTICE. *The British Journal of Criminology* 16 (1): 48–55.

Coad, David. 2008. *The metrosexual: gender, sexuality, and sport*. SUNY Press. Albany.

Connell, Raewyn. 2005. *Masculinities*. Polity Press.

Christie, Nils. 1986. Crime control as drama. *Journal of Law and Society* 13: 1–8.

Flower, Lisa. 2021. Rumbling stomachs and silent crying: Mapping and reflecting emotion in the sensory landscape of the courthouse. In *Sensory penalities: Exploring the senses in spaces of punishment and social control* (pp. 159–174). Emerald Publishing Limited.

Flower, Lisa. 2018. Doing loyalty. Defense lawyers' subtle dramas in the courtroom. *Journal of Contemporary Ethnography* 47 (2): 226–254.

Goffman, Erving. 1959. The presentation of self in everyday life: Selections. Doubleday.

Goffman, Erving. 1986. *Stigma: Notes on the management of spoiled identity*. Simon and Schuster. New York.

Hearn, Jeff, Nordberg, Marie, Andersson, Kjerstin, Balkmar, Dag, Gottzén, Lucas, Klinth, Roger, Pringle, Keith., and Sandberg, Linn. 2012. Hegemonic masculinity and beyond: 40 years of research in Sweden. *Men and Masculinities* 15 (1): 31–55.

Heber, Anita. 2017. 'You thought you were superman': Violence, victimization and masculinities. *British Journal of Criminology* 57 (1): 61–78.

Hollander, Jocelyn. 2001. Vulnerability and dangerousness. The construction of gender through conversation about violence. *Gender & Society* 15 (1): 83–109.

Jon, Nina. 2014. Transforming cowboy masculinity into appropriate masculinity *Masculinities in the Criminological field*. Routledge, 19–38.

Karlsson, Jenny., and Pettersson, Tove. 2003. *Fokusgruppsintervjuer med ungdomar om genus och våld. Konstruktioner av gärningspersoner och offer*. Stockholm University. Stockholm.

Lander, Ingrid, Ravn, Signe., and Jon, Nina. (eds.). 2014. *Masculinities in the criminological field: Control, vulnerability and risk-taking*. Ashgate. Farnham, Surrey.

Levenson, Laurie L. 2007. Courtroom demeanor: The theater of the courtroom. *Minnesota Law Review* 92: 573.

Mattsson, Erik. 2014. *Rättens iscensättning: rum, framträdanden, gränser*. Dissertation. Stockholm University.

Messerschmidt, James. 2004. *Flesh and blood: Adolescent gender diversity and violence*. Rowman & Littlefield. Lanham.

Messerschmidt, James W. 2000. *Nine lives: Adolescent masculinities, the body, and violence*. Westview Press.

Modéer, Kjell. Å. and Sunnqvist, Martin. (eds.). 2012. *Legal stagings: The visualization, medialization and ritualization of law in language, literature, media, art and architecture*. Museum Tusculanum Press. Copenhagen.

Pettersson, Tove. 2021. *Kriminologiska perspektiv på genus & brott*. Liber. Stockholm.

Stevenson, Kim. 2000. Unequivocal victims: The historical roots of the mystification of the female complainant in rape cases. *Feminist Legal Studies* 8: 343–366.

Törnqvist, Nina. 2017. Att göra rätt: en studie om professionell respektabilitet, emotioner och narrativa linjer bland relationsvåldsspecialiserade åklagare. Stockholm university. Stockholm.

Uhnoo, Sara. 2011. *Våldets regler: ungdomars tal om våld och bråk*. Dissertation. Gothenburg University.

Index

L. Flower and S. Klosterkamp (eds.), *Courtroom Ethnography*,
https://doi.org/10.1007/978-3-031-37985-7

SPRINGER NATURE

GPSR Compliance

The European Union's (EU) General Product Safety Regulation (GPSR) is a set of rules that requires consumer products to be safe and our obligations to ensure this.

If you have any concerns about our products, you can contact us on ProductSafety@springernature.com

In case Publisher is established outside the EU, the EU authorized representative is:

Springer Nature Customer Service Center GmbH
Europaplatz 3
69115 Heidelberg, Germany

The manufacturer's authorised representative in the EU is Springer Nature Customer Service Centre GmbH, Europaplatz 3, 69115 Heidelberg, Germany. If you have any concerns regarding our products, please contact ProductSafety@springernature.com

Printed and bound by CPI Group (UK) Ltd, Croydon, CR0 4YY

28/09/2026

02224072-0020